# TALK, TOOLS, AND TEXTS
## A LOGIC-IN-USE FOR STUDYING LIFESPAN LITERATE ACTION DEVELOPMENT

## Practices & Possibilities

Series Editors: Nick Carbone and Mike Palmquist

Series Associate Editors: Karen-Elizabeth Moroski, Aimee Taylor, and Aleashia Walton

The Practices & Possibilities Series addresses the full range of practices within the field of Writing Studies, including teaching, learning, research, and theory. From Joseph Williams' reflections on problems to Richard E. Young's taxonomy of "small genres" to Adam Mackie's considerations of technology, the books in this series explore issues and ideas of interest to writers, teachers, researchers, and theorists who share an interest in improving existing practices and exploring new possibilities. The series includes both original and republished books. Works in the series are organized topically.

The WAC Clearinghouse, Colorado State University Open Press, and University Press of Colorado are collaborating so that these books will be widely available through free digital distribution and low-cost print editions. The publishers and the series editors are committed to the principle that knowledge should freely circulate. We see the opportunities that new technologies have for further democratizing knowledge. And we see that to share the power of writing is to share the means for all to articulate their needs, interest, and learning into the great experiment of literacy.

### Other Books in the Series

Jessie Borgman and Casey McArdle, *Personal, Accessible, Responsive, Strategic: Resources and Strategies for Online Writing Instructors* (2019)

Cheryl Geisler & Jason Swarts, Coding *Streams of Language: Techniques for the Systematic Coding of Text, Talk, and Other Verbal Data* (2019)

Ellen C. Carillo, *A Guide to Mindful Reading* (2017)

Lillian Craton, Renée Love & Sean Barnette (Eds.), *Writing Pathways to Student Success* (2017)

Charles Bazerman, *Involved: Writing for College, Writing for Your Self* (2015)

Adam Mackie, *New Literacies Dictionary: Primer for the Twenty-first Century Learner* (2011)

Patricia A. Dunn, *Learning Re-abled: The Learning Disability Controversy and Composition Studies* (2011)

Richard E. Young, *Toward A Taxonomy of "Small" Genres and Writing Techniques for Writing Across the Curriculum* (2011)

Joseph M. Williams, *Problems into PROBLEMS: A Rhetoric of Motivation* (2011)

Charles Bazerman, *The Informed Writer: Using Sources in the Disciplines* (2011)

# TALK, TOOLS, AND TEXTS

## A LOGIC-IN-USE FOR STUDYING LIFESPAN LITERATE ACTION DEVELOPMENT

By Ryan J. Dippre

The WAC Clearinghouse
wac.colostate.edu
Fort Collins, Colorado

University Press of Colorado
upcolorado.com
Louisville, Colorado

The WAC Clearinghouse, Fort Collins, Colorado 80523

University Press of Colorado, Louisville, Colorado 80027

ISBN 978-1-64215-038-4 (PDF) | 978-1-64215-039-1 (ePub) | 978-1-64642-025-4 (pbk.)

DOI: 10.37514/PRA-B.2019.0384

Printed in the United States of America

Library of Congress Cataloging-in-Publication Data

Names: Dippre, Ryan J., author.
Title: Talk, tools, and texts : a logic-in-use for studying lifespan literate action development / by Ryan J. Dippre.
Description: Fort Collins, Colorado : The WAC Clearinghouse ; Boulder, Colorado : University Press of Colorado, [2019] | Series: Practices & possibilities | Includes bibliographical references.
Identifiers: LCCN 2019057967 (print) | LCCN 2019057968 (ebook) | ISBN 9781646420254 (paperback) | ISBN 9781642150384 (pdf) | ISBN 9781642150391 (epub)
Subjects: LCSH: Creative writing (Higher education) | English language—Rhetoric—Study and teaching (Higher) | Literacy. | Haecceity (Philosophy) | Agent (Philosophy)
Classification: LCC PE1404 .D56 2019 (print) | LCC PE1404 (ebook) | DDC 808.02—dc23
LC record available at https://lccn.loc.gov/2019057967
LC ebook record available at https://lccn.loc.gov/2019057968

Copyeditor: Don Donahue
Designer: Mike Palmquist
Series Editors: Nick Carbone and Mike Palmquist
Series Associate Editors: Karen-Elizabeth Moroski, Aimee Taylor, and Aleashia Walton

The WAC Clearinghouse supports teachers of writing across the disciplines. Hosted by Colorado State University, and supported by the Colorado State University Open Press, it brings together scholarly journals and book series as well as resources for teachers who use writing in their courses. This book is available in digital formats for free download at wac.colostate.edu.

Founded in 1965, the University Press of Colorado is a nonprofit cooperative publishing enterprise supported, in part, by Adams State University, Colorado State University, Fort Lewis College, Metropolitan State University of Denver, University of Colorado, University of Northern Colorado, University of Wyoming, Utah State University, and Western Colorado University. For more information, visit upcolorado.com.

For Lindsey and Joe

# Contents

# TALK, TOOLS, AND TEXTS

## A LOGIC-IN-USE FOR STUDYING LIFESPAN LITERATE ACTION DEVELOPMENT

# Introduction. Seeing Literate Action with a Lifespan in Mind: A Disciplinary Opportunity, a Theoretical Reconceptualization, and a Methodological Challenge

In August 2016, a group of international scholars met for the 50th Dartmouth Institute and Conference, *"College Writing": From the 1966 Dartmouth Seminar to Tomorrow.* Through a focus on methodology, the presenters, working paper authors, plenary speakers, and participants of this institute and conference addressed, from a variety of perspectives, a concern of central importance at this point in the continued growth of Writing Studies: What is the state of the art of higher education writing research today, and where must it go next?

In his working paper talk at the Dartmouth Institute, and his closing plenary address at the conference, Charles Bazerman suggested that Writing Studies might benefit from turning its attention toward the lifespan—exploring writing, in other words, with an eye toward the ways in which writers go about writing from cradle to grave. He argued in his working paper talk that "Writing takes a lifetime to learn" and that it "is a part of life, and accordingly intertwined with [a] way of life at different points in life, including reading and literacy engagement." He elaborated on this further at his closing address, pointing out that, as we can see through research on writers at various points in their lives, "Things really do change across the lifespan," and that these changes are worthy of further examination by Writing Studies scholars.

Bazerman's working paper and closing plenary brought to light a small but growing trend in Writing Studies research. Lauren Marshall Bowen's work, for instance, acknowledges that "the perspective of a lifespan can reveal otherwise hidden complexities of literacy" (Bowen, 2011, p. 586). Likewise, Paul Prior (2018) and Kevin Roozen (Roozen & Erickson, 2017) have embarked on long-term studies of their own that explore, in Lemke's (2000) words, how "moments add up into lives" (p. 273). Bazerman himself has headed up a Lifespan Writing Development Group (Bazerman et al., 2017, 2018), an interdisciplinary, international collection of scholars, to begin stitching together knowledge of writers and writing at different points in the lifespan and identify new directions for furthering this knowledge.

This growing emphasis on writing across the lifespan comes at an opportune time: as Brandt (2015) has noted, "For the first time in history, masses of humans have keyboards under their hands that connect them to people at a distance and screens that shine back at them the public look of their own written words"

(p. 159). The rise of what Brandt refers to as *mass writing literacy* on the back of proliferating technology and shifting economic development has transformed the way that people across all ages now engage with the written word. Our students' literate development is not our parents' or grandparents' literate development, nor is it ours, and we need a way of understanding that development on its own terms. Now more than ever before—as writing continues to be reshaped by breakthroughs in technology and economic transformations—the field of Writing Studies needs to understand not only how individuals are writing, but how they shape their writing (and how their writing shapes them) across the course of their lives and amidst the continually-developing swath of human history that they are caught up within.

Brandt, like Bazerman, has participated in the Lifespan Writing Development Group (LWDG). Arguing that writing, like "all complex arts," will necessarily "take a long time to learn" (Bazerman et al., 2017, p. 352), the LWDG suggest that this complexity and the lifetime it takes to work through such complexity need to be respected. In order to begin seeing writing through the lens of the lifespan (in research, pedagogy, and policy), the LWDG proposes eight principles to begin framing "a multidimensional picture of development that respects the complexity and individuality of writing" (Bazerman et al., 2017, p. 353):

1. Writing can develop across the lifespan as part of changing contexts;
2. Writing development is complex because writing is complex;
3. Writing development is variable; there is no single path and no single endpoint;
4. Writers develop in relation to the changing social needs, opportunities, resources, and technologies of their time and place;
5. The development of writing depends on the development, redirection, and specialized reconfiguring of general functions, processes, and tools;
6. Writing and other forms of development have a reciprocal relation and mutual supporting relationships;
7. To understand how writing develops across the lifespan, educators need to recognize the different ways language resources can be used to present meaning in written text; and
8. Curriculum plays a significant formative role in writing development (pp. 354–357).

These principles have been put into action by the *Writing through the Lifespan Collaboration*, a group of international scholars with a shared interest in responding to Bazerman's challenge to think longitudinally about writing across sites and over time. The *Collaboration* defines lifespan writing research as the examination of "acts of inscribed meaning-making, the products of it, and the multiple dimensions of human activity that relate to it in order to build accounts of whether and how writers and writing may change throughout the duration and breadth of the lifespan" (Dippre & Phillips, in press).

The *Collaboration*, in their shared work, has demonstrated that these principles can be useful heuristics for thinking about teaching, researching, and performing writing amidst their work to "build accounts" of changes in writers and writing throughout the lifespan. But while the principles are necessary components for usefully envisioning writing across a broad span of time, they are, on their own, insufficient for directing a research agenda. These principles represent useful configurations of multidisciplinary knowledge, but in order to be useful in the performance of research, they must be *operationalized*; that is, they must be put to work in the construction of new knowledge that can extend, complicate, and refine them.

In this text, I draw from ongoing discussions of sociological method—as well as their enactments in Writing Studies—in order to conduct research that operates with these guiding principles in mind, that mobilizes them toward accounts of lifespan writing development. I identify strategic and perspicuous research sites, materials, and methods that enable me to

1.  Construct a logic-in-use for studying literate action development through the lifespan;
2.  Study literate action development throughout the lifespan via that logic-in-use; and
3.  Extend and complicate contemporary approaches to writing development and transfer research with findings from such a study.

The studies at the heart of this text take a lifespan perspective on the writing development of eleven writers from ages 12 to 80. Through observations, interviews, and document collection, I trace the literate action that these writers performed for various purposes in order to determine how their participation with and through literate action transformed over time. By articulating a portable logic-in-use that I refer to as the *totality of the literate experience* (Chapter 5), I develop a lifespan perspective on the work that these writers were doing, and connect my findings from them to ongoing discussions in Writing Studies about writing through the lifespan, writing development, and transfer.

The *totality of the literate experience*, which I work out in Part I and articulate fully in Chapter 5, is aimed at creating a *lived reality* perspective on literate action development. The lived reality can generally be thought of as the entirety—conscious and unconscious, typified and untypified—of literate action as it is happening *in the experience of the person performing that literate action*. In other words, the lived reality directs attention to the understandings that writers bring to literate action in order to "keep writing or reading going" (Brandt, 1990, p. 8). It is this reality that the *totality of the literate experience* is used to uncover.

The lived reality of development is a different focal point than much other work on the subject. Research on writing development is often place- or community-bound, showing people developing as writers for particular kinds of writing in particular social organizations, such as postsecondary settings (e.g., Beaufort,

2007; McCarthy, 1987; Nowacek, 2011; Thaiss & Zawacki, 2006). In these kinds of studies, we see individuals writing themselves into organizations, transferring some writing knowledge and not others, and developing new understandings of writing based on their stances (e.g., Reiff & Bawarshi, 2011; Sommers & Saltz, 2004). Other studies have also shown the development of genres in those places, as social organizations have evolved to meet the needs of its members. These changes happen across widely varied periods of time—some over a period of centuries (e.g., Bazerman, 1988), and some over shorter periods involving the introduction of new technology (e.g., Spinuzzi, 2003).

In all of these studies, we see individuals being introduced to social structures and, to an extent, structurating (Giddens, 1984) a social organization further. But as Prior (1998), Roozen (2008, 2009a, 2009b, 2010), Woodard (2015) and others have noted, literate action does not observe the social boundaries we put around it—our literate actions regularly operate across various lifeworlds, with our understanding of ourselves, our artifacts, and our practices serving to co-construct social situations across what Prior refers to as *functional systems*, or "a process that links things happening within and between artifacts, people, and the world" (1998, p. 29). We are constantly drawing on knowledge, both explicitly and implicitly, across social boundaries, repurposing (Roozen, 2010) our literate practices to meet the demands of new situations in new times and places, which in turn shapes the interiority of our consciousness. Paying attention to the enculturation of actors in and across specific social organizations has highlighted the complex ways in which contexts shape and are shaped by the persons constructing and perpetuating those contexts, as well as the impact that this interaction between individual and context has on the performance of literate action.

However, if we are to understand the development of individuals' literate actions and practices across a lifespan, then tracing the contours of literate activity through functional systems is problematic as a central object for analysis. The lives that we live are constructed by (and, in turn, construct) laminated, co-present, and heterogeneously developed functional systems of activity, and to understand a *lifespan* of development through the lens of functional systems would require the tracing out the complexity of both the assemblages that constitute these systems and the transformations of consciousness that emerge from such social engagement. The complexity of such tracing—and the enormity of the records that would emerge from such tracing—may lead us to lose sight of the individuated development underway. Prior's recent project of studying literate activity through the lens of *flat CHAT* (Prior, 2008, 2015, 2018; Prior & Olinger, 2018; Smith & Prior, 2019) has begun taking on this challenge with new ways of exploring the "laminated assemblage" (Prior, 2008, p. 13) of literate activity. For Prior (2008), flat CHAT "means not taking for granted some form of the social, not discourse communities, not communities of practice, not bounded activity systems, not accepting the official maps of the social world that our everyday language offers us as complete" (p. 13). Prior's tracing of the *sociology of associations* in particular moments of multimotivational literate activity suggest some potential paths forward for usefully reducing data and tracing the moment-to-moment work of literate activity, but such laminated assemblages, in the tradition of Actor-Network Theory, run the risk of overloading moments of literate activity with the agency of actants, which may negatively impact data reduction. This may be a particular problem when trying to examine literate action through the entirety of the lifespan.

This is what the perspective of lived reality offers this text: a way to focus attention on the individuated actor engaged in a literate act that acknowledges the laminated assemblage that composes the act while, at the same time, accounting for the ways in which the individuated actor will use that act for a different purpose in another context (i.e., a different assemblage that also pulls together multiple sets of functional systems). In short, the lived reality serves as a lens that can examine individuated development as it is caught within the situated, social character of literate action. This can allow the field to understand how literate action develops for writers across times and places and, by extension, how the complex work of organizations and cultures shapes and drives (and is, in turn, shaped and driven by) the lifelong development of literate action.

Attending to the lived reality, as I show in Chapter 1, requires attending to the daily, ongoing, moment-to-moment actions of literate actors under study—because it is the momentary decisions, the short-term tactical work, from which writing development emerges. To do this, I need to explore not the lived reality of writing development but the lived reality of *literate action* development. Rather than paying attention only to the words that appear on the page and how those words change over time, I attend to the ways in which writers organize their material actions around and for writing, and how that—in tandem with the final written product—changes over time.

As part of attending to these material actions, I leave behind internal, psychological explanations of social action for much of this text. This can best be thought of as a data reduction, or methodological move: it is a way to highlight the ongoing work that people to do keep literate action going, and the developmental moments that occur amid that work. I am not suggesting that psychological explanations of social action are not useful, or that they are not important to understanding the complexity of literate action. In fact, the reader will note several opportunities to connect the materially-oriented work I am doing in this text to concepts in the Vygotskian tradition of psychology, such as the zone of proximal development. Rather, I intend to create a materially-oriented approach to lifespan literate action development from which lifespan-oriented psychological insight can later emerge. Once such an orientation is firmly established, we can—as I suggest in Chapter 9—shift our attention to the internal plane. In other words, I aim to construct, through a close look at the lived reality of literate action development, a materially-oriented framework for studying lifespan literate action development from which accounts of interiority can later be built.

The logic-in-use that emerged from this close look at the lived reality of literate action development is the *totality of the literate experience*. The totality is way of thinking through the mass of actions, movements, tools, and people that construct each moment of an individual's engagement with literate action. Through the lens of the totality, it is possible to see that each moment of literate action is bursting at the seams with potential—potential that is taken up by a literate actor through the experience of their lived reality one moment at a time.

Using the totality of the literate experience can focus attention on the moment-to-moment work, the lived reality of individuals as they take up talk, tools, and texts to engage in literate action development. This focus can serve as the framework for, the foundational infrastructure of, seeing writing and how it operates across the lifespan. This infrastructure serves as a starting point for linking the interactional work of the moment to what Prior (2018) refers to as *trajectories of becoming*, and what I refer to in Chapter 9 as *renovations of worlds*.

The idea of renovating our worlds can be considered as a way of understanding how people come to construct and, in turn, be constructed by social situations. The language of renovating our worlds is an attempt to pull away from an understanding of development as on any sort of trajectory. The word renovation suggests a re-working of the materials that we encounter as our understandings of literate action (both tacit and explicit) develop. Any encounter with language or activity always carries with it an element of newness, even if we have done the thing thousands of times before. It is this element of newness that the phrase "renovating our worlds" attempts to capture. As we go about operating in our various social worlds, we are always operating in them, in Garfinkel's (1967) words, "for another first time" (p. 9), transforming both our worlds and ourselves in the ongoing reproduction of both. Considering development as part of the ongoing renovation of worlds also highlights the history of our experiences as well as our flexibility in using them for another first time—it suggests not a trajectory, but a range of options that our continued action takes up to carry ourselves and our worlds forever into the future.

Attending to the ways in which writers renovate their worlds via literate action poses interesting extensions and complications of recent literature on development and transfer. Research on development treats development as being oriented toward a particular end state. Haswell is particularly clear about this in *Gaining Ground in College Writing*. He separates *growth*—a change in the way one goes about writing—from *maturation*, which is growth "toward a fixed standard" (1991, p. 117). *Development*, for Haswell, denotes maturation in terms of a broader culture. To develop for Haswell, then, is to change one's writing in relation to fixed standards that are attendant to the ongoing development of culture. Such a perspective on development suggests concrete future situations—that is, particularities of unfolding culture—that developing writers will engage in.

Likewise, work on the transfer of writing suggests that there will be future situations—in the case of much college-based transfer research, these situations are other classes—in which certain kinds of learning about literate action can be triggered and mobilized in order to successfully accomplish tasks. Hayes, Ferris, and Whithaus (2016), for example, take up the concept of prior knowledge and the new resources that students encounter equally as constants, rather than two mutually transformed aspects of the lives of those engaged in transfer. The students know what they know, and new situation is what it is, and the act of transfer involves the movement of one into the other.

Both of these approaches are assuming a social world that developing writers enter into and write into in some future time and place. Through the lived reality, however—and through the totality of the literate experience, which allows for the disciplined exploration of that lived reality—we can see that the social world that writers enter into is, at least in part, of their own making. Writers, as they go about writing and developing as writers, are also developing the world around them, responding to and making responsive their contexts as those contexts unfold with them from one moment to the next. In other words, the perspective of the lived reality removes the assumption of future situations that development and transfer take up, putting in its place an emphasis on the uncertainty, in the lived reality of the developing writer, of the unfolding moment—what I will come to refer to as *What-Comes-Next*.

As I explain in Chapters Six, Seven, and Eight, research on writing development and transfer does not necessarily stand against this uncertainty. Instead, this uncertainty is framed within the structures that shape the world now and will, because of their durability, shape the world for the foreseeable future. For example, while transfer researchers may agree that there is an element of uncertainty to the way in which a future class will unfold on an interactional level, there are certain material forces at work—the curriculum required by a department, the demands of accrediting agencies, the options afforded by the very shape and structure of the buildings, the financial commitments for yet another semester of courses by students, faculty, private organizations, and government—that provide us with some degree of certainty as to what will happen next. The uncertainty that is left, in other words, is of little consequence—researchers can get far more from taking up the certainty that they do have about what comes next than they can from embracing the uncertainty of *What-Comes-Next*.

In this text, I argue from the opposite position: that the uncertainty of *What-Comes-Next* needs to be at the foreground of understanding of how writers develop their literate action, because it is that uncertainty that is central to them, that directs their attentions and actions. Literate action is an attempt by actors working together to harness the uncertain, to put down as *decided* that which is, in the moment of literate action, *undecided*. To leave out this kind of complex social work is to ignore some of the most powerful ways in which writers develop not only as literate actors but as social beings in their cultures.

*Talk, Tools, and Texts* offers insight into the power and possibilities of a lifespan perspective on literate action development. Even in short bursts of time, in seemingly one-dimensional sites of study, a lifespan perspective on the ways in which writers are going about writing and how researchers might be able to study those methods has a great deal to offer Writing Studies. It extends and complicates commonplace understandings of writing, development, and transfer while, at the same time, underscoring the importance of some of Writing Studies' most closely held beliefs about all three.

## The Nonlinear Challenge: Constructing and Reporting a Research Methodology

The lived reality of literate action development—treating the unfolding experience of the developing writer (and the uncertainty that is central to that experience) as the focus of a research investigation—brings with it some interesting methodological challenges. My answers to these challenges have been recursive and iterative in nature. The nature of a manuscript encourages a linear progression of a research story: identifying an emerging problem in the field, proposing a research plan, selecting a site, carrying out the research, and producing results. However, the work that I performed for this project is decidedly nonlinear. This project has emerged gradually, as I came to understand my research sites more and more deeply. This work went on as new conversations in writing across the lifespan, writing development, and writing transfer were unfolding in Writing Studies, and as my own interests, concerns, and questions drove me more deeply into the ethnomethodological, phenomenological, and sociohistoric grounds for these unfolding conversations.

In order to account for this recursive and iterative work in ways that are both honest and communicable to a wider research community, I have intertwined my methodological choices within my search for data throughout the chapters, which I foreground in the section below. In what follows, I provide an overview of my site selection as a way of helping the reader make sense of why my sites—particularly when situated in relation to one another—are particularly effective at considering writing development with a lifespan in mind. It will also aid the reader in drawing connections from the logic-in-use uncovered in Chapter 5 to the empirical work demonstrated in Chapters Two, Three, Four, Six, Seven, and Eight. In those chapters, I elaborate on some of the methodological difficulties presented by my sites and my emerging logic-in-use.

## Constructing a Research Project: Pursuing Strategic and Perspicuous Research Sites

This text looks across research subjects at various ages and in various social circumstances. The first four chapters of empirical work consider the moment-to-moment literate action of students in two seventh-grade, language arts classes across an entire academic year. Chapter 6 considers the changing literate action of two under-graduate students in their first two years of college. Chapter 7 considers the past and present literate action of two creative writers completing an MA program in creative writing. Finally, Chapter 8 considers the literacy history and chronotopic construction of literate action by two older writers in their 60s and 80s.

The contexts of these studies—which I detail in the following chapters—serve as strategic research sites (Bazerman, 2008; Merton, 1987) that enable a founda-tional infrastructure of lifespan writing development to be established not be-cause any one site covers the entire lifespan but because those sites offer revealing moments that serve as a "microscope of Nature" (Merton, 1987, p. 11) for seeing literate action *in action*. These research sites offer a place where the complex so-cial realities of learning to write and participate in literate action are not only present but central features of discussion and collaborative work, an object to work with and toward. In other words, studying these writers in action gave this study a seat closer to the action of the lived reality of these writers.

But these research sites are not strategic merely because I placed a camera in the classroom, or turned on a recorder for a conversation. The writers I present in this text are encountering a shift in the way in which they engaged in literate ac-tion. The seventh graders, for instance, have just moved from elementary school to middle school. They had more than one teacher, more homework, different kinds of writing, etc. This is enough of a shift in the life of these students and their understanding of the grammar of schooling (Tyack & Cuban, 1995) that, particu-larly early in the year, a good deal of their literate actions were questioned by the students themselves and, by extension, those literate actions came to the level of discursive awareness for further discussion and examination. The other research subjects in this text were in similar positions, and found themselves encountering writing in ways that brought the particularities of their literate practices to the surface more often than in other times and places, offering a variety of moments that served as a "microscope of Nature" to work with.

A second criterion I attended to in my selection of sites was that they were *perspicuous* settings of the ongoing production of social order in some way. Garfinkel (2002) claims that a perspicuous setting "makes available, in that it consists of, material disclosures of practices of local production and natural ac-countability in technical details *with which to find, examine, elucidate, learn of, show, and teach the organization object as an* in vivo *work site*" (p. 181, emphasis in original). This relates to Brandt's (1990) attempt to study the acts of readers and writers—perspicuous settings make visible *how writers make sense of their actions* amidst the production of writing. A *strategic* research site reveals literate action in action, but a *perspicuous* site renders the sense-making activity of the actors in that setting visible for study.

Strategic research sites and perspicuous settings work together in this text to identify particular sites that will help me build an understanding of literate ac-tion development through the lifespan from the perspective of the lived reality.

These two components act as axes in a decision-making continuum (Figure 1). Research sites must be *strategically* selected so that they appropriately answer research questions, and *perspicuous* enough that the detailed picture of the lived reality can be kept at the center of attention while answering those questions. The process of answering those questions must balance the demand of capturing a phenomenon of interest longitudinally—that is, across significant swaths of time in the life of the developing writer—with the demand of production of social order that literate action is caught up within at any given moment in time.

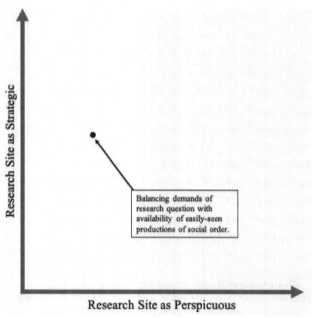

*Figure 1. Research site decision-making: A continuum.*

Throughout Part I, these two criteria overlap significantly. The middle school classroom that I select for study has a wide variety of writing (strategic) that can be easily viewed as it happens through participant observations (perspicuity) in order for me to pursue my phenomenon of interest: that is, locate and characterize literate action development through the lived reality. In Part II, however, as I study literate action development among different populations, I have to make decisions about where and when to sacrifice the perspicuity of the production of social order to take advantage of otherwise strategic research sites.

## Outline of Talk, Tools, and Text

This text is organized into two parts. In "Part I: Transformations amid Recurrence," (Chapters One through Five) I turn the reader's attention to the untypified aspects of recurrent social situations and, in doing so, respecify literate action development through the lens of *ethnomethodology*, or the study of how people work together to create social order through interaction. In "Part II: Tracing Development through the Totality," (Chapters Six through Eight) I draw on the logic-in-use of the totality that emerges from Part I to examine literate action development at various stages in the lifespan. In my conclusion, I further develop my logic-in-use, and outline the consequences of treating that logic as an infrastructure for studying literate action development through the lifespan.

In Chapter 1, I build on the argument for attending to literate action that I begin in this introduction more specifically, arguing that literate action as a coherent theory (Bazerman, 2013) must be oriented toward development and, in that act of orientation, its center of gravity shifts from typification and genre to the social construction of meaning, practices, and action. Since contemporary notions of "development" are insufficient for studying transformations of literate action through the entirety of the lifespan, I respecify development through the sociological tradition of ethnomethodology, aligning it tightly within a development-as-participation-in-social-action perspective (Applebee, 2000). Drawing on the example of candidate developmental moments of one seventh-grade student in a language arts classroom, Alice (pseudonym), I identify several concepts for thinking through literate action development as a phenomenon arising from interactions with talk, tools, and texts, and begin a search for a well-articulated framework that can attend to Alice's development.

In order to begin tracing literate action development, I produce a description of the practices that constitute a seventh-grade, language arts classroom throughout an academic year in Chapter 2. Because of Emily's focus on writing in her lesson planning and the degree to which writing is involved in daily classroom life, Emily's classroom serves as *strategic research site*. Since so much of Emily's students' writing happened in the class—where it could easily be observed—Emily's class also serves as a *perspicuous setting* for revealing literate action development as a part of the ongoing production of social order. I identify the locally-available organizing features of the practices in Emily's class throughout the year in order to develop an actor-oriented perspective on social order in Emily's classroom. Then, turning to ethnomethodological (Garfinkel, 1967, 2002, 2006, 2007, 2008) research, I develop two concepts—*What-Comes-Next* and information—that will support the conceptualization of an individuated perspective on literate action development.

In Chapters Three and Four, I use examples of particular literate action by four students: Marianne, Nick, Holly, and Don. Through the work that these students accomplish, I show the ways in which individuated literate action constructs opportunities for development, as well as what that interactional work of development looks like. In Chapter 3, I use the literate action of Marianne to trace the ways in which the intersubjectively accomplished classroom outlined in Chapter 2 can create the conditions for individuated understandings of a given social action. Nick's group work activity, which I trace through intertextual ties to an eventual blog entry, allows me to elaborate those claims. Holly's "Do Now" activity, and Don's writing in Chapter 4 carries this issue of individuated intersubjectivity further forward, showing the ways in which it can accrue into a rambling path of development across a wider swath of time and activities.

The findings of Chapters Two, Three, and Four lead me to develop a logic-in-use in Chapter 5, what I refer to as *the totality of the literate experience*. The totality is a way of making sense of the intense, laminated assemblage that constitutes each moment of literate action from the perspective of the individuated actor engaged in literate action development. In other words, in each moment of an unfolding experience, a literate actor has a range of past understandings and actions to draw upon which are made materially available in the unfolding moment, and the ways in which that range is drawn upon provides another step in the rambling pathways of literate action development. Considering each moment of literate action like this is a way of re-framing the writing that we observe in our classrooms, our research sites, and our literate lives, and sets the stage for further clarification with cases in Part II.

In Chapter 6, I investigate the literate action of two college-aged writers, May and Lilly, through the totality to explore the possibilities that this logic-in-use has to offer the study of literate action development through the lifespan. By exploring how May and Lilly co-construct social order with and through literate action for school, work, sport, and personal communication, I demonstrate the usefulness of the totality and reveal a concept for thinking through future lifespan writing research: agency. Drawing on this concept as it is revealed throughout May and Lilly's work, I extend and complicate current work on writing transfer.

Chapter 7 draws on two more cases—those of two creative writers with histories in industry and academia, John and Tom—to further extend the reach of the totality and develop another concept: identity. The cases of John and Tom highlight the ways in which subtle transformations of literate action in a given moment can be sustained over long stretches of time, to undergird new patterns of literate action that transform the lifeworlds we participate in throughout our literate lives.

In Chapter 8, I draw on the final two cases in this text—two writers in their 60s and 80s, Michelle and James—to productively complicate agency and identity through the totality. The cases of Michelle and James, who have significantly more control over their time, money, and resources than the previous cases, underscore the analytic power of the totality while also productively complicating the concepts that emerged in the previous two chapters. By attending to the writing that these writers do, and the histories of literate action that brought them to it, the totality of the literate experience as a logic-in-use is further refined, and the case for using such a logic as a starting point for a foundational infrastructure of lifespan writing research is made.

Drawing on the findings presented in Chapters Six, Seven, and Eight, I articulate a summary of the lived reality of literate action development and its attendant concepts. With this understanding of the totality and its connections to the concepts of Part II in place, I then outline the next steps in treating the totality as an infrastructure from which an interdisciplinary understanding of literate action development can build. I suggest potential sites of future interdisciplinary work that attend to interiority, broader systems of activity, and intergenerational cohorts.

# Part I. Transformations Amid Recurrence

It is my contention throughout this volume that an understanding of literate action development through the lifespan needs to have, at its center, the *lived reality* of that development—that is, the ways in which moments of development are experienced by those doing the developing. I attend to the lived reality in a material sense: how do actors work with talk, tools, and texts around them to engage in different kinds of writing over time? How, in other words, do individuated actors co-construct new practices that propel them into future situations.

But this positioning brings with it a number of questions, at the heart of which is the meaning of "recurrent" and "different." As Miller (1984) argues, material situations are not, in and of themselves, recurrent—rather, each situation is unique in a range of ways. Just as no person can step in the same river twice, no one situation can actually repeat. Actors grow older, new materials are introduced, the organization of material is slightly altered. Rather, that which is *recurrent* is an intersubjective accomplishment: a situation is the same as a previous situation because we define it as such.

Research emerging from rhetorical genre studies (RGS) focuses on the recurrence of social action: how and when recurrence is recognized, why, and how people make sense of that recurrence. In Part I, I do indeed attend to that which recurs. However, my focus is not so much on what *does* recur, but rather how meaningful transformations emerge amidst acts of recurrence, and how those transformations endure in future recurrences for individuated actors. It is in this site—individuated novelty amidst a perceived recurring social situation—that I locate literate action development.

To guide my attention toward such individuated novelty, I draw from research in ethnomethodology (Garfinkel, 1967, 2002), which I elaborate in Chapter 1 and throughout the text. Ethnomethodology, as the etymology of the word suggests, is the study of members' methods—in particular, members' methods of constructing social order. Ethnomethodologists see social order as emerging through interaction with both people and objects. Ethnomethodologists look to the ways in which social order is not pre-existing, but rather emergent as people interact with one another and their environments. The idea of recurrence—that is, a situation involving literate action perceived as "happening again" for the actors involved—will, throughout Part I, direct me to particular moments of literate action, which I can then study for signals of transformation.

## A Note on Methodology for Part I

The pursuit of the novel within the recurrent begins with understanding the recurrence of particular social actions with particular groups of social actors.

This "particularity" is important in the search for individuated transformations. Even simple acts of development, such as handing—that is, giving an item from one person to another (see Scollon, 2001)—cannot be seen without some sort of history of the individuated actor engaged in that work. Consider, for instance, my child, a toddler who has learned to hand things to his parents. The act of handing something to one of us to begin an activity—a book to read, for instance, or food to open—can be understood developmentally only in context of the earlier work that my son did to learn to put objects from his hand into mine: the novel experience of handing something to me, followed by multiple experiences of handing *anything* to me regardless of whether I needed and/or wanted it, serve as some of the many stepping stones upon which his current practice of handing is built. I can recount the development of my infant son's process of "handing," and can articulate particular moments when handing became more complex for him (such as handing me several objects in quick succession), became laminated with other activities (such as handing me a toy to put in the tub for later use once the bath was ready), and served as a starting point upon which more complex social actions were constructed (such as handing toys to other children at daycare as part of "sharing"), but any given snapshot of that work would not yield insights about developmental moments to a researcher who lacks an understanding of that history. My methodology undergirding the analysis in the following chapters, therefore, begins by attending to the broader emerging histories of the students and the classroom that they co-construct with one another and their teacher.

I articulate the ongoing work of the classroom in Chapter 2, largely through terminology repurposed from ethnomethodology. However, my understanding of this classroom world began with the orienting questions of interactional ethnography (Green, Skukauskaite & Baker, 2012). After understanding *what counts as writing* in these classes, I was able to begin articulating the ways in which these social actors came to orient themselves and others toward the act of writing in coordinated ways throughout the academic year. Understanding this work set the stage for the individuated attention that I develop in Chapter 3 and Chapter 4. Throughout this process, I paid close attention—through notes, interviews, documents, and video—to what these students did with and through writing throughout the academic year. By attending to these students' writing as the year progressed, I was able to see the consequentiality of particular moments of literate action for these students: that is, I could see the ramifications of a particular decision with and through literate action across future instances of "recurrence."

This longitudinal perspective allowed me to identify the transformations that occur amidst recurrence. In the coming chapters, I frequently turn back to that knowledge of what students are doing and how they have been doing it to make sense of candidate moments of literate action development. No doubt some readers may see this emerging attention to a single site of overlapping lifeworlds (that is, the classroom) as "thin" data. However, in unpacking the complexity of literate action in a given moment, particularly in the early stages of developing a robust conceptualization of tracing the lived reality of literate action development, this becomes a necessary data reduction move (and one that, as we shall see, incorporates multiple lifeworlds anyway, given the laminated nature of them). The analyses in Part II will move more directly into multiple lifeworlds across wider swaths of time once the initial framework has been developed.

# Chapter 1. Respecifying Literate Action Development Ethnomethodologically

Writing, as Prior (1998) suggests, is an insufficiently robust unit of analysis, particularly for researchers interested in understanding writing development. Rather, researchers must be aware not just of the text itself but of the circumstances of a text's production and, furthermore, the histories within which that textual production is caught. This local social ordering of activity to and through textual creation can be understood as *literate action*, a term that is central to Bazerman's (2013a, 2013b) theory and rhetoric of how writing works.

Bazerman's comprehensive theory of literate action draws on a number of generalized accounts of writing, development, society, and technology to develop a robust, multidimensional understanding of language use. In his conclusion to *A Theory of Literate Action*, Bazerman (2013b) argues that his volume "provides an account of the local production of purposeful meaning within textual interaction" (p. 191). Such an understanding of how writing happens and what it does, neither exclusively through static objects such as texts nor through "abstract, out of time conceptions of language, society, knowledge, mind, or thought," draws attention to the materially and historically situated work of writing (p. 191). Bazerman suggests that this focus "position[s] the writing self within historical circumstances to unpack the psychological complexity of someone attempting to produce effective texts for his or her circumstances and developing into a competent writer adequate to the opportunities and demands of the time" (2013b, p. 191). Bazerman's multidisciplinary approach enables a detailed, historically located, and material examination of how writers write and, to an extent, the ways in which these writers come to engage in writing differently in response to new circumstances. Such a theory of literate action is productive in accounting for the multidimensional complexity of human activity that makes up and accompanies the work of writing, and a productive starting point for understanding the ways in which writers work their way into new textual ecologies over time.

Bazerman's theory is rich with connections to theories of development in sociocultural psychology, interpersonal psychiatry, and pragmatism. These theories have generated useful insights for Bazerman both in their situated uses as parts of particular studies and as his studies accumulated into a broader, generalized understanding of literate action and how it works. In my work of turning literate action to the lifespan, however, I found it premature to turn to these theories and Bazerman's take-up of them. These theories have a great deal to say about interiority, about the ways in which the social becomes translated into the internal planes of our experiences. But before we can think about this complex interior work throughout the lifespan, we need a framework for envisioning the deeply social nature of literate action as it materially occurs in particular situations, and how those situations materially interconnect across space and time. Developing a complex, coherent, and usable account of the material work of literate action development can serve as the launching point for orienting theories of development (particularly as Bazerman takes them up) toward the lifespan. In this chapter, I draw on ethnomethodology—that is, the study of members' methods of producing local, social order via interaction (talk, gesture, tone, etc.)—as a starting point for tracing the material work of literate action and its transformation over time. Starting my account from an ethnomethodological perspective will allow me, by Chapter 9, to articulate a foundation for studying lifespan literate action development from which later research, using Bazerman's (2013a, 2013b) uptake of developmental theory as a guide, can explore the interior landscapes that transform as part of the process of literate action development. My account begins by *respecifying* literate action development in ethnomethodological terms, which means locating it in the production of local social order. The first step in this accounting is attending to development, and engaging with its limits and possibilities as a concept.

## Development: A Conflicted but Usable Term

Development, as a term, often goes undefined, or remains broadly defined, in its use. On the surface, the term seems self-evident: i.e., that we can recognize when development has occurred because things are not as they were before. Often, this term is tied up with the concept of improvement, of progress, of evolution. In this chapter, I highlight a particular way to go about considering development, one that is consonant with lifespan writing research.

Before moving into that explanation, however, I would like to clearly separate what development is *not* by outlining two terms that are often used interchangeably with it: learning and transfer. While I will, in some later chapters, draw on transfer literature, my attention remains on *development*. In my pursuit of the concept of development, I am exploring how people become different writers over time, and the mechanisms through which that difference emerges. Terms like learning and transfer fail to fully account for those changes. *Learning* often refers to the acquisition of knowledge or skills. One can learn the names of the planets or the rudiments of hitting a baseball, but this may not significantly impact the way in which the person interacts with the world around them. Learning may be involved with development, but the connotations of the word fail to capture the lived experience of enacting such knowledge, leaving it inadequate to capture the breadth of the phenomena that I am pursuing. We must know the *impact* of learning—the ways in which a writer engages in activity differently—and "learning" as a term does not carry that weight sufficiently.

Likewise, *transfer*, as it is traditionally taken up, does not adequately frame the work that the individual under study is taking on. *Transfer* implies two concrete situations—the one in which the student learns the writing skill, and the one in which the student uses that writing skill again. What is left out of this implication is the role of the student to *construct* that situation—and, furthermore, to *continually* construct a situation, to participate actively in the building of "English class" or whatever the situation may be. When we talk about transfer, then, we are leaving out the agency of the individuals in the construction (and identification) of the situations that they find themselves in. The work of various scholars on both of these terms informs my pursuit of development, particularly in Part II, but is not the center of my interests.

The term "development" is hardly in better shape, and has been a fraught one for well over a century. Kessen (1986) traces the interconnections among the words "development," "evolution," "growth," and "progress" since the rise of Darwin's theory of evolution in the mid–1800s, suggesting that such interconnections have troubled the ways in which we think about development for individuals and societies. The tendency to think of development through the lens of evolution and progress has also impacted literature in the fields of Education and Writing Studies. Fallace (2015) has outlined how the impact of thinking about development through Deweyan terms has incidentally also perpetuated racist understandings of childhood development, complete with subtle shadings of the "white man's burden" and the "great chain of being."

In their work to develop an interdisciplinary perspective on writing development, the Lifespan Writing Development Group (Bazerman et al., 2018) offered a potential path forward for defining development. They note in the introduction to their edited collection that "We generally agreed on associating development with a reorganization or realignment of previous experience that registers through writing or in a changed relationship to writing" (Bazerman et al., 2018, p. 7). This orientation, they argue, "resisted strongly teleological or linear conceptions of writing development" and located development "not merely in an achievement of change but also in actions or efforts toward change" (Bazerman et al., 2018, p. 7).

The LWDG provides a productive starting point for examining development in ways that separate the term from some of its problematic histories of use. Their focus on change allows researchers to negotiate the boundaries of that change, the threshold through which such change earns the label "development." But in that negotiation, researchers can think about where such change is located—in the text, in the process of creating text, in the social arrangements within which text is created, etc. The LWDG also provides several ways to orient our researcher's gaze as we "look" for writing development:

- Look to the embodied act of writing;
- Look to the medium of written language(s);
- Look to contexts of participation; and
- Look to the historical and cultural catalysts of writing development (pp. 8–10).

These orienting directions guide researchers to locate writing development in the cognitive work of producing material texts within complex social organizations amidst a particular swath of history. The LWDG used these directions to determine multidisciplinary intersections, and that very multidisciplinarity avoids prioritizing any of these ways of "looking." Additionally, their avoidance of teleological, linear, and normative conceptions of development have opened up new ways of thinking about development without articulating a particular way of envisioning what writers develop *toward*. Since writers are developing throughout their lives, it is unclear what they might develop toward. Each writer, as they change as writers throughout their lives, will be taking different, rambling paths of activity that co-construct new situations demanding the deployment of literate actions which, through such deployment, propels those writers into new (and not always predictable) situations.

Without the sense of an end goal for writers, what we are left with is the idea of simple "change," or what Haswell (1991) would refer to as *growth*. Growth, while a useful concept to explore, is hardly the goal that writing instructors and writers wish to witness and foster. It is a necessary but insufficient aspect of the overall transformations of writing that is expected through consistent work with and through the written word. In what ways, then, might we go about framing an understanding of development that is more than simple growth, but while continuing to avoid the teleological commitments that many understandings of development have taken on?

The start of such an understanding of development may usefully begin with Applebee's (2000) overview of alternative models of writing development. Applebee categorizes different approaches to writing development as "emphasizing purposes for writing, fluency and writing conventions, the structure of the final product, or strategic knowledge" (2000, p. 92) and goes on to consider the impact of those categories on curriculum design and instruction. However, Applebee concludes, at the end of his chapter, that "writing development remains ill-defined and difficult to assess" (2000, p. 103). In response to this issue, Applebee draws on recent research in writing across grade levels to show that the models he identifies "have treated writing development outside the contexts within which that development occurs" (2000, p. 104) when, in fact, "writers negotiate their place within the many communities of which they are a part, with a variety of resources and competing demands" (p. 104). Applebee takes up this attention to context and argues that "we must judge [student] development as writers in terms of their ability to participate with increasing effectiveness in an increasingly wide array of culturally significant domains for conversation" (2000, p. 106).

This approach—which Applebee calls "writing as participation in social action" (2000, p. 103)—provides a broad suggestion for studying writing development that suggests a potential lens for defining, bounding, and tracing development. Seeing development as participation widens attention away from merely the written word, or the act of writing, and to the complex social worlds within which that writing is happening—and through which that writing, by the participant, is understood. Essentially, writing as participation frames writing development as *literate action development*, and posits that individual writers develop within responsive contexts. Such a perspective on development would prioritize the "contexts of participation" orientation that the LWDG identifies, and make that the leading edge of an investigation into development.

With Applebee's (2000) work as a starting point, we can envision a way in which *development*—despite its problematic history—offers a focused and appropriate approach to understanding how writers transform themselves and their writing throughout their lives. It allows us to examine the ways in which individuals construct and are constructed by situations via material interactions with talk, tools, and texts activated in those situations. Below, I build on Applebee's framing of development to make a case for an *ethnomethodological respecification* of the term when considering literate action through the lifespan. This case begins in the literate action that one seventh-grade student, Alice, performs in the writing and reflection of her "river teeth" writing. This simple example will call our attention, in the following chapters and with the orientation that I develop, to the ways in which seemingly insignificant difference can serve as a driver of powerful change in literate action.

## Alice's River Teeth

It is a warm spring day, and the sun is shining outside of Emily's classroom as her students complete a "river teeth" activity in class. This "river teeth" activity is an attempt by Emily to encourage her students to write about the experiences in their lives. Based on *River Teeth: Stories and Writing*, by David James Duncan, the "river teeth" activity asks students to think about their memories from the past that stuck with them for one reason or another. This initial activity is a ten-minute period that allows students to write down a few notes about experiences they remember.

During this ten-minute period, Alice worked quietly but diligently on her sheet. She is able to identify five experiences to draw from—one more than the amount provided by Emily's sample worksheet. During this work, Alice spoke to no other students in the class. She paid attention to her own work, identifying interesting "river teeth" and then illustrating them slightly—with pencil only—before the writing period was up. A look at Alice's work in Figure 1.1 will show that at no point does she make her work chronological—even though she is writing in pencil, and the flow of the "river" in the middle of the page seems to encourage the writer to do just that.

A closer look at the writing that Alice does shows that the "river teeth" moments that she focuses on are not positive, by a long shot: she is pushed off of a trampoline, she is hit in the head with a toy by her brother, and she falls off of her bike. Two memories are positive—or, perhaps, at least not negative: her memory of snorkeling and her memory of using a zip line. These are not clearly positive in the prewriting activity that Alice completes. In fact, the zip line is marked as an experience that had her "scared," although there is not sufficient context to fully understand what Alice meant by that in only this activity. Perhaps the experience was at first scary but eventually thrilling—the text alone does not let us know this.

Alice's preoccupation with negative "river teeth" moments is the result of several elements that align in various ways. First, Alice does not look to her peers for ideas about writing—what she decides to write is based on her own experiences and her understanding of the task as presented by the teacher, Emily. Emily, actually, had provided a few examples of her own "river teeth," and two of these moments were noticeably negative (falling out of a moving car, catching fire). Alice's peers had turned to positive moments in their lives for their "river teeth" moments, and Alice could easily have turned to them for inspiration, advice, or further ideas. However, Alice—just as she had done throughout the school year—kept to herself, doing what she thought the teacher was asking for her. Alice, of course, was able to do what the teacher asked of her—she wrote down memories that could serve as a starting point for constructing a story. What I want to focus on here is not the writing that she does but the ways in which she organizes herself for that writing.

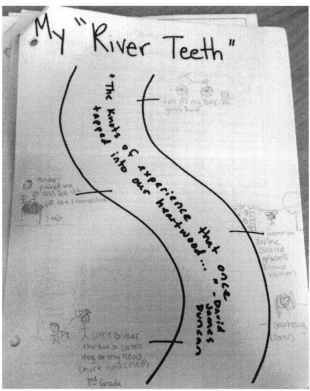

*Figure 1.1. Alice's River Teeth.*

Alice was silent in class—she did not speak unless spoken to or told to speak by Emily's instructions. I was intrigued by her silence, and I asked Emily about it. Emily noted that Alice was a hardworking student who did all of her work and participated when called upon, but who was curiously silent throughout the rest of the class period. When she did speak, it was in almost a whisper. This quietness did not seem to hamper Alice's success in the class.

Once provided with directions, Alice focuses on her work, following the directions given (and clarified) by Emily in order to complete her tasks. While her fellow students discuss their projects with one another, add color to their designs, and further develop their ideas, Alice mimics the sample moments that her teacher provided, providing a few drawings before the writing period ended.

One could reasonably assume, at this point, that Alice is writing as she has always written: that she is bringing her understandings of the world to bear as she always has, and completing the work in a manner that her teacher finds satisfactory, as she always does. And yet, if we look further into the future, we see a potential incongruity when Alice writes her reflection piece at the end of the "river teeth" unit (see Figure 1.2). If we compare Alice's end-of-unit reflection entry to her previous reflection entries, we can see that she is doing something slightly different than she has before. While she is, indeed, writing a rather short entry, this entry is actually one sentence longer than her other reflections. Furthermore, unlike previous reflective writing at the end of units, Alice expresses a desire to keep something with her at the conclusion of the unit. Instead of recapping the work that she has done throughout the unit, as she has done in previous reflective writing, Alice points out her favorite activity and says "I want to remember my river teeth moments."

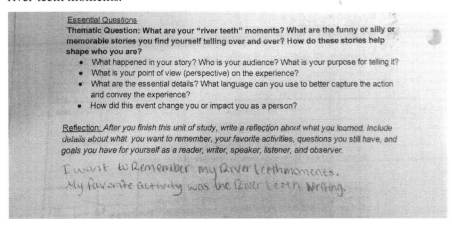

*Figure 1.2. Alice's reflection on the River Teeth unit.*

Of course, the instructions above Alice's writing suggest that she "Include details" about what she wants to remember, and her favorite activities. However, this chunk of text on the sheet is not unusual or new for Emily's reflective activities—

Alice has seen them before and has not responded to them. What can be made of this difference, then? Is Alice a different writer now than when she started her "river teeth" unit, and is that difference in any way noticeable? If so, does this small difference mean anything in terms of the wider span of Alice's development as a writer?

These brief moments of literate action suggest that some kind of transformation may be afoot. On the surface, this bout of writing by Alice might seem inconsequential. As I will argue throughout this text, however, these seemingly inconsequential moments of alteration in literate action add up into the larger transformations that we can see with the broader instruments of text analysis and retrospective accounts—and, by extension, are moments that we as researchers and teachers of writing must pay attention to if we are to understand lifespan literate action development in all of its complexity.

## Attending to the Novel within the Recurrent: Ethnomethodology

As the above example suggests, there is a great deal of difference between the moments of literate action I describe above and the previous (and subsequent) moments that I put it in conversation with. In fact, if we attend strictly to the materials involved in the construction of each situation, we will find that the similarities across instances are slim indeed: even the structure of the reflective activity (perhaps the most repetitive aspect in each of these moments) differs from one instance to the next. Miller (1984) notes that the situations we define as recurring cannot be recurrent in the materials themselves: "What recurs cannot be a material configuration of objects, events, and people, nor can it be a subjective configuration, a 'perception,' for these, too, are unique from moment to moment" (p. 156). Miller instead claims that the recurrent rests in the realm of *intersubjectivity*: it is "a social occurrence," and "cannot be understood on materialist terms" (1984, p. 156).

The disconnect between the material and the social creates the space for the novel to emerge within what might be otherwise considered recurrent events. Consider, for instance, the work of communicating with a spouse about dinner. As I begin to type a text message to my wife to ask what she wants to eat, I am creating a recurring intersubjective understanding (i.e., that we need to eat another meal and discuss what that meal might be), even if most of the materials—such as where we are in relation to one another, the circumstances we are in at our respective locations, the clothes we wear, the chairs we sit in—change dramatically. A number of things can change in the production of the recurrent. The challenge for researchers is to understand the changes, the novelty, in the recurrent that can "add up," over time, into sustained patterns of changes in literate action. To do that work, I turn to ethnomethodology (Garfinkel, 1967, 2002, 2006, 2008) and the attention that it pays to the material production of social order.

Ethnomethodology has long influenced the fields of Writing Studies, Education, and Literacy, both directly—in ethnomethodological publications—and indirectly, in the take-up of ethnomethodological insights across a range of theories. For instance, Latour (2005) argues that Actor-Network Theory is "half" Garfinkel in its nature. Brandt (1992) describes ethnomethodology as "a radical form of analysis that studies the methods that people use for 'doing everyday life,' including 'doing talk'" (p. 317). Ethnomethodology has as its goal "the explanation of how everyday activities achieve their organization or order" (Brandt, 1992, p. 318). Brandt separates the work of ethnomethodology from ethnography, suggesting that ethnography *uses* the everyday accomplishment of social order in order to understand a group, but ethnomethodology examines the accomplishment of that everyday social order. Ethnomethodologists have demonstrated (i.e., Garfinkel, 1967; Liberman, 2013) that the mundane is indeed something that is *accomplished*: "A fundamental insight drawn from these and other projects is that as actors in the world we spend a lot of our time (and language) *making ourselves accountable* for what we are doing and *accounting for* what other people are doing" (Brandt, 1992, p. 319). This focus on accomplishment in a local sense (that is, in the moment of producing text) can transform how we understand literate action: as not simply participation in far-flung organizations of social action, but also tactical responses to an unfolding, local social order.

Ethnomethodology has its roots in early- and mid-twentieth century sociological discussions. Harold Garfinkel, the founder of ethnomethodology, received his Ph.D. from Harvard in 1952, working directly under Talcott Parsons, then the giant of the sociological scene. Parsons' work, structural-functionalism, was of interest to a young Garfinkel, though he came to see that the organization of structural-functionalism raised problems in several ways. In his thesis, *The Perception of the Other: A Study in Social Order*, as well as his dissertation prospectus (published as *Seeing Sociologically: The Routine Grounds of Social Action*, edited by Anne Warfield Rawls, in 2006), Garfinkel challenges some of the assumptions of Parsons' approach, drawing on the phenomenology of Gurwitsch and Schutz to work though his problems with those assumptions.

Garfinkel's issues with Parsons' work stemmed from a divergent reading of Emile Durkheim's *Rules of Sociological Method*. Durkheim (1895) suggests that "the objective reality of social facts is sociology's fundamental principle" (p. lvii). A "social fact," for Durkheim (1895), is a "category of facts with very distinctive characteristics: it consists of ways of acting, thinking, and feeling, external to the individual, and endowed with a power of coercion, by reason of which they control him" (p. 3). As Bazerman (2004) points out, people come to believe social facts are true, and those facts then shape how they define the situations they find themselves in.

The ways in which Parsons and others traced the production of social facts was, in Garfinkel's view, misguided. Parsons and many of the structural-functionalists who followed saw social facts as emerging from a broader system of values that individuals act out in their lives. Social facts, then, are part of an over-arching social world that shape individual actions. Garfinkel (1967) suggests that the models of structural-functionalism create an image of a human being "who produces the stable features of the society by acting in compliance with preestab-lished and legitimate alternatives of action that the common culture provides" (p. 68). This unreflexive character of the actor, Garfinkel argues, is inaccurate, because it leaves out the ability of the actor to do their own sense-making and leaves them as a "cultural dope" (1967, p. 68), unable to do anything but follow sociological rules (see Lynch, 2012b for more on the development of 'dopes' in Garfinkel's writings).

Garfinkel hoped to attend to an *actor-oriented perspective* that would high-light the reflexive capacities of social actors, revealing their powers as "cultur-ally astute agents" (Lynch, 2012b, p. 224) and the ways in which their actions *produce* social facts in particular situations. Toward that end, he did two things. First, he turned to the language of phenomenology, initially through the work of Schutz and Gurwitsch but later expanding his reading to other phenome-nologists (Merleau-Ponty, for instance) and the intellectual descendants of the phenomenological movement, such as Derrida. Drawing on the interaction of self and object, of intention and object, Garfinkel (drawing in particular on the phenomenological sociology of Schutz) realized that the broad searches for social order evident in the statistical analyses of the structural-functionalist school were, in effect, losing the phenomenon of social order (Garfinkel, 2002). Social order was not to be found in aggregates, pulled together through socio-logical techniques applied to an unordered plenum.[1] Rather, social order was an ongoing accomplishment of social actors: in any given moment, people work together to make sense of both what is happening in a given moment and what is going to happen next. The production of social order, Garfinkel came to see, is always local, always *scenic* (that is, constituted from objects at hand—*just-here, just-now, with-just-these-tools,* and *just-these-people,* or what Garfinkel would come to call *haecceities*), and always constituted "for another first time" (1967, p. 9).

Several texts have traced the features, principles, and assumptions of ethno-methodology since its inception (Hammersley, 2018; Hilbert, 1995; Livingston, 2003; Sharrock & Anderson, 2012), and considerable effort has been made, par-ticularly with the rise of the International Institute for Ethnomethodology and Conversation Analysis in the late 1980s, to further these features, principles, and assumptions. Below, I articulate several of the key assumptions of ethnomethod-ology that are central to understanding how I operationalize ethnomethodologi-cal work toward the study of literate action development.

---

1. Garfinkel (2002) would come to refer to this as Parsons' Plenum, which was a shorthand to reference the inherently unordered social activity that structural-func-tionalist methods assumed of social action.

Ethnomethodology must be understood, in this work, as a *radically empirical* project: it attends to the material production of social order as that production happens. The pursuit of a radical empiricism eschews, for many ethnomethodologists, cognitive explanations of social action. Coulter (1991) productively frames the cognitive in the world of the ethnomethodologist: "Rather than construe memories as *themselves* neurally-encoded phenomena, we should instead think of neural structures, states or events as enabling, facilitating *the situated production of memory-claims* (to oneself and others) in all their variety" (p. 188). Much like it is for Hutchins (1995) or Latour (2005), cognition for the ethnomethodologist is deeply *scenic*, occurring with and as part of the material surrounding it, and the production of social order remains scenic right along with it. Explanations that remain cognitive in nature (or rooted in the individual—see Rawls' editorial introduction to Garfinkel, 2006) end up reifying the individual, obscuring social order, and therefore losing the very phenomena that ethnomethodologists hope to study.

An ethnomethodological study is *radically empirical*, then, because it attends so closely to the scenic production of social order. This social order is not theorized, or even historicized: the objects involved in the production of social order are treated in and of the production of a given situation among co-actors. Theorizing and historicizing can also lead to the loss of the phenomenon of interest. Ethnomethodologists are interested in the ongoing work of *immortal, ordinary society* (Garfinkel, 2002, p. 92). According to Garfinkel,

> *Immortal* is borrowed from Durkheim as a metaphor for any witnessable local setting whose parties are doing some human job that can range in scale from a hallway greeting to a freeway traffic jam where there is *this* to emphasize about them: Their production is staffed by parties to a standing crap game. Of course the jobs are not games, let alone a crap game. Think of freeway traffic glow in Los Angeles. For the cohort of drivers there, just this gang of them, driving, making traffic together, are *somehow*, smoothly and unremarkably, concerting the driving to be *at* the lived production of the flow's just thisness: familiar, ordinary, uninterestingly, observably-in-and-as-of-observances, doable and done again, and always, only entirely in detail for everything that detail could be. (2002, p. 92)

Attending to the situated production of order—in traffic jams, in restaurants, at intersections, in queues, etc.—offers a useful focus into the *local* work of actors to perpetuate social order. This focus on locality works hand-in-hand with attention to the scenic: because ethnomethodologists pay attention only to particular scenes of social action, and because they attend to the scenic aspects of the production of social order in those scenes, the ways in which social facts become established can be highlighted for ethnomethodologists.

Ethnomethodologists attend closely to language use, albeit in particular ways. Language, as Garfinkel (1967) claims, is deeply indexical: even words that are commonly understood to have a fixed meaning are deeply dependent on context in order to be understood, to create meaning into a productive communicative act. The indexicality of language reinforces the ongoing work of actors to produce local social order. By considering language as having its meaning contextually grounded, ethnomethodologists can avoid abstracted understandings of language and instead see how it operates in the production of a given social situation.

Throughout the rest of Part I and, to some extent, the rest of this text, I will continue to draw on ethnomethodological concepts and elaborate on those listed above, but these initial assumptions provide a sufficient orientation to begin ethnomethodological work, and will be the building blocks on which a perspective of the *lived reality* perspective is constructed. Ethnomethodology's *radical empiricism* calls attention to the *local* production of social order via attention to the *scenic* features of that locality. Part of those scenic features involves an inherently indexical language, which is brought to bear both in the pursuit of broad goals and in the work of maintaining social order.

## Identifying and Resolving Concerns for an Ethnomethodological Orientation

Though ethnomethodology has a productive set of concepts and assumptions for thinking through the lived reality of literate action development, the particular focus of the ethnomethodological project is rather distanced from writing research—or research on writing development—and this distance creates some inconsistencies and issues that need to be resolved as the respecification of literate action development continues. The primary issue with bringing ethnomethodology to bear on writing research is, as Brandt (1992) and Prior (2017) have acknowledged in their work, that ethnomethodologists have traditionally paid little attention to writing and the production of it (but see Lynch, 1993). Ethnomethodologists traditionally identify *perspicuous settings* (Garfinkel, 2002) that enable the production of social order to be effectively identified and traced. These settings do not attend to the production of writing, and they certainly do not trace the production of writing through *multiple* settings, which would be required in order to work out the ways in which literate action develops.

The focus on particular, perspicuous settings is linked to another disconnect between the aims of this research project and ethnomethodology. Ethnomethodology is the study of *members'* methods—that is, members of a group who are working together in order to make social order happen. Tracing the production of freeway traffic, or the flow of pedestrians across crowded intersections, has a fundamentally anonymous character to it when examined ethnomethodologically: the practices of drivers and pedestrians are interchangeable, and, once described, can be taken up by others involved in constructing social order in that setting. Take, for instance, Liberman's (2013) study of pedestrians at a crowded intersection: the acts of pedestrians to make themselves known to drivers, to move along crosswalks in ways that are accountable to other members of that group, are not dependent on particular members. It is for this reason that ordinary society is referred to by Garfinkel (2002) as *immortal*: there is no one person that it depends upon and, indeed, there is no whole, complete *person* available in the production of social order, anyway (see Rawls in Garfinkel, 2006). Rather, individual *actors*— socially-constructed and constructing aspects of individuals—work together to make a situation happen. The whole of the person is unavailable in any given situation, and so is not of interest to ethnomethodologists.

One final concern remains for the work of respecifying literate action development ethnomethodologically. The phenomenon of respecifying is, fundamentally, done through the practices and language of actors in a particular social scene. As Davidson (2012) notes, respecification "treats some concept, problem or notion as a local matter for members to address rather than a problem for sociologists" (p. 32). Zaunbrecher (2018), for instance, ethnomethodologically respecifies "spontaneity" in order to see how particular actions are co-constituted in the ongoing production of social order to *count* as spontaneous to the actors in the situation. "Development," however, is a *second-order* phenomenon—it is something identified by an observer (that is, a sociologist) looking at a situation, not something that emerges as an accountable phenomenon among members of a situation. So, in purely ethnomethodological terms, it is not possible to respecify development ethnomethodologically, at least not for those engaged in the act of writing.[2]

None of these concerns are insurmountable. The starting point for resolving them is, of course, that the object of my study is not the ongoing production of social order but how literate action develops within, through, and as part of that production. First and foremost, this is writing research, and is focused on the production of writing (or, more specifically, literate action). My intention in this work is to bring ethnomethodological insights, assumptions, and concepts to bear on literate action development. Attending to the above limitations is not intended to make this a fundamentally ethnomethodological study, but rather to avoid appropriating ethnomethodology against the grain of its own principles and, by extension, losing the advantages that Writing Studies stands to gain from such an approach.

With this positioning of the study in relation to ethnomethodology in mind, I can now turn to these problems one at a time. The primary issue at work with ethnomethodological studies of writing is that ethnomethodology has not tradition-

---

2. One could, of course, study the situated production of responding to student writing in order to understand how teachers came to understand development. Though an incredibly interesting research site, that is beyond the bounds of this particular project, as it loses the perspective of the developing writer as they are writing.

ally attended to writing, and so there is little prior work in ethnomethodology to build from with regard to writing. This is connected to the search for perspicuous settings by ethnomethodologists: the performance of literate action often does not occur in perspicuous settings, particularly for older writers. Writers tend to write in at least partial solitude, and to do so without the visible kinds of collaborative work akin to, say, negotiating a crosswalk. Prior (1998), Prior and Hengst (2010), and Pigg (2014a, 2014b) have begun the work of attending to writing in a more material and ethnomethodological way, but understanding what counts as a perspicuous setting for those interested in literate action development remains an open question.

My focus on literate action *development* calls attention to multiple settings: that is, it is important to see not just literate action once, but across multiple occasions to identify meaningful, measurable, and enduring change. So however these perspicuous settings are identified, they need to be multiple and connected—the practice of watching a traffic jam will be insufficient for tracing such development. This is not to say that a recurrent site of literate action—such as a classroom—cannot be attended to, but rather that such work needs to attend more closely to particular actors than ethnomethodologists have traditionally been willing to. In the coming chapters, I select a classroom as a recurrent site of literate action with a stable collection of specific students throughout an entire academic year. By selecting a recurring site that the same people return to again and again, I can begin the work of stitching together moments of literate action across instances of situations that may "add up" into developmental work.

Of course, turning to *people* seems, on the surface, to turn away from an ethnomethodological rejection of individual persons and a focus on anonymous group members. Throughout Part I, I focus not on *individuals*—that is, whole, discrete persons—but rather *individuated actors*, participants in producing social order with unique footings in the social space that they are co-constructing. The language of *individuated actor* allows me to focus on the contingent, situated, and locally-produced aspects of participants, as well as keep my attention on that which changes. *Individuals* encourage me to see people in a situation as complete beings who may change, whereas *individuated actors,* as a concept, allows me to see people as always in-process, always engaged in some kind of change.

Such a distinction is important to get at the situated production of literate action development. Ethnomethodologists have never argued that individuals do not exist, but rather that the concept of the individual occludes the production of social order. Taking this as a starting point, I focus on the work that members are doing (see Chapter 2, for instance) to create ongoing social order and, from there, trace the work of individuated actors as they contribute to that production—and, by extension, how those productions change through future instantiations of social situations involving the same individuated actor. My attention is thus to the singular work of a developing writer as understood through the unique-to-the-group contributions to ongoing social order over time.

The final concern addressed above is that of development as a second-order concept. Since members' methods in the situations I am interested in examining (that is, literate action through the lifespan) do not attend to development in the sense that I mean it, it cannot be respecified in a true ethnomethodological sense. However, beginning with the framework (Applebee, 2000) of development as participation in social action, I can render the concept of development more ethnomethodological. I call this rendering a respecification, not to conflate the similarities of it to traditional ethnomethodological respecification, but rather to highlight the tradition of turning to members' methods that it builds upon. This take on respecification follows Garfinkel's tradition of deliberate misreading. Below, I articulate this respecification, drawing on the assumptions and concepts above.

## Respecifying Development Ethnomethodologically

*Deliberate misreading* is a term that Garfinkel used when reading (or encouraging others to read) phenomenological literature. Husserl, Merleau-Ponty, Schutz, and Gurwitsch were regular components of Garfinkel's reading, and often assigned to his graduate students, as Liberman (2013) points out, but Garfinkel read these texts *as if* they were talking about the local production of social order. Such a deliberate misreading allowed Garfinkel to develop insights that he could then follow up on through a careful study of perspicuous settings.

The key word in *deliberate misreading* is "deliberate." Based on my reading of Garfinkel's work, I read "deliberate" as *cautious*, not simply *intentional*. Garfinkel certainly intended to misread these phenomenologists, but he did so in a cautious manner, with a particular view in mind. Perhaps another word for "deliberate" might be "disciplined." Garfinkel's misreading was a disciplined misreading. My misreading of respecifying, in turn, is also disciplined in nature.

Since the respecification of development in a purely ethnomethodological sense is not available, it may be useful to begin with an understanding of what respecifying does for ethnomethodologists and, drawing on the particularities of the phenomenon of interest in this study, extrapolate from that work. Respecification returns attention to the work and understandings of members of a particular social situation. Attending to the ways in which actors make themselves accountable to themselves and one another in the co-construction of a situation allows researchers to develop an actor-oriented perspective on the joint production of social facts, and respecifying research questions toward that cooperative, local work—what Garfinkel (1991, 2002) refers to as *haecceities*—allows researchers to attend to that work without obscuring it in broader theoretical frameworks or methodological techniques.

Respecifying development ethnomethodologically means attending to these haecceities in order to find transformations that endure beyond those haecceities. Seeing such development, however, requires multiple situations, each with its own haecceitic production of social order—and, by extension, attending to the individuated actor across those situations. Therefore, a respecification of development begins with attending to the ongoing production of situated social order by following an individuated actor across multiple situations.

Understanding development as emergent from the sequential production of social order keeps the focus on social order even if the term *development* is, itself, not fully respecified in a strictly ethnomethodological manner. And the distinction between the novel and the recurrent—that is, what of the infinite changes in the (re)production of social order come to count as "development" for an individuated actor—has yet to be fully articulated. At present, the conditions required are sketchy: the change must be involved in the production of social order for an individuated actor, and that change must endure through future recurrences of that production of social order. In order to begin filling in this sketch—something I will continue to attend to across the next four chapters as I build up a picture of the *totality of the literate experience*—I turn back to Alice's literate action from earlier in this chapter. How might an examination of Alice's work through an ethnomethodologically-respecified understanding of literate action development highlight potential development in the literate action of Alice?

## Pivoting to an Ethnomethodological Respecification: Alice's Literate Action Re-Examined

With this broad overview of an ethnomethodological respecification in mind, we can turn our attention back to the work of Alice in her "river teeth" writing. I want to treat this work as a *candidate moment* of literate action development for Alice: that is, a potential site of literate action development that is worthy of further study. Two ethnomethodological tools will be used to work out this respecification: the *unique adequacy requirement* and *ticked brackets*. These concepts, working together, bring the researcher's attention to the constructed orderliness of events, enabling the lived reality to emerge from that orderliness for closer examination.

The *unique adequacy requirement* is a central concern of ethnomethodologists. Because "a phenomenon of order* is only available in the *lived* in-courseness of its local production and natural accountability" (Garfinkel, 2002, p. 175, emphasis in original), researchers attempting to uncover unfolding social order must be adequately competent in the unfolding situation at hand. This is what ethnomethodologists mean when they refer to the *unique adequacy* of a research study. Unique adequacy comes in a weak form and a strong form. The "weak" form of the unique adequacy requirement requires that the researcher "must be *vulgarly* competent to the local production and reflexively natural accountability of the phenomenon of order* [s]he is 'studying'" (Garfinkel, 2002, pp. 175–176). The strong form of the unique adequacy requirement goes one step beyond vulgar competence: "It demands that the methods of analysis used to report on a setting should be derived from that setting" (Rooke & Kagiolou, 2007, p. 11). The strong form requires "a refusal to evaluate, describe or explain the activities that constitute the setting using criteria, concepts or theories that are not a part of that setting" (Rooke & Kagiolou, 2007, p. 11).

I address the details for meeting the weak form of the unique adequacy requirement in Chapter 2, but I can briefly summarize my meeting this requirement by noting that I was an observer in Alice's class from the first day of school to the last, that I spoke with Alice and her students on a regular basis, and that I had access to the worksheets and activities that Alice, her classmates, and her teacher (Emily) did. I also arrived at the scene with five years' experience teaching in a public secondary school in the United States. The strong form of the UA requirement is somewhat more complicated, particularly since my ethnomethodological respecification of literate action development pulls away from the situated orderliness and into the serialized, situational orderliness of social action. But the second concept I am using—ticked brackets—are needed to indicate the effectiveness of and need for UA.

Garfinkel (2002) uses several figures to suggest the difference between ethnomethodological work and what he refers to as "formal analytic" (FA) work. The working assumption of FA is that "there is no order in the concreteness of lived everyday activities (Garfinkel, 2002, p. 135). It is the job of FA, in Garfinkel's eyes, to establish order in the *plenum*, or "the plentitude; the plenty of it; the more than you or anyone can say or hope to say; the endless chaotic circumstantiality of lived, living, lebend, uhr, um, etcetera, and etcetera" (pp. 136–137). Garfinkel describes the plenum as -[ ]-. Within these brackets is the unorderliness of lived experience. FA studies use methods, which Garfinkel characterizes with an arrow, to develop ordered understandings of the world, which Garfinkel puts in parentheses. An FA approach to a research site then looks like this:

$$-[\ ]- \rightarrow (\ )$$

Garfinkel takes a different approach by beginning with a different assumption. Garfinkel assumes that there *is* order in the plenum, and makes uncovering that orderliness the task of ethnomethodology. Garfinkel expresses the difference between the FA assumption of an unorderly plenum—that is, the -[ ]- —with a different set of ticked brackets:

$$\{\ \}$$

Such assumed orderliness can also lend itself to formal analytic method, which Garfinkel represents through the following expression:

$$\{\ \} \rightarrow (\ )$$

Garfinkel argues that while the → ( ) can allow for various observations and generalizations, they lose the phenomenon of "the lived phenomenal properties" of ⦃ ⦄ (2002, p. 151). In my examination of Alice's work, I'll be drawing on a uniquely adequate understanding of both Emily's classroom and Alice's literate action to develop an account of how social facts are produced in the "river teeth" writing activity, and how development emerges from witnessably concrete practices amidst that activity. I will be using the ticked brackets to indicate how orderliness is produced in and through Alice's work—just-here, just-now, with just-these-tools and just-these actors. The labels within the ticked brackets, then, operate as more than simply codes: they call attention to the ongoing work, the methods of interaction, through which social order (and, by extension, the flow of classroom life as it may be described ethnographically) is perpetuated. The labels, in other words, describe the work through which the reality of the classroom is co-constructed, the ways in which students and teachers work to make sense of what is going on—and, as a result, what they should do next.

On May 23, after the class finished its daily warm-up and announcements, Emily and her class performed a ⁅desk organizing⁆ activity, which oriented them all to the work of their "river teeth" writing. The act of ⁅desk organizing⁆ in Emily's classroom is an interrelated set of responsive practices through which Emily and her students come to build and make sense of a transition between activities. Throughout the year that I observed Emily's classes, ⁅desk organizing⁆ emerged as a stable, coordinated practice.

Emily began ⁅desk organizing⁆ after she finished some announcements. "All right, for class today what you will need is . . . this packet that says 'river teeth' on it," said Emily, holding up a blank packet of assignments for the "river teeth" unit. "If you were absent," she continued, "it's probably in the mailbox," referring to a space at the back of her classroom where students who were absent in the previous class could pick up copies of their assignments.

After Emily made this announcements, students began taking their "river teeth" packets out of their backbacks. Some engaged in brief conversations with neighbors, while others, like Alice, remained silent. Emily answered a follow-up question about a previous announcement amidst the rustle of paper and the quiet hum of conversation. After answering the question, Emily said "All right, clear your desks except for this, please. And a pen or pencil." Students continued to put away materials and carry on quiet conversations while Emily helped a student looking in the mailbox for a packet. At this point, the ⁅desk organizing⁆ is well underway. Emily used a projector to show her table of contents for the "river teeth" packet, announcing "All right. So we're just going to catch up on this a little bit. Um. This should be the only thing you have out. This is it." Emily then said she would "remind you of what we were doing, because it's been a little while."

Although Emily has done the entirety of speaking to the entire class, the act of ⁅desk organizing⁆ is a collective act, begun, developed, and concluded via the material, physical, and social action of the members of the classroom. Emily's direction to "clear your desks" did more than clear desks: it set in motion a series of material interactions that led both Emily and her students to orient their attention to the work of the "river teeth" packet.

Emily built upon ⸠desk organizing⸡ with another haeccetic feature of social order in her classroom by beginning ⸠instruction reading⸡. Emily first directs students to a particular page in the packet with spoken language: "Down here are the essential questions, and I want to remind you what we're doing." The "down here" is accompanied by a gesture to the packet that is projected on to her television screen at the front of the room. Emily directs them further, down to "thematic questions." She repeats her instruction again, followed by a request for a specific student to begin reading: "I need everyone to look here where it says 'thematic questions.'" She then calls on a particular student, asking "will you read them to us?"

I begin my review of Alice's "river teeth" writing with ⸠desk organizing⸡ because we can see this as the beginning of a clear pattern of social ordering *just-here, just-now, in-just-this-classroom,* and with *just-these-tools.* Emily and her students produce an interactional order, a back-and-forth set of activities in speaking, movement, and material use that allow them to create joint meaning out of a particular segment of a large packet of activities during the ⸠instruction reading⸡. This order is an accomplishment, an achievement that effaces the conditions of its own creation. But it is from this accomplishment that Alice participates in the co-construction of the "river teeth" writing activity. By a continued reading through assignments and small writing activities in the packet, Emily and her students (including Alice) come to understand the page in Figure 1.1 as a site for recording important experiences in particular ways—through writing, illustrations, and color.

In the movement from ⸠desk organizing⸡ to ⸠instruction reading⸡ to ⸠writing activity⸡, the purpose of the writing activity—in this case, the "river teeth" writing—becomes sensible to both Emily and her students. Alice, when faced with a blank river and ten minutes to generate writing to fill it, understands her task not merely through the words on the page or the instructions of the teacher as the ⸠writing activity⸡ gets underway, but also through the way that Emily and her students have ordered themselves socially toward the writing task. By attending carefully to the haecceitic construction of social order, as evidenced in ⸠desk organizing⸡, ⸠instruction reading⸡, and ⸠writing activity⸡, we can see the production of social facts that led Alice to the "river teeth" writing that she did. Furthermore, we can begin to identify what triggered her work with the reflective writing, and whether or not we may consider it to be a sign of development.

As the ten minutes of the ⸠writing activity⸡ unfolds, Alice keeps her attention on her page, rarely looking up to acknowledge students as they walk by, or to look at Emily as she occasionally makes suggestions for "river teeth" ideas. Furthermore, there is no evidence in Alice's subsequent writing hinting that she took any of Emily's suggestions, such as focusing on the first days of school, or birthday parties. A close look at the pace of her writing activity, however, and the work on the page suggest that a slight shift in Alice's pattern of literate action begins here, and endures across the remainder of her "river teeth" writing.

Alice's ten-minute writing activity can be broken into two segments: an initial, consistent flow of writing for approximately five minutes, followed by a gradual taper with a brief flurry of writing in the final five minutes. The bulk of Alice's attention seems to lie at the start of her writing, as her later "river teeth" narratives focus on falling off of her bike and being pushed off of a trampoline, which she wrote about early on. Though unpleasant moments, Alice values recalling them in her writing and remembering them long-term, based on the reflection she wrote (see Figure 1.2).

Attending to the ordering practices of the classroom leading into the "river teeth" writing activity, as well as the material work of Alice during the ten-minute {writing activity} shows how Alice's activity was oriented to the task of writing "river teeth" ideas. Alice, to this point, has acted how she has always acted in the classroom: she silently participates in the co-construction of social action in the classroom, and she uses the aligned understandings that emerge from that work as a tool to accomplish the tasks at hand. But if we turn to the writing that occurs between the {writing activity} and the reflective writing that later happens, a subtle change in Alice's literate action emerges.

Figure 1.3 shows the result of a later {writing activity}, one that builds off of the May 23 {writing activity}, at least in part. In this sample, Alice recalls her sister pushing her off of a trampoline at a young age. This is something she drew and wrote about in her "river teeth" idea writing on May 23, but here Alice follows it up with an entire story. She closes the story with an interesting sentence: "My sister came up to me and apoligized, and she realized that it is all fun and games until you do something dum." This sentence is uncharacteristic of Alice's other writing in that she subverts a common expression to signal a criticism of another person—in this case, her sister and her actions in pushing Alice off of the trampoline. Though it appears to have been in part motivated by an option in the left-hand column, this is still a second unexpected move that emerges from the fairly ordinary activity that Alice performed during the May 23 "river teeth" writing.

If we locate this sentence between Alice's initial "river teeth" writing and her subsequent reflection, a pattern begins to emerge that distinguishes itself from the other writing that Alice has done. Alice begins by engaging in "river teeth" writing in what has become a fairly typical manner for her. Her pattern of literate action during the {writing activity} suggests focused early writing followed by a tapering of activity, and the writing done in those first five minutes correlates with the extensive later writing she would do. In this writing, Alice takes on some tasks that she hasn't taken on previously: she repurposes a common expression to underscore her own claim, and she engages more explicitly with a reflective activity than she has in the past. Alice demonstrates, in this series of writings, that her attention toward the series of tasks she co-constructs with her fellow students and her teacher may be changing in some subtle way. The {writing activity} does not stand on its own as the isolated activity Alice has treated it as in the past; rather, the text that emerges from the activity carries forward into the narratives that Alice creates. These narratives are artifacts of other ⟨writing activity⟩ moments, of course, but they suggest that, within them, Alice privileged particular ⟨writing activity⟩ moments in her past (which was made materially present by the "river teeth" text) in order to shape her writing. Furthermore, the final product of this writing (that is, the narratives) became documents that she valued in her reflective work on the unit. Alice, in her "river teeth" writing, has begun to stitch together the products of her ⟨writing activity⟩ throughout the unit, resulting in a final product (i.e., "river teeth" narratives) that she expresses as being valuable.

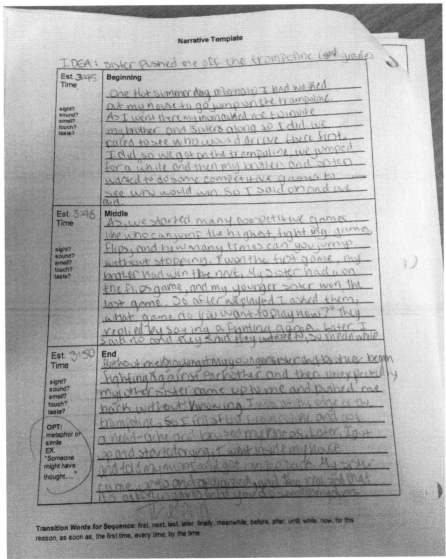

*Figure 1.3. Alice's "Trampoline" river teeth moment.*

Turning back to the issue of respecifying writing development ethnomethodologically, we can trace in Alice's interactions and writing a slowly shifting coordination of the talk, tools, and texts around her. Alice begins the unit with the same solitary focus on her writing as she has in previous units, but as the "river teeth" writing experiences develop, she attends to the material world around her differently, materially drawing on particular past ⁅writing activity⁆ moments to develop the more complex texts that are being socially ordered into relevance.

## Following the Phenomenon: Building on Alice's Developmental Candidacy

In the above section, I draw on Garfinkel's (2002) concept of ticked brackets to highlight the social construction of the initial "river teeth" activity and build, from that, an understanding of how Alice's literate action may have developed. Attending to the production of social order in Emily's room set the stage for understanding how Alice shifted her patterns of literate action—how she came to see the interconnected nature of multiple assignments and respond with her writing accordingly, and how the products to emerge from those shifted patterns came to be valued by her during a ⁅writing activity⁆ that she has historically done little writing in. We can identify this as a transformation in her serial production of local social order while producing the texts required for an academic unit. According to my earlier ethnomethodological respecification, this would seem to be a candidate moment of literate action development. But the tools available for this analysis do not provide sufficient insight for making a determination for or against development on their own. For now, then, I am going to leave this as only a candidate. In the next three chapters, I will further articulate a logic-in-use through attention to more moments of literate action with some of Alice's fellow students. In Chapter 5, I'll bring this logic-in-use to bear on Alice's literate action and make a case for whether this "counts" as development. First, however, I would like to articulate the differences between the ticked brackets and what Garfinkel (2002) labels the formal analytical brackets—( ).

Garfinkel's ticket brackets continually brought attention back to the way in which a given activity, whether it be clearing desks, reading instructions, or engaging in writing, were socially produced accomplishments. Doing so revealed Alice's participation in those accomplishments and, through that revelation, the ways in which her literate action was beginning to change. Formal analytic methods and their attendant sociological abstractions—which, as Garfinkel argues, ignores the order inherent in the plenum—may have lost both the accomplishments and the developmental transformations that came along with those accomplishments. This is not to deny the obvious value of such methods in other research studies, but rather to suggest that, when it comes to understanding literate action development—particularly through the lifespan—such methods run the risk of losing the very phenomena they hope to describe. It is my argument that such methods *do* have a place in studying lifespan literate action development—indeed, as I argue in Chapter 9, we would not be able to grow as a subfield without it—but that they need to be repurposed, respecified, and misread in order to enable researchers to adequately and effectively follow the phenomenon of literate action and its development through the entirety of a life.

# Chapter 2. The Haecceitic Production of Writing in Emily's Classroom

In Chapter 1, I argued that, if we are to look through the lifespan at writing development, we need to see development as participation in social action. Toward that end, I suggested an ethnomethodological orientation may serve as an appropriate base from which to build a complex, coherent theory of lifespan writing development—or, more specifically, lifespan *literate action* development. Using the example of Alice, I identified a *candidate moment of literate action development* that highlighted both the possibilities of such an approach and the questions that arise when we attend to social action as the centerpiece of our understanding of development. In this chapter, I expand the ethnomethodological framework I began in Chapter 1, introducing several new terms to fully bring researcher attention to an actor-oriented perspective—and, more specifically, an *individuated* actor-oriented perspective through the serial production of social order.

## The Scenic Aspects of Literate Action Development: Focusing on Practice

Alice's example in the previous chapter underscores the importance of attending to the *scenic* aspects of literate action. Instead of attempting to frame Alice's decision-making as internal—that is, the result of cognitive work—I instead traced the material work of Alice: the way she organized her desk, the pace of her writing, the ways in which she seemed responsive to her colleagues and the language of her teacher, her patterns of interaction with both the writing on her desk and the writing on the classroom television, etc. Ethnomethodologists argue that social action is located in these *haecceities*: the just-here, just-now, with-just-these-people, just-these-tools, and just-this-talk (Garfinkel, 2002). Turning to an internalized series of choices, an identity of a *whole person* (Rawls, 2005), or structures standing independent of interaction is a turning away from the constitutive work of social order, social action, and—by extension—individuated participation in that social action. In other words, other "turns" away from the constitutive work of social order risks *losing the phenomenon* of that order, and creating understandings of social action (and, by extension, *literate* action) that obscure the sites of its accomplishment.

For these reasons, ethnomethodology has been understood as radically empirical, as it attends to that which is scenic—that is, available at the scenes of the co-construction of social order. Alice does not compose her drawing of falling off of a trampoline in her mind and realize it through her pencil: she engages in the practice of drawing to participate in the social action of the classroom and, by extension, sets the stage (that is, creates the product) for her later literate action when she is writing her "river teeth" stories. Her co-constitution, with her class-mates, of the ⧘writing activity⧙ in Emily's class that day was an accomplishment of social ordering and, perhaps, a springboard for her own literate action develop-ment. As Alice engaged in the ⧘writing activity⧙, she made her actions intelligible to both others and herself, and they did the same. The mutually-recognizable, interactive work that these actors did is expressed in ethnomethodological lan-guage as *practices*.[3] Practices are the ways in which we make our actions recogniz-able to others as well as ourselves; likewise, practices make others' actions sensible to us. Alice, in her co-construction of the ⧘writing activity⧙ in Emily's class, was engaging in practices with others in order to engage in that co-construction.

The observability of practices is what allows ethnomethodology to remain rigorously empirical in its studies, as well as what allows it to move beyond the focused studies of specific sites of traffic stops, debates, etc. For ethnomethod-ologists, what matters is not whole individuals but *actors*, aspects of individuals brought to bear on moments of social action that have competence in creating situated order through mutually intelligible actions. A good launching point for thinking about this—though it perhaps risks too-easy (and, later, obfuscating) connections with Goffman's work—is to consider actors on a stage. An actor on a stage is playing a particular role, participating in a scene in order to move along a production of a particular play or show. What we see of the actor in the instance of the scene of a play is analogous to what we see of a person in any given social interaction. It is a particular aspect of an always-in-process person. Ethnomethodologists aim to see what this actor does to produce social order through practice. Practices are the means through which mutually intelligible actions are accomplished, and the ability of readers to make sense of particular sites of study—i.e., the rendering of these actions as *intelligible*—carries with it more general implications for social order.

But the use of practice in this text has a different purpose than ethnomethodol-ogists: in this text, I am interested in using practices to highlight how individuated actors *transform the practices they engage in* while performing literate action. To continue the theatre analogy above, while an ethnomethodologist might look at the performance of an actor in a given scene, but a focus on development would encourage us to look across multiple scenes, to identify the ways in which an actor can transform their acting in one performance and carry that transforma-tion into future performances. Practice, then, is an important term in our grow-ing understanding of literate action development. Individuated actors work with other individuated actors in groups through *practices* to form those groups and create situated social order in those groups. Tracing the practices at work in Em-ily's classroom can bring to our attention the production of social order, such

---

3. "Practices" is a frequently-used term in Writing Studies and the research tradi-tions that much of Writing Studies draws from. I have avoided these connections to the moment in order to treat "practice" as it is ethnomethodologically understood.

as {writing activity} and other social orderings like it, and bring forward from those social orderings acts of individuated development. Balancing an analysis of the production of social order with individuated, enduring transformations is a difficult act, and practices is the mechanism that can support such difficult work.

In this framework, the concept of practice solves one of the issues raised at the end of the introduction to Part I: how to identify moments of change when any given moment of literate action is, in so many ways, unique to that particular moment. It resolves the contentiousness between difference and repetition (Pennycook, 2010) in terms of literate action as a next move toward an *actor-oriented perspective*. Through practices, we can identify the repetition of action by the mutually-identifiable practice that emerges in members' co-construction of social order. As Alice engages in {writing activity}, then, we can turn to the ways in which other actors in Emily's classroom sequentially (Rawls, 2005) coordinate their own literate actions in order to identify her work as another instantiation of the practice of {writing activity}.

Practice solves the problem of how to identify repetition, so that an actor-oriented frame for identifying and describing literate action development can be further articulated. But the issue of repetition was only one part of a two-part problem. The second part is identifying the ways in which differences become meaningful, come to transform a social practice for an individuated actor so that (a) mutual intelligibility remains and (b) the actor is able to act *through* that mutual intelligibility in "new" ways that endure, whatever "new" may mean. The second part of this problem will emerge after an actor-oriented perspective on practice is more fully articulated.

In order to engage in this articulation, I turn to a description of Emily's classroom. Emily's classroom will be a site through which I examine, in Chapters Three and Four, several instances of candidate literate action development. From these candidate moments, I will be able to draw, in Chapter 5, a concept of the *totality of the literate experience*, which we can then use to make sense of the lived reality of literate action development. In this chapter, I provide an actor-oriented perspective of the ebb and flow of social ordering in Emily's classroom, based on my year of observations in her room. Emily's classroom offers a strategic and perspicuous site for tracing literate action development through an ethnomethodological lens: strategic because it provides a wide range of literate action that is new for the writers engaged in it, and perspicuous because the writing often happens in the classroom, making it easily available for view via participant observation.

Below, I provide an outline of the social order produced with, for, and through literate action in Emily's classroom. This detail will inform the individuated acts of literate action development that I articulate in Chapters Three and Four. I begin this detailing with the work of Emily, the teacher in the classes that I observed. I do this in order to highlight the material decisions that Emily makes, which will in turn shape the production of social order in the classroom. Emily has a very material power to produce social order in her class that her students to not: she can be in her classroom before the start of the academic year; organize the desks, posters, books, and other materials; decide what copies of which materials will be made and available to students; and organize seating assignments.

To be sure, the students in Emily's classroom talk and act Emily's organizational attempts into being, but they do so as a response to the work that Emily has already done. If we think of the academic year as a continuing series of interactions, Emily takes the first move in the work that she does to organize her classroom at the start of the academic year. Because of this initial move by Emily, I begin detailing the production of classroom order with her. From there, I work my way into how the classroom is further talked and acted into being, which I use to frame the literate action development I witness in later chapters.

## Emily

Emily is a fifteen-year veteran of the classroom. A graduate of the University of California system with a BA in English, Emily earned her teaching credential and M.Ed. through the UC system as well before moving into the classroom. Emily is a National Writing Project fellow who frequently participates in her local NWP branch. The year before the current study, Emily completed her submission for the National Board of Professional Teaching Standards (NBPTS). She was awarded National Board Certification during the winter of my data collection, which she earned on her first submission—an accomplishment that only 48% of NBCT candidates accomplish in any given year (MacKenzie & Harris, 2008).

The start of Emily's career, by her own account, had been rather difficult, particularly in terms of classroom management issues. This difficulty led her to focus on developing her classroom management skills, which can be easily observed in action: students have clearly demarcated rules for participation and activity, neatly defined times for assigned reading and writing activities, and regularized routines that students have learned throughout the day.

In addition to her extensive classroom management skills, Emily is well-versed in the English Language Arts subject matter. Emily possesses the outward credentials (NBCT, M.Ed.) to signal that she understands how her subject matter works and how to teach it to her students in multiple, effective ways, and her activities within the classroom realizes those credentials. During her time as a classroom teacher, NWP Fellow, and leader within her department, Emily has constructed a set of understandings about teaching her craft that she would deploy in order to deal with the constant reforms that she has endured throughout the duration of her teaching career.

## Sequences of Activity in Emily's Classroom

Activity in Emily's classroom is organized collaboratively around a series of timed activities. When students walk into the classroom at the start of the period, they can see a list of activities on the board directly ahead of them. They can also see, on the television screen above the board, the ⦃Do Now⦄ activity that they are to begin class with. This is normally an activity to build what Emily refers to as *sentence sense* among students, although students use the ⦃Do Now⦄ to copy tasks in their agenda at the start of each week. Regardless of the activity, however, Emily greets the class with a "Good morning" or "Good afternoon" (what I label, in ethnomethodological terms, as ⦃Good Morning⦄) once the bell rings, and gives students between three and four minutes to complete the activity. Emily uses a timer at the front of the room to track the time. Emily normally provides students with some guidance before starting the timer. When time expires, Emily checks on the progress of her students. Occasionally, she gives them an extra minute or two if they need it. During most of the observations, however, students had completed the activity and were ready to move on.

After the students finish the ⦃Do Now⦄, Emily discusses the ⦃Do Now⦄ activity with the students, calling on students either randomly or by taking volunteers. The number of volunteers that Emily takes varies with the complexity of the exercise and the problems that students have with it, although most ⦃Do Now⦄ activity reviews involved two to five students.

Once the ⦃Do Now⦄ was discussed, Emily holds a brief ⦃Review⦄ of the class objective and the schedule of events for the class. The discussion of lesson activities normally expanded into the larger assignments of which they were part. For example, a discussion of a writing task that would turn into part of a larger blog writing assignment would lead to a discussion of the blog writing assignment in general. During this period, students often asked clarifying questions about assignment content, due dates, and specific requirements. Occasionally, students would also interject their own interests into the conversation, which Emily welcomed but also continually brought back to the review of classroom activities.

When Emily finished reviewing the tasks for the day, she engaged in ⦃Desk Organizing⦄, which was structured by Emily's sense of timing. Emily would tell students what they had to have out on their desks, and sometimes even where on their desks it needed to be. She would also give students a set amount of time to do this, often 42 seconds. Forty-two seconds is the usual amount of time (according to Emily) between the start of a pop song and its first chorus. Emily often played music during this time, and expected students to be prepared at the start of the chorus.

After the students completed their organizing activity, Emily began the ⦃Activity⦄. These activities would vary widely, from reading to writing to watching video or even moving around the room. But the ⦃Activity⦄ was itself an accomplishment, a haecceity through which social order was perpetuated in the class. The chain of interaction—the teacher providing instructions, the students taking up those instructions both at the moment they are given and the moment they are left to take up those instructions—occurred as a manner of these individuated actors moving toward the end of class.

Near the conclusion of class, Emily would often provide students with an ⟨Exit Ticket⟩, or a writing activity that encouraged students to reflect on their activities from the day's lesson. Exit tickets were not offered every lesson, and sometimes a planned exit ticket was scrapped from the lesson plan if Emily ran out of time. The above description provides a general overview of how Emily's class operated in a given class period. While there were quite a few varieties of class action that emerged from the ⟨Good morning⟩, ⟨Do Now⟩ – ⟨Review⟩ – ⟨Desk Organizing⟩ – ⟨Activity⟩ – ⟨Exit Ticket⟩ unfolding of a class period, the interactional pattern was observable throughout all of the lessons that I attended throughout the academic year.

## Emily's Classroom

Emily's classroom is located in the far back corner of the school, nestled between another English teacher's classroom and a hallway leading to an attached charter school. Outside of the classroom runs a sidewalk that winds across a small grove of trees and classrooms to the auditorium, computer lab, offices, and a massive common area that the students use for lunch. A set of windows in the back of Emily's classroom looks out over the trees, walkways, and other classrooms.

*Figure 2.1. Emily's Library.*

Students enter Emily's classroom in the back right corner of the room. To their left runs, beneath the windows, a combination of bookshelves and class materials.

Next to the door sit a garbage can and a set of shelves dedicated to school-related texts. Just past that, Emily has put a large cart of class materials. On top of the materials rests a large set of cubby holes that Emily uses to put spare worksheets, handouts, and other materials from the week's lessons. Students who are absent can draw their missing materials from here. On top of the cubbyholes are baskets for returned work and late work.

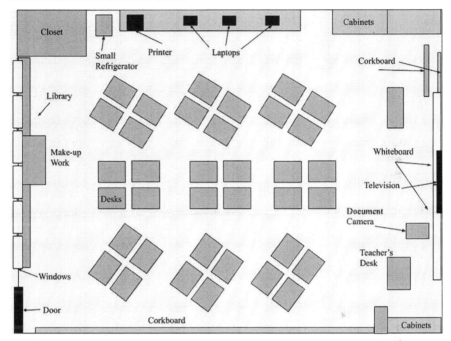

*Figure 2.2. Emily's classroom layout.*

Another set of shelves for school-related texts rests on the other side of the class materials. Next to that is Emily's personal library, which contains a set of young adult literature that students can sign out if they wish. Emily has a set of boxed books (presumably also course-related) next to her library. The corner that connects the back wall to the far left wall contains a small closet that I have never seen Emily use.

The far left wall is dedicated largely to technology. Emily has three Apple laptops in the classroom, two of which she acquired with a grant and one of which she brought from home. These laptops are locked in a closet every night, but are left out during the school day for students to use. The laptops are on long, low tables that occupy the middle space of the wall. Behind them rest more course textbooks that students rely on for certain units. To the left of the laptops rests a printer. This printer is for Emily's use but is also linked to other teacher computers in Emily's hallway, as teachers regularly enter the room to pick up printed material. Between the printer and the closet there is a spare desk, where I regularly sat during my observations.

*Figure 2.3. Outside of Emily's classroom.*

To the right of the laptops, running all the way to the corner between the left wall and the front wall of the room, is a set of closets that Emily keeps locked. These closets contain benchmark writing assessments, and, at night, the laptops. The closets also contain more of Emily's class supplies, such as glue sticks and colored pencils.

The front of the room is taken up almost entirely by Emily's white board. A small blank space between the closet and the whiteboard is taken up by a rolling bulletin board. The whiteboard runs from the bulletin board to Emily's desk, which takes up—along with another closet and a set of filing cabinets—the corner of the room between the front wall and the right wall. Early in the year, Emily's desk faced the left wall, which allowed her to come out from behind her desk more easily and work with students. Later in the year, however, Emily moved her desk to face away from the front wall, so that she could sit behind her desk and look out over the students in the classroom. Behind Emily's desks are several small bulletin boards with various personal and public items tacked on to them.

Above the whiteboard and bulletin boards are a large-screen LCD television, which Emily uses frequently through her AppleTV and her document camera. Emily also has several posters scattered along the upper edge of her walls, not just in the front of the room but on the left and right walls as well. These posters contain directions for classroom activity, definitions of important terms, examples of student work, and posters of literature, poetry, movies, etc.

The right wall of Emily's classroom, which runs back to the door, is largely covered with student work. The closet, filing cabinet, and desk of Emily's take space away from the corner of the wall, but the rest of the wall, at eye level, is dedicated to large bulletin boards containing student work. Emily changes these boards every few weeks, giving many different students the opportunity to have their work displayed. However, she rarely references the boards during her work in class.

Above these boards are more guidelines for students. She has several handwritten posters that describe the purposes of English, entry and exit routines, group work reminders, and reminders of "how to earn an A" for small writing assignments. This wall also contains the clock, which ran about a minute ahead of the official school time (and thus the bell schedule) for most of the school year.

Inside of these walls sit, in addition to Emily's desk and two smaller desks that she uses to collect student work and organize her handouts prior to a lesson, thirty-seven desks. These desks are arranged in nine groups of four. The nine groups are also aligned in three rows of three. The desks of the middle row point straight ahead, while the desks on either side of the middle row are angled slightly to allow students to see the front center of the board while looking straight ahead.

## Progression of the School Year in Emily's Classroom

Emily's class moved through several units throughout the course of the school year. Each of these units was deliberately marked off by Emily in several ways. Primarily, this marking was accomplished through the use of the English section of students' school binders. Goodland Middle School asked all students to purchase a large, three-ring binder for the start of the school year. Students organized these binders by class, with each class getting a separate section. Emily's students, then, arrived in class with a section reserved for Language Arts in a three-ring binder. Emily took advantage of this opportunity by organizing her handouts (and leading the students' organization of the handouts) around this binder section.

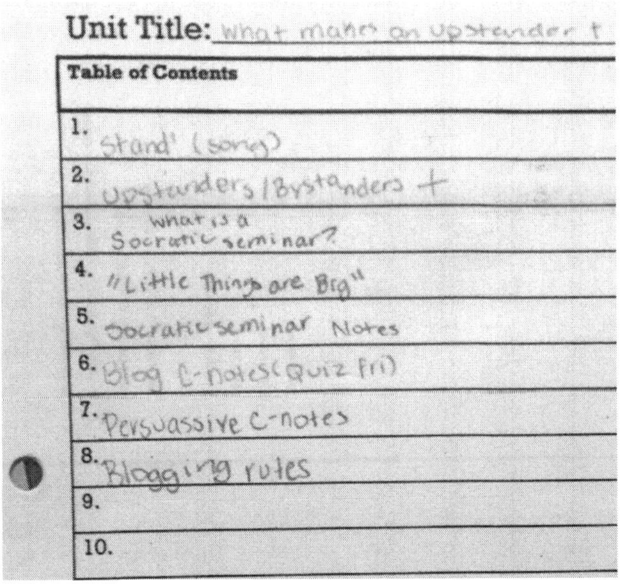
**Unit Title:** What makes an upstander t

| **Table of Contents** |
|---|
| 1. "Stand" (song) |
| 2. Upstanders/Bystanders + |
| 3. What is a Socratic seminar? |
| 4. "Little Things are Big" |
| 5. Socratic seminar Notes |
| 6. Blog C-notes (Quiz Fri) |
| 7. Persuassive C-notes |
| 8. Blogging rules |
| 9. |
| 10. |

*Figure 2.4. A sample table of contents sheet.*

First, students were provided, at the start of each unit, with a new Table of Contents sheet and some introductory materials. Emily used this, as well as the process of collecting older Table of Contents packets, as a signal that the class was moving into a new set of activities with a new theme. As the class continued activities in the unit, they were given additional material to add to their Table of Contents. Once the unit came to a close—either with a benchmark exam or some other culminating activity—Emily had her students read through their sheets, highlight the key points, and write a short reflection on their learning on the back of the Table of Contents sheet. The students then removed all of their sheets from the English section of their binders, stapled them together, and handed them in for a grade. This reflective act not only signaled the end of a unit, but the start of a new one, as students came to understand that this activity led them directly into the introduction for their next unit.

Emily's units varied widely in their length and amount of recorded sheets. Some units, in fact, required two separate packets with Table of Contents sheets in order to keep all of the writing organized. These Table of Contents sheets, as well as their organization, provides a clear pattern of the unit organization of Emily's classes throughout the school year. Each unit title represents a theme that tied all of the work that students completed in Emily's class together during that unit. Emily felt that the organization of units according to themes helped students make sense of the activities that they were completing, and gave the many, disparate activities that students completed some sort of direction throughout the course of a given unit.

Some assignments, of course, were persistent throughout the school year without reference to the unit themes. The writer's notebooks, for example, always followed the same framework regardless of classroom activity. The "Do Now" activity was also structured in very similar ways throughout the year, rarely connecting to a unit theme. When a unit theme connection was brought in to a "Do Now" activity, it was a coincidental moment: Emily did not try to bring the theme of the "Do Now" activity into the unit activities.

The above description of the units and the Tables of Contents used to organize them outlines the way in which classroom writing activity was organized throughout the school year. This classroom writing activity, of course, was also tied to student activity as they attempted to participate meaningfully in the unfolding structure of class. The genred forms of writing that students participated in also shaped their participation in many ways.

## Turning toward an Actor-Oriented Perspective

The social ordering power of the practices of ⟨Good morning⟩, ⟨Do Now⟩, ⟨Review⟩, ⟨Desk Organizing⟩, ⟨Activity⟩, and ⟨Exit Ticket⟩ have, together, constructed a rough orientation of an actor's perspective on the everyday production of Emily's classroom for a next first time. This is as the ethnomethodological breakdown is intended: the mechanisms through which social order is produced and maintained are articulated so that others may understand how to make sense of that articulation.

It is important to remember that the six practices identified in Emily's classrooms are not concepts for understanding what Emily's students did—rather, they *are* the activities that these actors co-constructed together, time and again, throughout the entire academic year. These practices *created* Emily's classroom, made it sensible for students and for Emily, even as this sensibility-construction allowed those in the room to likewise make sense of themselves. Each next-first-time instantiation of these practices was an accomplishment of the students in that classroom, an accomplishment that was the classroom itself.

One drawback to the practices identified above is that they give the mistaken impression, at times, of a concreteness that, while existent in practice, is not actually there. In other words, these practices are not as taken-for-granted as their invisibility in the eyes of the actors would lead one to believe. Their constructed nature, social as it is, leaves room for uncertainty in the co-constitutive work of individual group members. In other words, in the scenic production of social order, much may be left undecided. An actor may engage in ⸨writing activity⸩—that is, an ⸨Activity⸩ oriented toward writing—in one particular class period and, while engaging in practices that co-constitute that activity, be faced with uncertainty in the unfolding of that co-constitution due to the specificities of the scenic accomplishment of the work.

A rather straighforward example might be a student who co-constitutes the early stages of a ⸨writing activity⸩ by turning to her backpack to take out the required forms. In her work to take out those forms, she misses Emily's instructions and has to steal glances at her classmate's forms to see which one they have oriented to. This instance of uncertainty is neither long-lasting nor difficult to overcome through attention to different scenic features of the situation. But uncertainty and its role in the ongoing production of social order can be much more complex—and, as we will see below, can be a site of developmental moments for the writers being studied. Garfinkel's *Toward a Sociological Theory of Information* provides some useful framing about uncertainty and how we cope with it. Below, I trace out Garfinkel's conception of information and repurpose it for the demands of the study of literate action development, which I can then use to think through the complexity of Emily's classroom and the development captured within it.

## A Sociological Perspective on Information and the Concept of What-Comes-Next

*Toward a Sociological Theory of Information*, as Rawls points out in her extensive editorial introduction, "represents a significant piece of work . . . that has been essentially lost to scholarship since it was first written" (2008, p. 7). The focus of his work is, as the title indicates, an attempted sociological theory of information. At the heart of this theory is the idea that information—and the people who take up and make sense of that information—is always incomplete.

The work that individuals do to make sense of the world around them, to make themselves sensible to others, is always done with and through incomplete understandings. This basic insight is key to understanding the very different approach that Garfinkel takes toward understanding information and how it is shared (or, in perhaps more specific language, co-constructed) with others. This idea of incompleteness is what makes Garfinkel's text such a useful addition to understanding uncertainty.

Garfinkel's understanding of how information is created and shared, revealed in an early text, is at odds with many of his contemporaries, and indeed it is at odds with many theoretical framings of information today. Rawls describes Garfinkel's theory as belonging "to the classic period in the development of information theory—1935–1955—but as a heretofore unrecognized alternative voice" (2008, p. 12). Framing information sharing as happening amidst incomplete knowledge turns the attention of the researcher from the flow of information and to the work that individuals do to attempt to maintain the flow of information. If our knowledge is always partial, how can we go about identifying and making sense of information?

Garfinkel's answer is to examine information exchange as something that is *constituted*, rather than done. Information is not shared but rather created by social actors at work. In the unfolding co-construction of social order, something becomes recognized (constituted) as information that can then be acted upon. This understanding of information as co-constituted carries an intersubjective framing: that is, what *I* call information in a given moment will also be information to *you* because we are co-constructing the situation together and locating information in it as we do that work. Below, I develop an understanding of this concept that is individuated in nature, which will allow us to see not just how information emerges for people in a given situation, but how what may be indexed as information for some will not be for others.

Central to Garfinkel's notion of information is the *anomaly*. Garfinkel argues that, without some anomalous aspect that the constitutive order of everyday life has to deal with, there can be no information. In other words, for information to be conveyed, there must be something that sense needs to be made *of*. The unexpected, the uncertain, is the ground from which information emerges. As actors constitutively create a situation to deal with the unexpected and uncertain, they generate practices that make the unexpected expected, the insensible sensible. The anomalous is co-constituted into something known, something that can be worked through in subsequent co-constitutions of social action.

Garfinkel develops his notion of information through the work of organizations—that is, he tries to understand how information gets recognized, taken up, and acted on by the co-constitutive ordering of social action by members of organizations in chains of local engagement. Anomalies develop in these co-constitutive interactions, and their resolution (that is, information) emerges from members' methods as they attempt to make sense of the anomaly. This anomaly can be pulled into the social order through constitutive practices, or it can fracture the social order, leaving actors with the work (and its accompanying moral indignation) of repairing it. Garfinkel's past work on breaching experiments (Garfinkel, 1967) provide evidence of this. Briefly, Garfinkel would ask his students to behave in ways that were counter to the social order as it was usually produced—continually asking follow-up questions, acting as a boarder in one's own home, etc.—and then to report on the results of these disruptions. These "experiments" highlighted the consequences of inserting an unable-to-be-resolved anomaly into the ongoing work of social order in particular times and places. The unwitting participants in these experiences (such a study would surely struggle to receive IRB approval today) were unable to resolve the anomalies, and in the end announced their indignation with comments such as "drop dead!" or some other such dismissive content.

Garfinkel's work on information sets the stage for taking yet another step toward an actor-oriented perspective on literate action. Information is introduced into the constitutive ordering of social action when anomalies arise among the work of members of groups to establish social situations. But in order to make sense of this introduction of information, we need a broader conceptualization of how constitutive order is established in the first place. We can understand, from an actor-oriented perspective, the practices through which social order comes to be established in the classroom, and the concept of information provides us with a lens to consider how newness is realized and acted through in that social action. By fleshing out further how we could conceptualize the ways in which information is introduced to social situations, we can move forward with conceptualizing an actor-oriented perspective of literate action.

This conceptualization begins with Garfinkel's (1963) notion of *trust*, and the ways in which that trust comes to be realized (and betrayed) in the ongoing work of actors. Garfinkel suggests that part of what makes the fragile work of social action *seem* enduring, available for use, and able to be taken for granted is the work that members do to *create* that seeming. Garfinkel (1963, 1967) makes the case that disruptions to this seeming-ness is a moral issue, with other actors involved in the production of social order reacting strongly and negatively to such disruptions. In his breaching experiments, Garfinkel showed how simple acts like asking for additional clarification, or revealing a tape-recorded conversation, can result in dramatic changes to the ongoing production of social order and strong emotions from those dramatic changes.

Trust, then, is an implicit requirement for producing social order: I act in a way that I believe you can understand, and I *also* believe that you will act on that understanding in ways that I can find sensible. The trust that we extend allows for us to have an idea, together, of what comes next in the work of producing social order. But though the practices we engage in may seem "durable" (Erickson, 2004, p. 140) as routines for producing social order, in fact each passing moment involves an array of what Erickson (2004) would call *tactical* work—adaptations of familiar routines to the production of the present (and unfolding) moment. As actors work together to constitute social action, they are working through the ongoing uncertainty of what the next moment will bring.

This uncertainty can best be characterized as *anxiety* in the first two of its dictionary definitions—an uneasiness about how the next moment will unfold, and a tense desire to shape that unfolding. I refer to this anxiety of the next moment conceptually as *What-Comes-Next*. Each passing moment in our lives is a moment of working through *What-Comes-Next*. The next moment, whether it be in an interaction, during writing, exercising, eating, or whatever, cannot be entirely expected. The practices that we engage in can *reduce* the uncertainty of *What-Comes-Next*, and many aspects of our lives may be co-constituted to do just that: we have morning routines, for instance, that pull us out of bed and to the car, office, and these routines, these practices, become deeply habitual in a very material sense. The location of the coffeemaker and the toothbrush, the earlier-in-the-week purchase of breakfast food, the remote starter for our car, etc., all co-ordinate, call out for action that pulls the actor through a specific set of practices that lead to arriving at work in a timely manner.

At other times, however, the production of social order becomes too different for our routines to bear: the anxiety of *What-Comes-Next*, in other words, becomes raised to a degree that our ongoing practices cannot account for. A first date, for instance, may be filled with pregnant pauses, repaired communication, and a tentative working-out of relatively straightforward activities such as walking through a doorway in a coordinated manner (Do I hold the door? Do I let her go first? She's gesturing that I go first—what do I do in response to that?). The next-first-time nature of our practices in these situations emphasize the *first*ness of the practice over the *next*ness, as opposed to the morning routine described above. In these moments of heightened uncertainty, our practices have the potential to change—sometimes in enduring ways, sometimes not. In certain situations such as the two cases above, the differences between heightened and reduced anxiety of *What-Comes-Next* is relatively obvious.

Adding *What-Comes-Next* and information to our list of concepts is a productive next step for framing our search for literate action development in Emily's classroom. By attending to practice, and seeing each instance of practicing as a way of managing *What-Comes-Next*, we can envision how novelty works its way into the ongoing production of social order. By attending to information, as a concept, we have some language for making sense of what happens when *What-Comes-Next* is so anomalous, uncertain, and unexpected that the practices we typically deploy to make sense of ourselves, others, and the objects around us struggle to meet the demands of the moment. What we do not yet have is a way to move into understanding when a difference in a given instantiation of a practice *endures* as a transformation of a practice. In the next section, I pull these three concepts together further and operationalize them for tracing development in Chapters Three and Four.

## Tracing Development through What-Comes-Next

The practices of Emily's classroom can be thought of as the tools for reducing the uncertainty of *What-Comes-Next* for the members in Emily's classroom. However, it would be incorrect to assume that these practices reduce uncertainty evenly across the student body. The actors in the classroom may have jointly co-constructed a practice to reduce uncertainty, but uncertainty may linger more for some actors than others. In other words, members' methods for reducing uncertainty in any given moment may differ. Tracing heightened uncertainty—identifying when information has to be wrestled with by individual students—is the starting point from which development can be traced.

With Alice's example in Chapter 1, I posited that a change in patterns of literate action could make a candidate for literate action development. A number of questions remain with this approach, but the concepts of practice, *What-Comes-Next* and information help us further round out this tentative concept of development and, by extension, further explore the consequences of such a label in the coming chapters.

*What-Comes-Next*, as a concept, brings attention not just to the work of members of a given social situation—in this case, a classroom—but additionally to the work of individuated actors within that set of members. Since all members are working, together, toward reducing the anxiety of *What-Comes-Next* in their moment-to-moment production of social action, the opportunity of attending to *What-Comes-Next* is everywhere, available with each passing moment of a social situation.

But the connection between *What-Comes-Next* and development has not yet been made clear. In Chapter 1, Alice's actions in her reflective writing activity and the work leading up to it seemed to be, based on a reading of development as participation in social action through writing that was established earlier in the chapter, a candidate for a developmental moment. Alice was clearly working through the uncertainty of *What-Comes-Next* in her writing, and making joint sense of the tasks being asked of her by Emily as the classes developed through the "river teeth" unit. *What-Comes-Next*, then, enables an actor-oriented framing of Alice's work, but does not, on its own, yield what is needed to be known about development. For that, we need to turn to information, and particularly, its relationship to *What-Comes-Next*.

If we are to think about development as emerging from the serial production of social order, then it follows that the serial production of social order is also, by extension, the ongoing reduction of anxiety in terms of *What-Comes-Next*. The ongoing work to establish the uncertainty of *What-Comes-Next* as known, rather than unknown, is the space within which literate action may develop. A central condition for this is elevated uncertainty: when a writer is unsure of what to do in the next moment, when the practice that sustains a fragile social situation breaks down, an opportunity arises to transform a practice in order to repair the situation and, in Brandt's (1990) words, keep writing going. It is at these moments that researchers must look in order to see development emerging. Moving forward, I will draw on Garfinkel's language and refer to such elevated uncertainty for an individuated actor—the point at which *What-Comes-Next* is so different that the practices a given actor normally engages in to make sense of ourselves and others struggle to contend with it—as *information*. Information, for our purposes in this text, refers to the anomalous aspects of an unfolding situation *for an individuated actor* that need to be rendered usable in the continued work of producing social order.

As noted above, however, any given change to the ways in which an actor resolves *What-Comes-Next* is not necessarily development, even with elevated levels of uncertainty. Say, for instance, that one of the keys on my keyboard begins malfunctioning as I engage in a writing task—a letter sometimes emerges on the Word document, but sometimes not. This elevates, to some degree, the uncertainty of my work as I go about finishing my writing task. I *may* get through writing a sentence that does not require the letter to be used, or used to a great enough degree that the malfunction becomes problematic—perhaps easier if the letter is "Q" rather than if it is a vowel. I might also stop my writing and attempt to fix the problem in some way. I could also just barrel ahead, striking the problematic key as often as necessary, and with as much force as necessary, to get the letter to appear.

Each of these options has me engaging in work to reduce an elevated uncertainty—a malfunctioning key on a keyboard. But none of this work is likely to result in developmental change in the production of literate action: at the very least, when I fix my keyboard or get another one, I will simply cease having an issue with it, and revert to the writing patterns I engaged in before. A change, then, is not in and of itself an instance of development. This change must *endure* across future recurrences of a practice—in other words, the practice must be altered, and that alteration must stand the test of future instances of a practice.

If we turn our attention back to the example of Alice in the previous chapter, we can perhaps make a case that this candidate instance of development has endurance, although not in the particulars of the case that I articulated alone. In reviewing my observations of Alice throughout the academic year, I noted that her work on her "river teeth" writing involved a configuration of references to earlier writing in her packet that she had not done in previous units. The text that she produces at the end of her packet comes to be heavily mediated by her drawings earlier in the unit. This re-orchestrated act of coordination, though occurring near the end of the year, happened across more than one "river teeth" writing episode, suggesting a kind of endurance across practices. While it would be more persuasive that this moment endured should Alice have had several opportunities over time to demonstrate such textual coordination, the work that she does with these documents may be sufficient to make a case that this candidate for literate action development is indeed an instance of it. Alice is participating in social action through a familiar practice, and doing so in a new way that persists across future instances of that practice-in-use.

Alice's example suggests that attending to the work of literate action through a lens that aligns practices, information, and *What-Comes-Next* may be a useful way of identifying an actor-oriented perspective on ways in which such practices change in lasting ways. Furthermore, the very nature of these concepts—that is, their endurance across the many stages of the lifespan—suggests a stable lens for examining writing not only at any point in the lifespan, but through multiple points in the lifespan. These concepts, in other words, may form a lens that can be a productive launching point for studies across ages, kinds of writing, and social situations.

Alice's example, however, has been insufficiently examined even within this framework. So far, what we know is that practices, information, and *What-Comes-Next* can serve as a lens to understanding changes in writing and identifying strong candidates for developmental moments in the lives of literate actors. In order to identify the limits and possibilities of this lens, I bring it to bear on other moments in the lives of students in Emily's classroom. Since Emily's classroom is a perspicuous setting for studying literate action development, there are many moments similar to Alice's that occurred to students throughout the academic year. In the next two chapters, I identify four moments of literate action that can serve as candidates for literate action development. Drawing on my knowledge of the ways in which these students continued to write throughout the academic year after these moments, I can confidently make the claim that their actions serve as developmental moments in their writing lives. These moments can show us more than just developmental moments of individual students, however: by looking across these sites, we can identify some additional characteristics that can fully flesh out the complexity of what it means to engage in a moment of literate action development.

In Chapter 3, I look at two students in Emily's fifth-period classroom: Marianne and Nick. Marianne shuffles—and, to some extent, has shuffled for her—the resources at her disposal when she engages in preparing to write a blog entry about Helen Keller. Nick re-orchestrates his interactional order with his colleagues as he attempts to finish his work during a worksheet activity in Emily's class. In both of these instances, these students engage in a new approach to participating in the ongoing social order of Emily's classroom, and these new approaches endure across future moments of literate action, future instantiations of particular practices. Through Marianne and Nick, we can see the ways in which objects around writing—in particular, books and individuals—can shape the practice of writing differently when they are ordered differently.

In Chapter 4, I look at two students in Emily's fourth-period classroom: Holly and Don. Each of these students also re-orchestrate their interactional order with the talk, tools, and texts around them, but do so in a more private space than either Marianne or Nick. The relative isolation of their literate action has increased relative to Marianne and Nick, and they offer an interesting site for identifying further characteristics of literate action development. Holly pulls together a revised blog entry on her grandfather, in part, through the knowledge she developed during a sentence-combining activity that Emily developed throughout the school year. Don orchestrates his work as a classroom points-manager and his writing tasks in order to develop new approaches to the desk-organizing and writing activity practices that the classroom develops together.

# Chapter 3. The Possibilities of Objects: An Individuated Perspective

In Chapter 1, I noted that current research, methods, and framings of writing development were insufficient for constructing a robust understanding of writing development through the entirety of the lifespan, although treating development as an act of participation (Applebee, 2000; Boscolo, 2014) seemed to offer the optimal starting point. My respecification of the concept of development through an ethnomethodological lens opened up new possibilities for reframing and expanding writing development as a matter of participation in social action (what I have come to call *literate action* development). In Chapter 2, I began working out some necessary concepts for enacting a new vision of literate action development, and detailed the mundane accomplishments of Emily's classroom in order to take on that work. Since I was working from previous ethnomethodological work, the focus of these chapters was the *joint* production of social order: that is, how the individuated actors in the classroom came to understand what was happening throughout the class period. In order to understand literate action development, however, we need to attend to an individuated perspective on that joint work. That is, we must turn our attention to how a single individuated actor might develop their literate action amidst, with, and through the joint accomplishment of ongoing social order.

In this chapter, I build on the concepts of practices, *What-Comes-Next*, and information to suggest two additional concepts that can help us see the complex work of an individuated actor in a social situation: the possibilities of objects, and adumbration. These two concepts, as we shall see in the cases of Marianne and Nick, offer a useful way to work the boundaries of the individuated actor and the social situation, so that we can adequately track the serial production of social order by an actor that leads to development.

Both the possibilities of objects and adumbration emerge from the ethnomethodological and phenomenological work that I have been touching on, either directly or indirectly, through the first two chapters of this book. The concept of "possibilities of objects" emerges from Garfinkel's *Toward a Sociological Theory of Information*. In that text, Garfinkel, drawing from transcendental phenomenology, develops a concept of the "object-in-general" (2008, p. 133), which he uses to think through the relationship between meaning-making and the objects that we make meaning of. Garfinkel suggests that objects themselves contain *possibilities*, which he (2008, p. 133) synonymizes with "candidacy"—that an object can be specified in a number of ways.

Consider, for example, my dining room table. This table can be a number of things. At the moment, as I type these words, it serves as a workspace, holding my laptop, several books I am referencing, and a drink next to my laptop. In several hours, it will be used as a place where my family eats a meal. Later in the evening, it may be draped with a blanket to serve as a "fort" while my son and I play some kind of game.[4] In each of these instances, a different "possibility" of the table is recognized: it is used as part of a broader social situation involving other people (myself, my wife, my son) and other objects (my laptop, dinner plates, a blanket).

The table has not changed in form, but we have recognized different possibilities in it, and acted upon those possibilities. Perhaps most importantly for understanding the production of social order, we have recognized these possibilities jointly. Through the constitutive ordering of talk and objects, we render the table into a particular kind of object—in Garfinkel's words, we *thingify* it. Looking to the possibilities of objects—and what Garfinkel calls a unifying principle, or the way that we come to shared understandings of what possibility we are taking up—allows us to see the social work that goes into recognizing objects as components of an unfolding social situation. From there, we can draw on the concept of *adumbration* to frame individuated perspectives on unfolding social order, and by extension maintain the delicate balance of the individual and the social the first two chapters of this text begin attending to.

## Adumbrated Perspectives on Social Ordering

The starting point of the lived reality, as I argue in the first two chapters, must be ethnomethodological: that is, it must orient to the joint production of social order. But this is only a starting point, as understanding literate action development through the lifespan has to be *individuated*, focused on the ways in which actors organize themselves for writing, engage in writing, and produce writing in different, but patterned ways over time. The lived reality, in other words, is social and individual—it sits at the complex intersection of social order and individuated understandings.

What remains absent from my account of this intersection so far is productive language for making sense of the ways in which the individual and the social meet. This intersection has been highlighted with Alice's example, but not adequately conceptualized. In order to make sense of this, I introduce the term *adumbration*, a term rooted in Husserl's transcendental phenomenology, which can frame our understanding of the upcoming analysis of Marianne and Nick's work. An object we encounter (including the production of social order) can only be seen as shaded—that is, we cannot grasp it in its entirety from a given perspective.

I draw on this term to make sense of how individuated actors perceive the production of social order in any given moment. A student may take out a pen or pencil when asked to, and by extension contribute to the production of social order in the classroom, but the particularities of taking out that pen or pencil from a backpack—if it is difficult to grasp, for instance, or if it is in a different pocket than the student expected—will lead to an individuated participation in that

---

4. I am rarely provided with all of the details of the games we are playing, thus my vagueness here. But forts are not an uncommon part of such games.

production, and by extension an individuated set of actions as the situation continues to be co-constructed. Perhaps dropping or being unable to find the pencil pulls the student's phenomenal field away from the teacher, and so they miss the instructions about what to do next. They must then complete other activities—such as following the lead of a nearby classmate—to continue participation in the expected production of social order.

As framed, this example may lead the reader to understand individuation as a push against a broader social norm, but this is a misleading effect of my simplified example. Each and every member of that group has individuated understandings, individuated participation, in the practices that co-construct the class. While one student may have dropped their pencil, another may be daydreaming, another may be talking to a fellow student, and another may be raptly taking notes. No one of these students is participating in social order more or less than the other—they are co-constructing social order in their individuated work. This individuated perspective, however, is *adumbrated* in the sense that each actor only sees so much of the production of social order, and must base their next actions only on what they perceive. It is this individuation that provides the opportunity for developmental transformation—and, as we shall see below, it is through the co-participative nature of ongoing social order that such small transformations by individuals are easily overlooked.

Adumbration can shape how we understand individuated actors to see the co-construction of possibilities in an object (or, as we will see below, a network of objects). Individuated experiences of the co-construction of social order are necessarily perspectival, necessarily shaded off by that which they do not experience in the complex work of the ongoing production of social order. This adumbration impacts not only the arrays of possibility they see at work in an object but how that operation is followed up in subsequent situations. To return to the student who dropped their pencil, let us assume that while reaching for the pencil, they missed a teacher's introduction of a new topic, and as a result assumed they were talking about the topic they were on when the pencil was dropped. The "unifying principle" of the co-construction of the social order has changed in the class, but the student is unaware. Now, should the student avoid saying or doing anything that gives away their obliviousness, they will have an opportunity to follow the continual unfolding of the situation, see that the "criterion of continuity of experience" (Garfinkel, 2008, pp. 137–138) no longer holds value for them, and can adjust their operator as needed to continue participating in and making sense of social order. This adumbrated aspect of participating in social order, as Marianne's case demonstrates below, can have interesting developmental consequences. We can think of the lived reality, then, as adumbrated co-participation in the practices of ordering an array of objects that reduces the uncertainty of *What-Comes-Next*. Development within the lived reality, as we saw in Chapter 2, may be located within elevated levels of uncertainty, which can trigger a revision of practices at work. The cases of Marianne and Nick provide some inroads into the

complexity of such development, and from them we can determine some characteristics of how development moves forward as part of a sea of ongoing practices.

## The Possibilities of a Fact: Marianne and Helen Keller

During a three-month span throughout the school year, Emily's students engaged
in blog writing. The blogs were relatively brief, isolated on the internet (via a blog-
ging site designed for young students in school), and written across the course of
several drafts. The work for the blog entry at the center of this analysis occurred
as part of a research day at the school's library. The students went to the library,
did some reading, collected facts, and used those facts to create a blog entry.

During their research day in the library, Emily provided students with several
resources—both paper-and-pencil and online—to go about finding information
that they would later use to contribute to their blogs. In the end, students collected much more information than they actually published. Marianne's work
during this period emerged as a *perspicuous setting* in this instance: the work that
she does to collect records on and do some writing that will later be repurposed
toward her blog entry become caught up in observable interaction, allowing the
unfolding social order that the writing is produced within to be visible.

Writing, for Emily, was a central tool of classroom management, learning, and
participation in her classes. She was particularly interested in using digital writing, bringing technology into the classroom to get students to understand how
the digital world worked in terms of writing. The work she does with her students
in this example is part of her "Upstanders vs. Bystanders" unit. It was a theme
promoted by the California Writing Project around the time that I observed her.
The students were writing a blog called "Who is an Upstander?" They had to
identify someone from history who was an upstander, not a bystander, and how
they changed the world in positive ways.

Marianne met with the rest of her class in the library on February 10. They had
two sheets to guide their work during that period: a white sheet for identifying who
they wanted to study, as well as questions they had about them; and a blue sheet for
recording facts as they found them in the library. Emily told students that they were
to collect ten facts on their blue papers by noon. They could use the books, maga-
zines, or the computers. They could also, if they chose to, work with a partner. Alexis
and Marianne, who had been developing a friendship throughout the school year,
decided to work together. They immediately got their sheets, found some books,
and cleared a spot at a table to work from. They started with writing down the information required for MLA citation, which was a requirement of the assignment.
At this point in the year—about six months in—this kind of activity is common in
Emily's class. Students are regularly given opportunities to take books and other
resources and record notes about them, always starting with an MLA entry.

As she is entering MLA information, Marianne realizes that one of the books
she collected contains an entire chapter on her subject, Helen Keller. She and

Alexis, at this moment, make the unstated decision that they have sufficient texts to begin their work (i.e., they stop collecting new books). They then settle into the kind of work that they've done before, which I referred to in my own notes as ⧸worksheet activity⧸ as I developed an ethnomethodological perspective on the incident. The students were given, by the teacher, a set of tasks to do, and some sort of place to record the work they do on those tasks. These worksheets were organizing objects for Marianne and Alexis: they were the sense-making mechanisms through which social order came to be established.

*Figure 3.1. Marianne's desk work.*

In Figure 3.1, Marianne's work is off to the left, with Alexis' work off to the right. The individuated actor that I am attending to here is Marianne, but Alexis' work became part of the distributed production of facts on the worksheet. Note that they have the blue sheets on top, and the books next to them. This configuration of objects enables them to construct facts through their reading, their discussion, and their writing in near-simultaneity. Essentially, they have organized their space, themselves, and their resources for and through the worksheet.

Alexis and Marianne discuss some of the facts that they find with one another as they read. The flow of activity involves one of them stating a fact aloud and receiving affirmation from the other about that fact—either a "cool" spoken aloud, or a quiet "uh-huh" as silence returns. The constitutive ordering of this activity, then, is organized across physical space, worksheet organization, and turns at talk. Figures 3.2 and 3.3 show Marianne's sheets in detail.

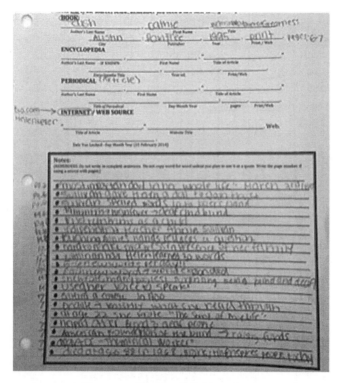

*Figure 3.2. Marianne's blue sheet.*

These texts participate in the unfolding production of social order in the class. Marianne and Alexis use the structure of the sheets to shape their reading of texts, and their understanding of their tasks during the class period. Note the ways in which the space of the lines in both Figures 3.2 and 3.3 shape, for Marianne, the ways in which she can translate the facts she uncovers in her reading. The space does not dictate completely what Marianne can write—at several points, for instance, Alexis allows her writing to flow into multiple lines as she elaborates the facts she uncovered—but it does influence the ways in which their individual reading is taken up.

After several minutes of this work, Marianne returns attention to the larger goal that Emily indicated at the start of class: accumulating ten facts. They each proceed to count how many they have. This talks the goal of the activity—completing ten facts before noon—back into their understanding of the actions they are performing. They realize they don't have enough, and so they go back to work accumulating new facts. It's at this point that a candidate moment of development begins to unfold in Marianne's work. In the space provided from the sheets that she has to work from (see Figures 3.4 and 3.5), Marianne transforms what she finds in her books to what she needs for the assignment. She writes first that Helen Keller, at a young age, nearly died of an illness, but survived without being able to hear or see. She states this fact, writes it down, and moves on. Later, she encounters the fact that Helen Keller also spoke, and so she builds that fact into the textual space of the worksheet activity as well. After slotting in that fact, however, she realizes the anomaly that has arisen. She doesn't see how both of those facts can be true of Helen Keller at the same time. How was she able to speak if she couldn't hear or see? What can she make of that?

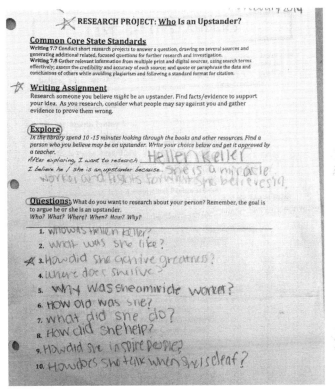

*Figure 3.3. Marianne's white sheet.*

This anomaly becomes socially available through Marianne's thinking-out-loud: "Oh, she could talk. No, she can't." Alexis, who appears to be engaged in her own work, responds "No, she can't," without turning to the reading that Marianne was working through. Marianne confirms Alexis' response with a "Yeah," as a moment of silence develops. Alexis, turning more of her attention to Marianne, then says "Everyone *can* talk—" which appears to be the start of a more complicated observation that is not completed by Alexis. At this point, the school librarian, who was clearly frustrated at the level of noise in the library, was walking by, and attended only to the word "talk" when she responded "There's no *reason* to talk!" This interjection by the librarian interrupted Alexis, but both the turn at talk by Alexis and the interjected turn by the librarian did not raise a response from Marianne, as she continued to read. Shortly after the librarian moves to another part of the room, Marianne says "She did." Then, reading aloud, she says "She used her voice to speak by imitating the sounds . . ." and trails off, turning away from the exchange with Alexis and more fully toward the chapter she was reading.

*Figure 3.4. Marianne's question (white sheet).*

We see, in this work by Marianne, new information emerging out of the unfolding orchestration of activity. Through the production of facts via social, physical, and textual ordering, Marianne realizes an anomaly that needs resolving in order for social order to continue: could Helen Keller talk, or not? This anomaly interferes with the production of her putting words on the page: the facts that she records lack a coherence that she has to work to construct. This anomaly, then, leads her to produce more writing in later social, textual, and physical orderings of the world around her. It is important to note that the ambiguity here rises above the always-present uncertainty of *What-Comes-Next*. What Marianne has been presented with here is what I am labeling *information*—an uncertainty in some aspect of *What-Comes-Next* that requires resolution via transformations of practices in order to continue co-constructing social order. If we zoom out to attend to the ongoing production of order in the classroom, then Marianne's work to continue classroom social order requires that she work through, in some way, this information. Marianne *could* do this by leaving the anomaly in place: writing down the two contradictory facts and leaving those facts untouched as she continues to fill in her sheet. This would resonate more strongly with the work that Marianne has done on multi-draft writing and research throughout the semester, which might be best described as acts of translation: that is, Marianne would read her texts through the language of the worksheet, using the space available, the verbal instructions by Emily, and the directions on the page to select what aspects of which texts should move from her reading to her worksheet. In this instance, however, the increased anomalous aspects of *What-Comes-Next* have disrupted Marianne's practices, and require new practices in order to take on further social order.

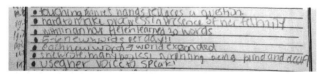

*Figure 3.5. Marianne's facts (blue sheet).*

The working out of this additional information enables Marianne to realize new possibilities in the objects that she is working with. Figure 3.4 highlights the aspect of the worksheet in which Marianne first calls attention to the anomaly she identifies. As she attempts to define Helen Keller as an upstander, she brings her understanding of how Keller learned to speak to bear on this, indicated in Figure 3.5. Throughout the drafting and publishing of Marianne's work as shown in Figures 3.6, 3.7, and 3.8, she maintains, from the start, the link between Helen Keller's disabilities and her accomplishments as a writer. This, according to Marianne, is what makes Helen Keller an upstander. This upstandingness gets underscored by the fact that Marianne accomplished to resolve the anomaly that she came across becomes the central understanding that Marianne uses to make sense of and then write about Helen Keller's life. Marianne makes her "hook," in Emily's words, the fact that Keller wrote books even though she was blind and deaf. Marianne also tries to wrestle into coordination with that point the speaking that Keller learned to do. She is showing how both of those accomplishments by Keller make her an upstander.

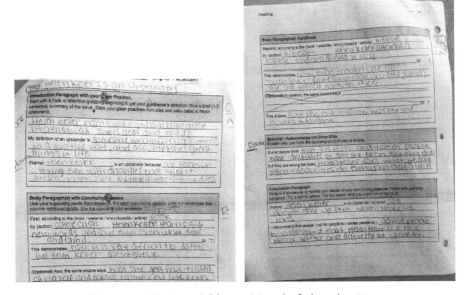

*Figure 3.6. Marianne's blog writing draft, hand written.*

If we put these pieces—the production of knowledge and the production of the blog—side by side, what we see is Marianne constructing a new understanding of subject matter that she is faced with through the orchestration of talk, tools, and texts in a particular situation. The results of this work become the central focus, and the central challenge, of the writing that Marianne finds herself doing later. The complexities that she pushes up against in the construction in her worksheet activity, in other words, have offered her an opportunity to orchestrate her writing practices around and through that fact in a future writing situation.

# Helen Keller Is an Upstander

TAGS: HELEN KELLER   INSPIRATION   TRYING   UPSTANDER   WHO IS AN UPSTANDER   WRITER
CATEGORIES: WHO IS AN UPSTANDER   FEBRUARY 20, 2014 @ 1:38 PM   3 COMMENTS

Helen Keller wrote many books and even talked while deaf and blind. My definition of an upstander is someone who influences others in a positive way and accomplishes great things in her life. Helen Keller is an upstander because she keeps on trying even with disabilities that make it almost impossible to do the things that she did.

6 new words and even said them while deaf and blind. This demonstrates how it is very difficult to do this but she doesn't give up. Also, the same source says that she became frustrated at herself and threw tantrums but she will keep on trying no matter what. This shows how Helen Keller is a miracle worker and wants it accomplish this.

Second, according to the website "Bio.com", Helen Keller attended a college and graduated in 1904. This demonstrates how even though she has "brain fever" (illness that made her deaf and blind), she still made it through college.

Some people may think that it is easy and a lot of people have disabilities so this one person isn't a big deal, but they are wrong because Helen Keller does what people without her disabilities do even when she can't see or hear.
Helen Keller is an upstander because she doesn't give up even when times are hard. I advise people to read her books and understand that Helen Keller is defiantly an upstander and is extremely intelligent.

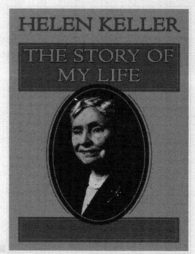

Image from:"globalresearch.com"    Image from:"mycreativepersuits.com"

*Figure 3.7. Marianne's published blog post.*

We can trace the flow of Marianne's writing about Helen Keller from her initial question to a blog post (Figure 3.7). Based on my observations of Marianne and her writing throughout the year, I see this moment as Marianne's first significant change from what we might call "reporting" in her research. Rather than reporting the facts from her texts (which focus largely on Helen Keller's development as an author), Marianne integrates her own interesting finding—Keller's efforts at spoken language—into those facts, using both to account for her "upstandingness." It is an early and uneven attempt, as we can see in her subsequent writing, but it is a first for her, and it is through the constitutive ordering of mundane action for another first time that we are able to see it.

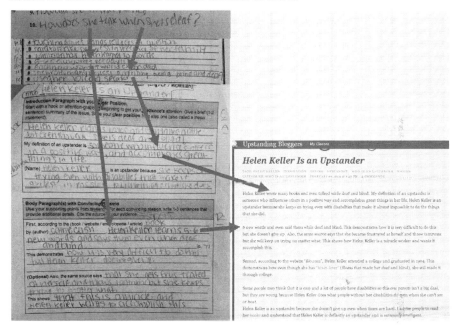

*Figure 3.8. Tracing a fact across drafts.*

We also need to examine the ways in which the possibilities of objects are realized in this work by Marianne. Her traditional work, to this point, has been to read the texts she is assigned through the ways in which she makes sense of the requirements that Emily provides her. But in this instance, the account of Keller's life cries out for closer inspection, leading Marianne to recognize new possibilities in the text than her recurrent practices would seem to have supported. The complexity of Keller's literate life raised the uncertainty in her work that transformed into information through her interactions with the talk, tools, and texts around her. In this transformation, Marianne established new configurations of objects around her that realized new possibilities in those objects, not only through individual objects (such as books about Keller) but through interactions between and among objects (such as how her new knowledge of Keller transformed her understanding of the structured assignment provided by Emily). The new possibilities opened up by the facts of Helen Keller for Marianne lead her to new and lasting configurations of objects (and, by extension, the realizations of possibilities of those objects). Nick's work, traced out below, articulates the ways in which these transformations can be realized not only in concrete objects such as books but in the configurations of interaction among actors in an unfolding social situation.

## The Possibilities of Uncertainty: Nick's Note-Taking Activity

Before the students had begun research in preparation for their own blog writing activities, Emily used a novel the students had read (*The Outsiders*) to introduce students to the concept of an "Upstander." On January 22, Emily had her students develop definitions of several terms in preparation for the "Upstanding" blog writing unit: upstanders, bystanders, victims, and bullies. Using a mix of modalities and examples from *The Outsiders* to get all students on the same page, Emily tasked students with reaching definitions of the terms as the class discusses examples and characteristics of each term.

Emily passed out the sheet shown in Figure 3.9 to help students orient their writing activity with what she was asking them to do. Emily had students box the word "definition," because she told students that they would be asked for that later on. Emily projected the sheet the students were working from on her television screen so that she could fill it in as they moved through it. In a back-and-forth among students and teacher, Emily and her students identified examples and characteristics of each term from the characters in *The Outsiders*. Once examples were provided for each term, Emily gave students three minutes to write their own definition of the terms down.

Throughout the activities outlines above, Nick engages with the instructions of Emily and interactions with his friends. In video of this classroom activity, Nick can be seen writing down what the instructor asks him to write down, and using the time between the end of his writing and the start of Emily's next instruction to interact with the students around him. It is this interactional pattern that I wish to trace in Nick's writing: his movement in ⸨writing activity⸩, from the interactional work of completing an in-class activity, to his interaction with his peers. This movement between these two sets of practices is interesting in my ongoing tracing of development not because of the pairing of both worlds but the sequencing of their presence in the unfolding social order in the classroom, and the consequences of that sequencing in Nick's literate action development.

The work Nick does here can be isolated from the ongoing flow of social action in Emily's classroom with the concepts previously articulated. Nick is engaged in what might be called note-taking practice: he is listening to his instructor, copying down the notes that she puts on the television screen, and doing so in a way that perpetuates the ongoing social order of the classroom. This practice of note-taking, of following along with the work that Emily is highlighting via the television, moves the ⸨writing activity⸩ forward, in part. Nick's movement from writing down notes to talking with his peers shows him participating in multiple kinds of social order through an anticipation of *What-Comes-Next*. That is, as Nick finishes copying down a portion of the notes, he can use (1) the remaining blank spaces on the page and (2) the continual instructions from Emily to determine that there will, soon, be other passages to copy down onto his worksheet. This reduction of uncertainty allows him to fill the space between note-taking events with unrelated talk amongst his neighbors.

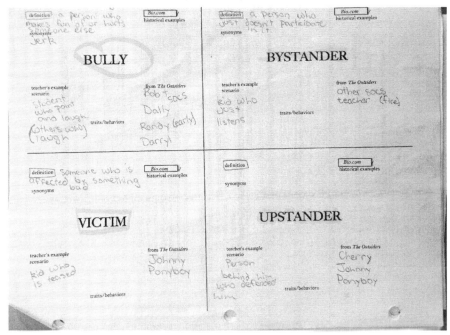

*Figure 3.9 Nick's notes.*

Nick's interactions with others do not keep him from participating actively in class in ways that "count," according to the class, as participation. Nick raises his hand on occasion when the teacher asks a question (though he is not called upon), and, as mentioned earlier, dutifully writes down what the teacher asks him to. Furthermore, near the end of class, when Emily asks students to define each of the terms at the end of class, Nick defines three of them. During this lesson, Nick engages in several literate acts, but it is most beneficial for our purposes to focus on the final minutes of the activity, when Nick draws from his available notes to write definitions about each term. During this sequence, which takes approximately three minutes, Emily gives students the chance to work with others in their group—Nick has two others at his cluster of desks—in order to come up with definitions and, if possible, synonyms for each.

Emily's encourages her students to "work together!," and Nick engages with one of his group members. Although he does listen in as Emily gives some clarifying examples to a group near him early on in his writing (the video shows him turning his head and leaning toward the group), most of what he writes under each "definition" emerges from talk with the neighbor to his immediate right as he works through the first two terms. By the time he has finished writing definitions on his sheet, however, his partner has left to speak with Emily at the front of the room, leaving Nick by himself to finish the remainder of the worksheet. This time "alone" does not preclude his interactions with other students in the class: he has several turns at talk with students in other groups, including Alexis, who is located several rows of desks closer to the front of the room than he is.

Nick's writing becomes a set of preparatory materials in the ongoing work of the class: he follows his instructor in taking notes so that he can later write definitions, which are in turn a preparation for prewriting about his blog entries. In each of these writing incidents, Nick manages to complete his assigned work—to participate in the ongoing production of classroom order—while also participating in the ongoing production of peer interaction with, through, and around the note-taking. At this point, Nick has not encountered anything anomalous in the unfolding of *What-Comes-Next* that leads him to shake up his normal production of social order. Nick's participation in this segment of activity remains similar to the kinds of participation he has engaged in throughout the semester: participating in classroom activity that count in the co-construction of social order while also engaging in what Brooke (1987) might call "underlife" practices that complement the ongoing flow of social order in the classroom.

This work on Nick's behalf is indeed *work*: it is time- and attention-consuming, and the orchestration of lifeworlds that Nick is engaged in here keeps him from engaging in some of the more long-ranged thinking that Emily has encouraged throughout the academic year. This work, for instance, is a stepping stone into later blog writing activity, but at no point does Nick cease to indicate that he is not attending to the work at hand as *merely* the work at hand: he does not make any rhetorical moves to step away from the immediacy of the issue to consider the larger issues to which this work of preparation is attached.

This is not to say that Nick is doing something wrong or incomplete, but rather to highlight the adumbrated perspective that Nick is working through. Nick sees the task before him, completes it in ways that are accountable in Emily's classroom, and does so while maintaining the pattern of peer interactions that he and his peers have come to expect. Much like Marianne, Nick's work to complete a worksheet is caught up within the local production of social order and, by extension, so is the candidate moment of development that emerges from this work in subsequent weeks.

Nick, being in the same class as Marianne, finds himself also writing several blog posts about upstanders and bystanders, and frequently turns to the work that he does in his worksheet in order to complete these blog entries. Essentially, this worksheet creates the underpinnings of complex intertextual ties that span a broad swath of Nick's school writings in the coming weeks. This was, in part, Emily's design, as her assignments are designed to scaffold students into a full blog post. Nick's work takes advantage of this scaffolding, and the language of his blog posts can be followed back along a material, intertextual chain that has its origins, in part, in his worksheet.

If we look at Figure 3.9, however, we note a topic that Nick fails to define in his worksheet: that of an upstander. The unfolding of the end of class in that period suggests that perhaps Nick ran out of time to complete the {writing activity}, and instead had to shift gears into the {Exit Ticket}. Whatever the reason, Nick does not have this paper to turn to in his own packet when the class co-constructs a {writing activity} that builds on the definition of an upstander to identify potential examples. Thankfully for Nick, a draft activity leading to the text shown in Figure 3.10 provides an opportunity for him to co-construct a new definition.

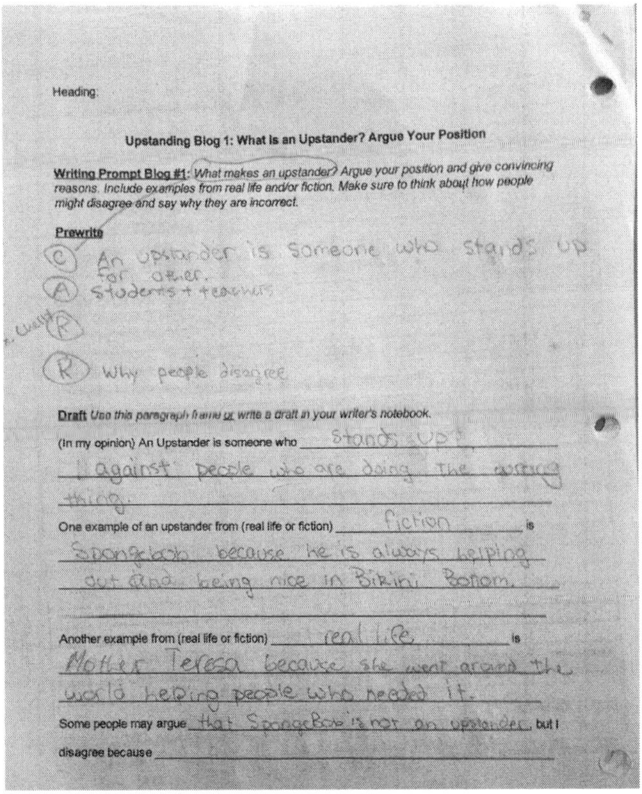

*Figure 3.10. Nick's blog draft.*

Nick is able to develop a definition of an upstander in the first step of this worksheet, which began as a {writing activity} in Emily's class and continued as a homework assignment. Emily and her students worked together to produce language for working through the demands of the worksheet. Nick develops this definition from its first iteration to the first sentence of his draft (Figure 3.10). In his initial definition, Nick writes that "An upstander is someone who stands up for other." In the first draft of his blog entry, Nick transforms that sentence into "An Upstander is someone who stands up against people who are doing the wrong thing." It is interesting that, although his definition changed from one entry to the next, his examples relate more closely to his first definition than his second. Nick doesn't talk about Spongebob Squarepants and Mother Teresa as those who stands up *against* others, but rather as people who are "always helping out," whether it be at Bikini Bottom or around the world.

Nick's examples—Spongebob Squarepants and Mother Teresa—are more common pairings than the reader might first surmise. Emily provided students with a list of people to research (this is what led Marianne to pick Helen Keller), so Nick was able to select Mother Teresa from that list, and Spongebob Squarepants from his television habits. But the mix of Spongebob and Mother Teresa is less important than the work that Nick seems to be doing to anchor examples to a somewhat-fluid definition of upstander. Note the lack of a definition of an upstander in Figure 3.9. Nick walks away from that series of textual activities without an artifact to turn to that had a definition of an upstander on it, and the lack of this intertextual tie correlates with his struggles to define an upstander as the blog activity develops. What had occurred without an elevated level of uncertainty in the {writing activity} captured in Figure 3.10 is now shaping an elevated uncertainty of what counts as an upstander in the ongoing production of social order that makes up the blog draft. As Nick attempts to keep writing going, in other words, he is working out his sense of a definition. Figure 3.11 shows Nick's actual blog post.

Nick's blog post demonstrates a third definition at work: "In My Opinion an upstander is someone who helps other people out when they are in need of it." Nick's third definition moves in the direction of his examples, and away from the language of standing up "against" people or standing up "for" others—helping is central to Nick's understanding of an upstander. The work that Nick does here to develop a new definition of upstander through his subsequent writing and discussion highlights a demand that his adumbrated work in the co-construction of social order created for him. Nick's work to balance both social participation and "official" literate practices in his classroom lead him to the need to produce a definition of upstander that will fit in with the Spongebob and Mother Teresa examples he has set up for himself in his subsequent worksheet activity. As Nick develops a definition in his later work, he finds himself in the position of having to revisit his definition multiple times—each time bring more tightly together the interpersonal work among him and his classmates and the writing work of the worksheets that he finds before him. Nick, in other words, orchestrates his lifeworlds a bit more tightly, and in doing so tweaks the history of his co-participation in Emily's classroom in durable ways.

# My Upstanders Blog

Tags: spongebob    upstander

Categories: What Is an Upstander?

February 6, 2014 @ 6:18 AM    o Comments

## What Is An Upstander?

In My Opinion an upstander is someone who helps other people out when they are in need of it.  One example of an upstander from fiction is Spongebob SquarePants because he is always helping other people out in Bikini Bottom.  Spongebob is always volunteering to test Sandy's experiments with her and always agreeing to work late for Mr. Krabs.  Another example from real life is Mother Teresa because she went around the world helping people out who needed it.  Mother Teresa even won an award for being an upstander.  The award was called the Jawaharlal Nehru Award for International Understanding.  Some people may argue that Spongebob is not an upstander, but I disagree because there is one episode where he says he will help Mr Krabs, Sandy and go to Patrick's birthday party but they are all on the  on the same night.  He ends up helping all of them but they find out about all the commitments he made and they said that it would have been fine if he said no to them.

imi

*Figure 3.11. Nick's blog post.*

Nick's literate action development—the pulling together of previously-disparate lifeworlds through the organization of material environments and patterns of social interaction—can be seen as an adumbrated modification of the "unifying principle" he shares with his fellow students in adumbrated ways. From the start of his worksheet activity described above, Nick participated in ongoing social action in Emily's classroom with the same operator: that is, his answer to the question "what is going on here?" remained "worksheet activity," and his answers to the question "what do I do next?" build on that answer. But in working out his answers to "what do I do next?" Nick transformed his literate action. Rather than completing his worksheet and turning to his peers to pass the time until the next required worksheet activity, or engaging in collaborative work when exhorted to by Emily, Nick made sense of information (a heightened uncertainty of *What-Comes-Next*) by drawing on the writing and discussion of his peers. The full implications of Nick's re-orchestration of his lifeworlds could not be seen over the long term—Nick ended up moving to another classroom late in the year—but the work that he did in subsequent classes, particularly as he worked on subsequent blog entries, suggests that this re-orchestration proved durable enough to be considered developmental.

## Insights into the Lived Reality: Recognizing New Possibilities in Objects

The examples of Marianne and Nick have provided interesting additional insight into the lived reality, and additional dimensions to think through when considering how literate action development might be understood from that perspective. Both of these students came to realize the new possibilities inherent in objects they were co-constructing with others from one moment to the next, and both carried those new sets of possibilities forward through the work of their blog writing. We can see that the ways in which they go about the literate action that creates texts has begun to change—Marianne in terms of the relationships she co-constructs with and through texts, Nick in terms of his interactional accomplishments during small group work.

Each of these students has an *adumbrated* perspective on the unfolding co-construction of social order within the class, and it is this adumbrated understanding that provides the individuated opportunity for literate action development in the ongoing production of what Garfinkel (2002) refers to as *immortal, ordinary society*. From these insights, we can take some tentative steps toward an integration of object possibilities, practices, *What-Comes-Next*, and adumbration into a framing of the lived reality of literate action development. The work of these students to reduce the uncertainty of *What-Comes-Next* highlighted several important aspects of the production of possibilities of objects when focusing on literate action. As Marianne demonstrated, textual interaction is an important site of constructing sites of literate action—not just the texts written, but the texts read and, perhaps even more importantly, the *way* in which these texts are read, co-constructed, in unfolding situations. Because Marianne was able to talk through the complications of Keller's literate life with Alexis, Marianne's understanding of Keller became a scenic feature of social order that would transform her notes, her rough draft, and eventually her blog post. Likewise, Nick demonstrated the role of interaction at sites of writing, and the ways in which those interactions also become scenic features of a moment that leave their imprint on the future production of text—in Nick's case, through a worksheet, to another worksheet, to a rough draft, and finally to a blog post.

These interpersonal and intertextual transformations are possible only when viewing practices as *adumbrated* in the eyes of participants, and when locating the mechanisms in that adumbration in the structuring of possibilities of objects in moment-to-moment interaction. That is, the "unifying principle" that

Garfinkel (2008) discusses is not entirely shared amongst members of a group in an unfolding social situation—each member's understanding of and action through unifying principles is individuated to a certain extent, and that individuation offers opportunities for a new approach to taking up the possibilities of objects that may not violate the unifying principle but still offers new individuated insights through it. In the next chapter, I follow this up with two additional cases: Holly and Don. Holly's transformation of her understanding of the "unifying principle" of revising a blog entry, and Don's transformation of how he follows the shifting "unifying principles" at work across a range of tightly-packed activities demonstrates the ways in which social order is both a shared achievement and an opportunity for individuated literate action development.

# Chapter 4. Building Lifeworlds, Developing Literate Action

Chapter 3 introduces two concepts (possibilities of objects; adumbration) that, along with the concepts of Chapter 2 (practice, *What-Comes-Next*, information), draw attention to the intersection of social and individuated understandings needed to view the lived reality of literate action development. The cases of Marianne and Nick in Chapter 3 also highlight what literate action development looks like from the perspective of the lived reality. These cases, while a useful starting point for envisioning the lived reality, are also located in a rather truncated period of time: throughout the blog writing unit. In this chapter, I look at literate action across a wider span of time and a wider swath of activities. Drawing on two further cases—Holly's sentence production and Don's work with "points" in class—I show how the productions of literate action, rooted as they are in the ongoing, local production of social order, contribute to and expand the lifeworlds that we come to find ourselves in. At the heart of this work is the claim that new chains of reasoning, new understandings of and work with literate action are always unavoidably scenic: that is, the ways in which we bring our understandings of the world to bear is always, in some way, materially present in the moments of literate action that we undertake. It is often possible, in other words, to chase down the ways in which past social situations that come to impact the present are made materially available in a given instance, provided that we know what we are looking for. Drawing on my yearlong knowledge of Holly's and Don's literate action, I am able to trace the material recurrence of objects upon which development rests through the moments under study.

## The Possibilities of the Sentence: Holly

The search for literate action development across a broader swath of both time and activities will begin with Holly's work in Emily's classroom to develop her literate action via attention to sentence-level work. In particular, I will be focusing on her work with the ₡Do Now₱ on November 13, and her revision work that I interviewed her about at the end of January. Holly's November 13 ₡Do Now₱ is a transformative moment for her: her work with the sentence structures and, later, sharing them with the class leads her to focus on what her teacher, Emily, will label "sentence sense" in her subsequent writing. Although this is of course later reinforced with future ₡Do Now₱ activities, what Holly shows on November 13 is the start of an increased engagement with and attention to sentence-combining activities.

### Antecedent: November 13 "Do Now"

The ₡Do Now₱ activity, in Emily's classroom, unfolds in a sequence of three interrelated moves. In the first stage, students were provided with handouts and

Google slides on a television at the front of the room and told to engage in sentence combining activity. Students were usually given between three and four minutes to work on this activity. During the second stage of the activity, students turned their attention to one another. In the third stage and final stage of the activity, Emily brought the attention of the class together and asked for volunteers to share the writing they did throughout the first stage.

Holly's work with sentence-combining on November 13 began like her other ⧘Do Now⧙ activities throughout the academic year to this point. Holly came into class, sat down, and looked to the slide on the big-screen television at the front of the room for guidance on what to do, coordinating that slide with the pages from Killgallon and Killgallon's sentence-combining text (see Figure 4.2). Using these texts in concert and with occasional instructions from Emily, Holly worked out two sentences (see Figure 4.3) that matched with what Killgallon and Killgallon (2000) (and, by extension, Emily's class) would label an "S-V split" and an "opener."

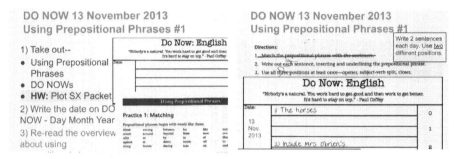

Figure 4.1. Slides with "Do Now" instructions.

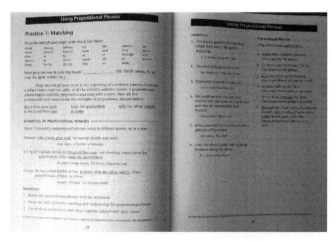

Figure 4.2. Killgallon & Killgallon Text.

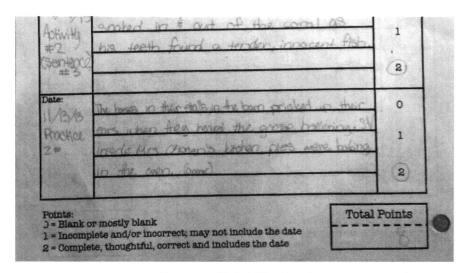

*Figure 4.3. Holly's "Do Now."*

The work so far—the written assignment, Holly's structuring of the task, and her participative actions—is no different than her work in earlier ⊄Do Now⊅ activities. Holly reaches an understanding of what is being asked of her by the teacher without noticeable hesitation or trouble—she completes her task at about the same time that those around her do, and she does not ask for clarification or help from either another student or Emily. Holly is making sense of her ⊄Do Now⊅ activity in ways that "count" in the ongoing production of social order.

The work that Holly has done to this point serves as a starting point for a change in her participation later in the class period. Throughout the first two and a half months of the academic year, Holly was a quiet student, participating when called upon and in small group work, but rarely speaking up voluntarily in class. During the third stage of the November 13 ⊄Do Now⊅ activity, however, Holly shifted her normal ways of participation, and in the process suggested a comfort with the sentence-combining activity that she had not displayed before. In order to more effectively guide the reader through the exchanges in the third stage of the activity, I present them in Table 4.1 (Holly's participation is in bold).

Holly's work during the third stage of the ⊄Do Now⊅ can be most effectively understood by centrally attending to two particular segments of the exchanges. The first segment is underscored in the "Initiation" column. During the opening of the activity, Emily ("T" in Table 4.1) asks a particular student to read their sentence aloud, adding that "if you [other students] had it a different way, please raise your hand." Other students began speaking, requiring Emily to re-start the exchange, and when she did, she reframed her structuring of participation. Instead of asking students to raise their hand only if they had written their sentence a different way, Emily adds that if someone "*knows* a different way," they may also participate.

**Table 4.1. I-R-E exchanges about the "Do Now."**

| Initiation | Response | Evaluation |
|---|---|---|
| T: Okay so um I'm going to have (student) start and then if you had it a different way I want you to raise your hand. | | |
| T: Wait, (student), until it's quiet | S: (starts to speak) | |
| T: Okay (student) did an opener one so he'll read and then if somebody did it a different way <u>or knows a different way you can read yours.</u> | | |
| | S: Inside Mrs. O'Brien's kitchen pies were baking in the oven | |
| | | T: Yep so the inside Mrs. O'Brien is opening it, now— |
| | S: Isn't Mrs. O'Brien a (???) | |
| T: All right who can do it a different way? How about Holly? Wait, wait until it's quiet. | | T: I don't know, it's unclear and I've never read that book so I don't know. |
| T: And which, which method was that? | **H: Pies inside Mrs. O'Brien's kitchen were baking in the oven.** | T: Okay |
| T: Did anybody know another way? So we heard S-V split, we heard opener, and could we do it one more way? How about (student)? | **H: I think that was S-V split.** | T: It is. |

This slight change in instruction opens up the possibility of Holly's participation. Holly raised her hand to participate in the activity when Emily asked for volunteers, but was not called upon. Another student read the same sentence structure (an "opener") that Holly had used, but because of Emily's extra instruction during her re-start, she had the opportunity for additional participation.

The second item to centrally attend to is Holly's response, which is boldfaced in the "Response" column of Table 4.1. After the first student response provides the answer that Holly had written about, she reviews her sentence and, without any writing, alters her sentence in an S-V split form to participate in the third stage of the ⁅Do Now⁆.

This work by Holly showcases two important elements of her work in the class. First, she is beginning to participate differently in class, suggesting a transformation of her perceptions of what is available to her in terms of class participation. Second, through her increased participation during this particular activity, Holly showed an understanding of and interest in sentence-combining activities that she had not demonstrated previously—though she has always completed her ⁅Do Now⁆ activity in the past, she had not previously constructed a new sentence extemporaneously in order to participate in a class discussion. In order to understand the ways in which Holly's literate action undergoes a developmental shift, we must turn to the next place that such attention to sentence-level work turns up: blog writing.

## Co-Constructing Developmental Moments: January Blog Writing

Several weeks after Holly's November 13 ⁅Do Now⁆ shift in participation, Emily began the blog-writing unit that I describe in Chapter 3. Holly's blog writing can be traced across several lessons, but it is perhaps easiest to see how Holly orchestrated her writing activity by working backwards from a finished post. Figure 4.4 shows Holly's first draft of a blog entry for her "What is an Upstander?" blog entry. In this draft, Holly's writing is directed by several factors. First, Emily has provided students with various sentence frames to shape their writing. While this is not necessarily a problem for students (in fact, many students use these as guides for their writing), it does limit some of the options that Holly has when she engages in writing. Second, Holly only has a limited amount of space for her entry: it is limited to a single page, and her answer to the "What is an Upstander?" question is broken into several pieces, each of which has a limited space to be described. This limitation is similar to the limitations that Marianne and Alexis' worksheets had as they pulled facts out of their books in Chapter 3—it shapes how she constructs a sense of the task demanded of her.

Figure 4.4 shows a draft of Holly's blog entry. Perhaps because of the sentence frames provided by Emily, the connection between the blog and the "Do Now" is not quite made in the initial draft. Neither in her writing or her organization around and for the writing does Holly appear to be drawing on her understanding of 'sentence sense' through the terminology established in the ⁅Do Now⁆.

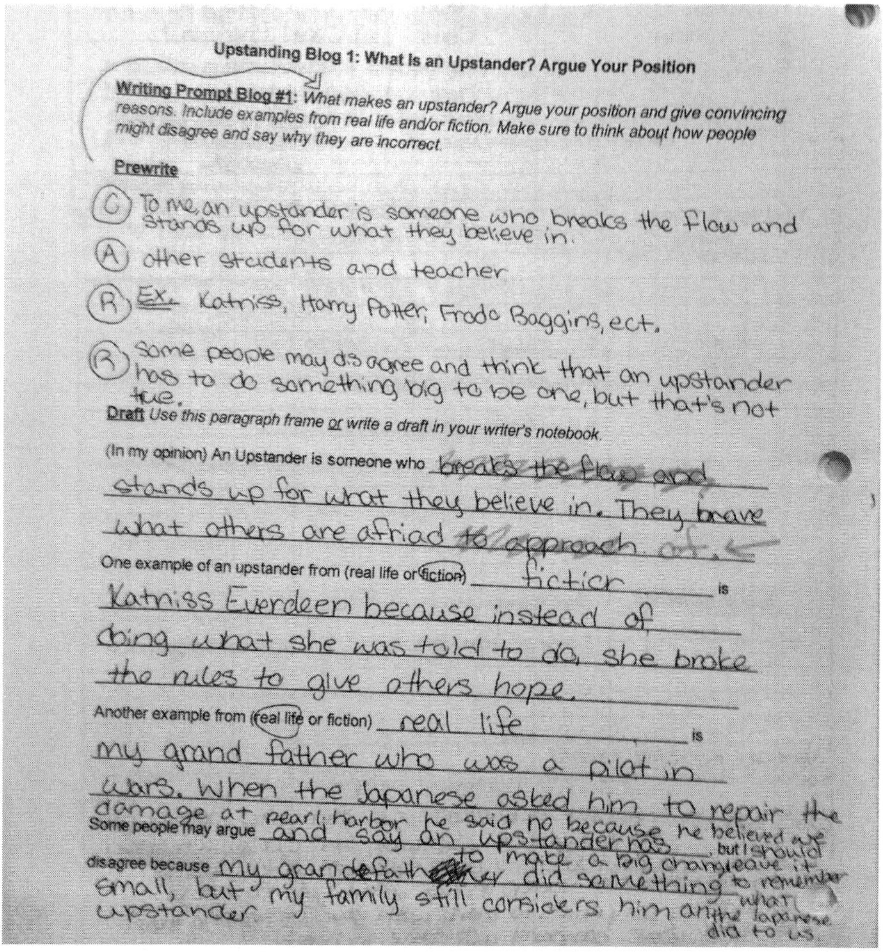

Figure 4.4. Holly's "What is an Upstander?" draft.

However, if we compare the revised blog entry (Figure 4.5) to what Holly wrote in her initial draft, a few important changes emerge. Holly's initial draft is organized into six sentences. Her revised draft—which emerged after several passes of revision—expanded into eight sentences. The additional words (as well as the word replacements) provide clarification for the reader, adding detail and specifying claims beyond the framework and space initially provided by Emily's worksheet. In this space, we seem to see Holly engaged in another project—that of transcribing (and, with it, revising) her blog work for electronic publication on *Kidblog*. However, it is at this point that Holly's attention seems to be changing. In the previous work, Holly is merely accomplishing specific kinds of work. As Holly moves her writing from the page to *Kidblog*, however, her attention to the text seems to change.

Upstanding Bloggers    My Classes

Picture from: tribune.com

LEAVE A COMMENT

## *What Is an Upstander?*

TAGS: BELIEVE   KATNISS EVERDEEN   UPSTANDER   WHAT IS AN UPSTANDER?   CATEGORIES: WHAT
IS AN UPSTANDER?   FEBRUARY 6, 2014 @ 6:33 AM   11 COMMENTS

picture from www.myhungergames.com

    An Upstander is someone who stands up for what they believe in. They brave what others are afraid of. One example of an upstander from fiction is Katniss Everdeen because instead of doing what she was told to do (which was killing Peta), she broke the rules and ended up saving Peta as well as herself. By doing this, Katniss gave hope to others and sparked a war. Another example from real life is my grandfather who was a pilot in wars. After the attack on Pearl Harbor, the Japanese asked him to repair the damage. He said no because he believed we should leave it to remember what the Japanese did to us. Some people may argue and say that someone has to make a big change to be an upstander, but I disagree because my grandfather did something very small and is the perfect example of an upstander because he stood up for what believed in which makes him a hero as well as an upstander.

LEAVE A COMMENT

*Figure 4.5. Holly's revised blog entry.*

Holly seemed to put in more extensive work moving her text to *Kidblog* than her peers did: she added 38 words to her text, rather than simply copying over her writing and making changes suggested by Emily. The additional 38 words came in a variety of forms: new sentences, parenthetic relative clauses, verbal phrases, compounded predicates, and additional clauses (as well as a Creative

Commons-licensed image) provide undeniable sentence variety compared to Holly's initial draft. But the sentence variety itself is just a symptom of a larger shift in Holly's participation in the production of social order. Holly, through her revisions, turned her attention from completing particular tasks to attending to the needs of a particular audience—in this case, Emily.

Holly, in response to my questions about her revisions, mentioned that she liked to "use the S-V splits and stuff" in order to "surprise" Emily, the audience that she has in mind. What is clear from her actual revisions is, of course, that she did not use prepositional phrases to open, split, or close the subject and verb of her sentences in any way that mimicked her work in the {Do Now} activity—either on November 13 or later. However, what Holly does indicate is an attention to two elements: the sentence-level details of her blog entry, and the needs of her audience. Furthermore, these two elements are co-constructed into being during the space of revision between drafting and publishing. Holly's perception of sentence-level activity as important is directly related to her perception of Emily as an audience, but only becomes mobilized as Holly wrestled with the opportunities that a shift between rough draft and final publication offered.

The available data does not suggest that Holly's syntactic flexibility has dramatically transformed, nor that her knowledge of sentence structures gleaned from the "Do Now" activity has helped her make sense of the sentence that she is writing. What she appears to have done is realize new possibilities for action at the sentence level in her work across multiple drafts: that is, the sentence has become something it is possible to revise, something that can "surprise" a reader. She seems to have taken up this value through the work of revising her blog entry while she transcribed it from page to *Kidblog* entry. Furthermore, we can trace similar work across future multi-draft publications in Emily's classroom, which suggests that the transformation of between-draft moments as opportunities for sentence-level revision has the staying power to count as literate action development.

## The Possibilities of the Points: Don

Contrast this activity with the activity of Don, the point-keeper for the class. Don is a very active student who regularly talks with other students throughout the class period. However, Don does not push at the edges of classroom boundaries. He is a strategic speaker, rarely addressed by the teacher for speaking out of turn. He also participates regularly in class.

Don is a capable writer and artist. His writer's notebook is littered with detailed sketches of people from some kind of cartoon or video with which I am completely unfamiliar. His writing is also regarded as superior according to classroom benchmarks, and he regularly receives high marks for his efforts. However, Don does not self-identify as a writer; rather, making stories is something that he does with friends. The link between academic writing and personal writing, for Don, has not yet been made.

Don had spent the second part of the lesson—the completion of the sentence-combining "Do Now" activity—awarding "points" to different groups who were participating in the activity. These group points could benefit student grades later in the year. After the groups finished and Emily moved on, Don was not quite done at the board, as Emily asked him to "add up all the points so [she] could see who the winner is." He was caught between the instructions to pull his agenda out of his backpack and revise the week's entries and tallying the points for the week. He chose to finish his point tallying before moving back to his seat and, as a result, had an entirely different experience than a fellow student seated not far from him. Examining this activity in the context of the broader classroom action that Don engaged in will reveal the developmental opportunities present.

Don's work at the board began as the class shifted to the third part of their daily warm-up, the class discussion. Emily called on her first student to read his answer. Upon hearing it, Emily said "So he did an S-V split and closer, and that worked perfectly. And then I've got to remember that group five gets a point" before calling on someone else. While she was saying this, Don got up from his desk and moved to the front of the room to start recording points, bringing his notebook and "Do Now" sheet with him. He walked up the middle aisle of the classroom, moved to the left-hand side of the board, spun, and picked up a marker to write down group five's point. As Emily calls on students, Don recorded points for different groups, interacting with nearby students and occasionally dancing as he does so. At one point, Emily remarks that Don is "doing a good job with that."

At the point in the year that this activity happened (May 21), Emily had elaborated her "Do Now" to include not just a sentence combining but an imitation: a chance for students to reproduce the sentence structure they discussed through their own experience. After providing an example of her own—involving her brother getting into trouble with her parents for staying out past curfew—Emily encouraged her students to take one minute and write down an imitation of their own. When she gives students this minute, Don put his marker down and returned to his desk. Once sitting at his desk, Don realized that he left his notebook and "Do Now" sheet at the front of the room, and got up again to retrieve it. By the time Don returned to his desk, Emily is ready to discuss the sentence imitations with the class. Back at his desk, Don took a drink of water from his water bottle and had a brief exchange with a student next to him. Before he could turn to his imitation activity, however, Don was called to the front of the room by Emily to continue awarding points. Don left his notebook and "Do Now" sheet at the table this time.

It is here that Don is asked to do two things at once: revise his agenda and add up his points. Don responds to the twin pressures by finishing his notes at the board and then returning to his desk to finish his agenda revising. While Don is adding up points, Emily reviews late library book returns, and resolves a time conflict between their "river teeth" activity and a National Honor Society event. Don's time lost on the new activity was somewhat attenuated by Emily's need to address two students who, in her view, were not attending to the assignment. Don arrived back at his seat at the end of that address, and was able to quickly fill in the changes to the week's entries in the agenda before Emily shifted the discussion to a survey that the GATE ("Gifted and Talented Education" program) sponsorship brought into the classroom. By the time Emily begins handing out the survey instructions, Don has completed both activities.

Don's orchestration of tasks allow him to prioritize the writing that he has to do in order to participate in a range of social action in the classroom. Don's actions in this literate act show a change in the prioritizing of activities that he carries with him into multiple writing opportunities (i.e., "river teeth," anthologies, etc.) throughout the remaining weeks of the school year. This shifted awareness of the importance of different elements of writing tasks makes itself known via the attention given to each of the final activities of the year. This attention reveals an increasing awareness of the interconnectedness of the kinds of writing that Don finds himself doing, as well as the management of social arrangements needed to accomplish each of them.

Looking at what Don does through our existing concepts, it seems that Don is using his practices to wrestle some new information—that is, a quick succession of writing tasks that he is faced with on a regular basis as the Point Keeper—into a more manageable *What-Comes-Next*. Don's rapid movement from Point Keeping to agenda-revising suggests that he has established a kind of synergetic production of practice that allows him to move forward and participate in class with practices that, though necessarily adumbrated in ways noticeably different from those of his classmates, are not problematically so.

Don manages this deeper integration of writing tasks by recognizing new possibilities in particular objects. Some of this recognition is not effective—such as when he brings his notebook and "Do Now" sheet to the front of the room with him, and forgets it there when he returns to his desk—but his attention to the integration of his activities follows from the relationships that he sees (i.e., the unifying principle) in the objects he works with. This unifying principle is not itself visible, but can be inferred from the interrelationships of objects that Don works with sequentially. Consider, for instance, Don's movement from his "Do Now" writing to his Point Keeper work. When the discussion begins about the warm-up, Don's sentences are written, and he is able to attend to the work of the Point Keeper without falling behind on a graded assignment (Emily scores warm-up activities) just before a high-stakes event about that particular assignment (there is a quiz at the end of the week on the sentence structures of the "Do Now"). When Don returns to his desk after the point-totaling is complete, he finishes updating his agenda before the next activity begins.

These new possibilities can also be seen in the work that Don chooses not to take up. Don's decision to forego reading his sentence as part of the group work suggests that he sees his writing—though a necessary component of participation at the time—as a problematic object to take up in his co-production of the social order of the classroom, not because of problems in the moment but because of problems that can arise in subsequent moments. In other words, Don is participating in specific ways so that he can see and act on a broader sequence of activity. Don also manages to maintain this work moving forward through the remainder of the academic year. Much like Alice in Chapter 1, Don's work to begin integrating a range of practices comes rather late in the academic year. As the "river teeth" unit develops in Emily's class, Don's practices remain more tightly knit in this unit than in previous ones, so his progression through the sequence of activities in Emily's classroom echo with the same preparatory purposes: Don continues to be ready for the next task by the time the current one wraps up for the class as a whole. This keeps Don from falling behind schedule in the flow of writing activity in Emily's class, to be sure, but it also suggests that Don is controlling for potentially problematic adumbration in his perspective on the unfolding social order of the classroom. The movement from being responsive to this problematic adumbration as it arises to taking steps to keep it from arising suggests that Don saw the competing demands on his time as elevated uncertainty, as information that he worked to reduce in his subsequent literate action. To do so, he turned to the scenically available talk, tools, and texts around him to coordinate his literate action and create a manageable *What Comes-Next* in these complexly-layered moments.

The literate action development that Don goes through here is, like Holly, a recognition of new opportunities in previously-unexamined spaces of social and literate action. Holly came to see the space between drafts as an opportunity for sentence-level attention in response to the needs of her audience. Don saw pacing his literate action in relation to the unfolding social order of the class as a way to meet the demands of consequential tasks that were competing for his attention. Instead of the space between drafts, Don looked to the space within tasks.

## Extending a Series of Moments: Stretching Concepts through Time and Lifeworlds

This chapter has explored the effectiveness of the five concepts established in Chapters Two and Three across broader spans of time and social activity. In Chapter Three, Marianne and Nick's candidate moments of literate action development occur in a tightly-scripted series of opportunities provided by Emily. Holly's and Don's literate action, though still rooted deeply in the co-construction of the classroom, ranges across multiple classroom activities such as classroom warm-up activities, readings, and agenda-writing. Additionally, these activities range far past the timespan covered in Marianne and Nick's examples. Whereas Marianne and Nick's work spans several weeks, the literate action development chronicled in Holly and Nick's work spans several months. Holly's and Don's literate action, in other words, enabled us to see what the concepts developed in

Chapters Two and Three uncover within a broader swath of lifeworld over a longer span of time.

So, how did these concepts hold up to such a task? Did they shed important light on the lived reality of literate action development? Have they continued to be useful ways of understanding the literate action that people engage in in a given moment of time and how that action contributes to the ongoing development of literate action over a broad span of time? Based on the findings that emerged from the study of Holly's and Don's literate action, the answer seems to be "yes." Below, I articulate the value that each of these concepts brought to the study of literate action development from the perspective of the lived reality.

The first concept articulated in Chapter 2 was that of practices—the socially recognizable work that enables writers to make their actions sensible to others and themselves. Practices are broadly used in writing research, but in the ethnomethodological respecification of my study the emphasis was placed on the tactical work of such practices: the way they emerged from scenically available materials and co-constructed social order. Attending to the practices of Holly and Don highlighted the ways in which transformations emerge and endure, just as they did with Marianne and Nick. The broader spans of time and activities are not blocked off by a focus on practices. Rather, attending to practices has shown how each of these writers builds a lifeworld and orchestrates those growing lifeworlds with others in their continued engagements with and through literate action.

One of the central tasks that practices performs is to reduce the uncertainty of *What-Comes-Next*. Recognizing the work of Holly and Don to tangle with *What-Comes-Next* through their practices across broader stretches of time (Holly) and increasing co-present activities (Don) highlighted the ways in which our practices and the transformations of them build upon scenically available material. Information, likewise, proved a generative concept, as it provided some language for what Holly and Don were working through when the uncertainty of *What-Comes-Next* increased beyond what recurring practices were capable of contending with. Working in tandem with the concept of practices, *What-Comes-Next* and information directed attention to the tactical work of any given moment, the incredible flexibility that such practices offer, and the conditions through which actors realize new possibilities for action that they make scenically available in the further ongoing, serial production of local social order involving literate action.

The final two concepts, adumbration and the possibilities of objects, rounded out an analysis that kept the lived reality both at the heart of studying literate action development and grounded in the materiality of unfolding social order. Adumbration proved up to the task of tracing the lifeworlds of Holly and Don through the ongoing revisions of their practices. This concept directed analytical attention to the practices that Holly and Don saw as scenically available to them in a given moment and, by extension, the ways in which they used that availability (or lack thereof) to build out their lifeworlds in enduring ways.

# Moving Toward Coherence: Building a Conceptual Framework

This chapter expands the initial work of Chapter 3, demonstrating the ways in which moments of literate action more distanced in time, space, and co-constructed purpose (such as Holly's sentence-combining activity) can be made scenically available in the present moment as key elements in the take-up of new possibilities of arrangements of objects as they are talked and acted into being in both individuated and intersubjective ways. The constellation of concepts tentatively finalized in Chapter 3 that drive toward an understanding of the lived reality—*What-Comes-Next*, practices, information, the possibilities of objects, and adumbration—prove up to the task of tracing literate action development across slightly broader spans of time than demonstrated in Chapter 3. The particularities of the moments in this chapter—such the ways in which they work across jointly-produced activities at various points in the past—make these moments perspicuous in revealing the reach and power of these operationalized concepts.

It would appear now that a set of concepts exist for envisioning and making sense of literate action development from the perspective of the lived reality. This approach has evaluated the candidacy of specific moments of literate action for being developmental in nature in a way that allows for a robust articulation of the features of that lived reality that might turn our attention more effectively toward development as occurring amidst the ongoing work of social ordering that participants are always already engaged in. The emerging understanding of these concepts and how to work with them, however, remains deeply rooted in the particularities of each of the four moments described in this chapter and in Chapter 3, as well as Alice's example in Chapter 1. In the next chapter, I take important steps to render the findings in these chapters and their implications for the concepts being brought to bear on understanding the lived reality of literate action development *portable*, able to be brought to bear on a wider range of situations involving literate action throughout the lifespan.

# Chapter 5. The Totality of the Literate Experience

The first four chapters of this text provided an exigence for an ethnomethodological respecification of writing development when considering writing through the lifespan and articulated a set of interrelated concepts to frame the *lived reality of literate action development*. This chapter brings these concepts together to form a portable logic-in-use for understanding the lived reality that I refer to as the *totality of the literate experience*. This totality is a lens that I will be using to make sense of literate action development at other points in the lifespan in Part II. Below, I tightly bound the lived reality of literate action development, articulating what needs attending to and what does not when researching writing through that lens.

## The Totality of the Literate Experience: A Conceptual Framework

As I indicated at the close of the previous chapter, the five concepts I've brought to bear on the lived reality of literate action development (*practices*, *What-Comes-Next*, *information*, *adumbration*, and *possibilities of objects*) appear to work productively with one another in certain ways. With the *totality of the literate experience*, I fully integrate these five concepts to build a productive and, as seen below, portable logic-in-use for understanding the lived reality of literate action development. The totality of the literate experience (or "totality") directs attention, through an integrated network of concepts, to each passing moment of literate action and the richness of each moment. Essentially, the totality begins with the assumption that any given moment of literate action is bursting at the seams with many dimensions of human activity.

The ways in which this opportunity is taken up in a given moment—the way in which the totality is operationalized, made real as the moment develops—can be followed through the concepts traced through the first four chapters of this text. These concepts are situated along a timespan (see Figure 5.1) through which the totality continually unfolds. Note how the practices, understood in an adumbrated manner by individual actors, lead into and shape the joint production of *What-Comes-Next*. The increasing uncertainty of *What-Comes-Next*, indicated to the right-hand side of the figure, is represented by the disconnect between the height of practices and the height of *What-Comes-Next* as depicted in the figure. It is this gap that may trigger literate action development.

I suggest that, in order to understand the lived reality of literate action development, we need to make the totality of the literate experience the center of our theoretical and empirical attention. Of course, it is impossible to see the totality of the literate experience in its entirety: no matter our social positioning, there is always a horizon of understanding beyond which we will be unable to see. Attending closely to individual moments of writing, how people co-construct order within those individual moments of writing, the dimensions through which that ordering carries to the next moment, and the ways in which unarticulated dimensions are dragged along through that ordering are all made possible with the totality of the literate experience, as a conceptual framework, acting as a central interpretive lens. Treating the totality of the literate experience as a concept for considering the literate action of individuals over time enables writing research to look toward the material, situated, and intersubjectively-aligned actions that contribute to the construction, perpetuation, and alteration of literate practices. Through attention to the totality of the literate experience, we can understand not just how individuals come to make sense of the world over long periods of time and retrospectively, but also how those literate practices come to be constructed from materially and temporally situated actions by individuals.

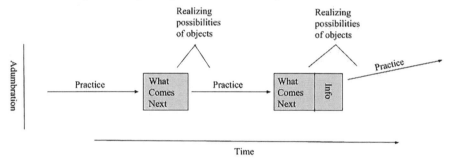

*Figure 5.1. Concepts in action: Focusing on the lived reality.*

## Revisiting Alice's River Teeth through the Totality

In Chapter 1, I indicated the first of what became five candidate moments of literate action development and, drawing on ethnomethodological insights as a starting point, asked whether such a moment might "count" as literate action development for the student in question, Alice. At that point in the text, I had not yet developed a sufficiently robust conceptual framework through which I could examine Alice's literate action to answer my question effectively. In the intervening chapters, I took a closer look at the classroom Alice was working in, traced out other candidate moments of literate action development, and articulated a working conceptual framework, the totality. In Part II, I will be bringing this totality to bear on other moments of literate action at different points in the lifespan, but I want to fully bring my Part I investigations to a close by bringing this completed conceptual framework to bear on the case of Alice.

This investigation begins, of course, with the practices that Alice brought to bear on her work with the "river teeth" writing. Alice was participating in the work of ⟨desk organizing⟩, ⟨instruction reading⟩, and ⟨writing activity⟩ in her work on May 23. Her participation, as I noted in the start of Chapter 1, began as unexceptional in regard to her past participation: she was silent, followed the teacher's examples, and did not converse with her fellow students nearby, even when others took advantage of the opportunity. So we can think of Alice's practices as largely meeting the demands of *What-Comes-Next*. What we need to find in the sequence of Alice's work is the increase of uncertainty, the rise of information that her scenically-available practices are incapable of meeting. There are two signals of a potential rise of uncertainty: Alice's reflective writing and her written-out "river teeth" story.

Alice's writing in both of these texts suggests a need to work through information with writing in ways that the scenic availability of past practices cannot account for. Much like Marianne, Alice has found something in the content of her work that makes it different from her previous writing. As Alice is constructing a text about her sister pushing her off of a trampoline, she sees the construction of the text not only as a series of moves to be completed according to the structuring that Emily provides, but as a place to work out the complexities of a past experience. Alice's literate action for and around the "river teeth" writing takes into account both the unfolding social situation of a ⟨writing activity⟩ and, at the same time, as an item in a broader series of situational moments stretching back into her interactions with her sibling. Alice's listening to her teacher's stories (which involved her interactions with her own family and her own injuries that emerged as part of those interactions) brought to mind her past experiences with falling off of the trampoline, which then became an artifact of her May 23 activity.

When Alice brings her "river teeth" packet out to engage in her story drafting, the trampoline story becomes scenically available to her, and is caught up in her practice of moving from pre-writing to outlining to writing and revising a text throughout a unit, which has become a common practice in Emily's classroom. In her work of co-constructing social order from an adumbrated perspective, Alice has blended the history of her interaction with her sister with the work of completing one of Emily's units, and this blending has not only extended the lifeworld of her schooling activity (bringing her family life at least partly into it) but also created additional information—the complexities of her past experience that need working out. This blending then leads Alice to her claim that her sister, in apologizing for knocking her off of the trampoline, "realized that it is all fun and games until you do something dum." Alice seems to face increased uncertainty again in her construction of her reflective writing, when she draws the conclusion that she would like to remember her "river teeth" moments.

To summarize briefly, Alice's practices led to two moments of increased information in the ongoing sorting of *What-Comes-Next*. This, in turn, led her to extend the lifeworld of her classroom activity in resolving the complexities of her past experience, which she came to see, in her adumbrated perspective, as central to the ongoing work of her "river teeth" story. This leads her to see new possibilities in the objects in front of her, which is as a place to work out such complexity. So it would seem that Alice, at this point, has had a transformative moment and that, just as before the conceptual framework was elicited, this is a genuine candidate moment of literate action development. But is it actually a moment of development?

One of the important signals that a candidate moment of development actually *is* a moment of development is the durability of the transformation. Drawing on the language we developed in Chapter 4, we can say that the transformation makes itself scenically available in the future production of literate action. Alice's literate action, occuring as it does late in the academic year, does not provide a great deal of opportunity for following the practice into the future. However, Alice is able, in her moment of "river teeth" writing, to extend her academic lifeworld to encompass stories about and from her family. As the "river teeth" writing moves on in the final weeks of the academic year, we see Alice continue to do the work of integrating these lifeworlds across another entry, culminating in her brief comment in the critical reflection. This suggests that Alice, in the construction of her "river teeth" writing, has had a moment of literate action development.

## Chasing a Phenomenon of Interest: Making the Totality Portable as a Logic-in-Use

The concepts of the totality are, as I indicate in these initial chapters of Part I, a productive one for examining literate action development from the perspective of the lived reality. At this point in the text, however, the phenomenon of interest—literate action development—has been located in the strategic and perspicuous research settings of a middle school. School settings are important aspects of literate and social development, not the least because of the sheer volume of time that it takes up at important phases in the lives of developing writers (but see Prior, 2018). Emily's classroom provided a more strategic and perspicuous research setting than most classrooms, rife as it was with many kinds of writing on a regular basis throughout the academic year. The conceptual framework as it stands, however, is tightly tied to the particularities of studying writing when the following resources are available:

1. Regular access to writing in all of its stages, both public and private;
2. Regular access to literate action as it is happening; and
3. Opportunities to observe transformations over time.

These resources are not necessarily available, depending on the goals of a research program. For instance, if I were interested in the development of literate action for writers throughout the twentieth century, none of these resources are available to me—I am restricted to writers as they develop throughout the twenty-first century, as I would need to witness the literate action as it happens. Yet research such as that of Deborah Brandt's (2001) still shows us a great deal about how people become different kinds of writers over time.

In order to give wider flexibility to my conceptual framework (and, as I will show in Part II, to use that flexibility to my advantage as I study literate action development throughout the lifespan), I suggest envisioning the framework not as merely a tool for investigation but as a *logic-in-use* (Green, Skukauskaite & Baker, 2012; Kaplan, 1964), one that focuses on the lived reality of literate action development and uses that focus to shape subsequent investigations of literate action with a range of methods, participants, and records.

The term logic-in-use has several roots. Kaplan (1964) separates a logic-in-use from what he calls reconstructed logic (p. 3). A logic-in-use is, as its title suggests, a logic that exists as it is used. In the writing up of research, this logic is often reconstructed in ways that fit neatly under separate banners of "methodology," "epistemology," and so on (see Lee, 2004 for a concise summary of Kaplan's position). The claim that Kaplan makes is that this reconstruction is not the logic-in-use. Our epistemologies, our ontologies, do not stand still for distillation into a particular section of a text. They are lived, enacted in the conduct of research, and only fragmentarily revealed via reconstructed logic. Reconstructed logics are, in Lee's words, *maps*, and maps, although helpful, are not territories.

In order to mobilize this framework into something more portable, I propose articulating not a methodology or an epistemology but a logic-in-use that is flexible in response to the needs of the research question and the research site. I draw particularly off of the language of Green, Baker, and Skukauskaite (2012) in this work. In their development of ethnography as a logic-in-use, they provide what they refer to as "principles of operation" (2012, p. 312) to guide the work of ethnographers in a "nonlinear" process of enacting "an iterative, recursive, and abductive logic" (p. 309). These principles of operation include

- Ethnography as a non-linear system;
- Leaving aside ethnocentrism;
- Identifying boundaries of what is happening; and
- Building connections.

These principles generate conceptual issues and implicated actions, which they articulate further through a *telling case* (Mitchell, 1984) that highlights the work of these principles in action.

Rather than offering principles and implicated actions, I offer, in Table 5.1, three *framings* for operationalizing the concepts of the totality into a logic-in-use that can be applied to new sites of study. These framings, available in Table 5.1, will enable researchers to ask new research questions, bring new methods to bear, and still keep the lived reality at the center of research.

**Table 5.1: Rendering a Portable Logic-in-Use**

| Concept | Framing |
| --- | --- |
| Practices | Ongoing, Joint Action |
| *What-Comes-Next*, Information, Adumbration | Individuated Actor |
| Possibilities of Objects | Scenic Reduction of Uncertainty |

I offer these framings as an alternative to a more rigid methodology in order to enable researchers to make methodological choices informed by my findings but still responsive to the needs of the actor under study. In Part II of this text, I bring these steps to bear on writers at other points in the lifespan, writing under very different circumstances, in order to examine the effectiveness of this logic-in-use.

## Framing Ongoing, Joint Action

The initial framing move in this logic-in-use is envisioning literate action as occurring among (and as part of) the ongoing, joint production of social order. People make meaning, make sense of the world around them in order to operate within it. Any given literate act occurs as part of a wider sequence of joint production of social order that carries on what we perceive as "broader," "larger," or "more distant" social structures. Social order only exists, in other words, because people work together to *make* it exist, again and again, always for another first time.

In framing any given literate action under study as participating in ongoing social order, researchers must see literate action as composed of *practices*—socially recognizable actions that allow people to orient themselves to one another and keep social order (and, with it, literate action) going. As we saw in the work of Nick in Chapter 3, practices in the ethnomethodological tradition help us to think differently about goal-directed human action. The goal of a practice, for instance, may be to do nothing more than continue social order: to maintain a line in a bookstore (Livingston, 1987), to maintain momentum in an awkward meeting among family members, etc. Through the concept of practices, researchers can attend to the ways in which members of a group engage in ongoing, joint action with, through, and from which literate action development occurs.

Researchers can begin framing ongoing, joint action by turning to the following questions to orient their work:

1. What signals are present in available records that might suggest practices in action?
2. How might the sequential development of such available records suggest practices of multiple actors?
3. In what ways might the records suggest an interplay among these practices in action?

Though broad, these questions and others like them can help researchers focus on to the work of ongoing, joint action by attending to individual practices and the work that those practices do to help people keep literate action going.

Early in Chapter 1, I articulated the need to attend to the *serial* production of social order—that is, literate action as it happens with, through, and around a particular actor over time. In the intervening chapters, this focus on the serial has become backgrounded, but it is a crucial aspect of the first step in this logic-in-use. Whatever the available records are—recordings of writers, interviews, existing documents, or some combination of the three—ongoing, joint action can only be productively framed if the joint action is seen as serial, as linked and historical in nature, even if the connection between one moment and the next (as was indicated in the studies in the earlier chapters) needs some analysis.

Beginning with ethnomethodological insights on social order in mind, the work of literate action must be framed as occurring amidst the ongoing work of jointly-produced social order. It is at this step that socially recognizable practices need careful attention: how do people act in ways that will be interpretable to themselves and others, and how does that action shape the situation as it unfolds—and, for those interested in development, how does one unfolding situation lead to the next?

## Framing the Individuated Actor

After framing ongoing, joint social action through an attention to practices (and the questions above), researchers can move toward an individuated orientation to those practices and their development over time. This is the second step, which frames individuated actors in the work of the ongoing, joint production of social order. As noted in earlier chapters, all individuated views of unfolding social order are *adumbrated*, and this adumbration is the condition through which development emerges. As groups work to reduce the uncertainty of *What-Comes-Next*, uncertainty will be raised higher for some actors than others. Their work to continue the fragile social ordering of everyday life has the opportunity to transform their practices, perhaps in enduring ways. Understanding the ways in which individuated views on an unfolding situation have been adumbrated enables the tracing of increased uncertainty when it arrives.

Researchers can uncover the individuated actor in the ongoing production of joint social action by working through the following questions:

1.  What threads of practices by a single individuated actor might be productively followed across records?
2.  How might such practices be envisioned as tactical responses to the problem-at-hand of producing social order?
3.  What instances of particular practices represent the start of a dynamic transformation for the individuated actor in question?

Through these questions, the individuated actor can be singled out of a series of records and their particular practice(s) can be traced across multiple instances over time. In this second step, the individuated literate actor is recognized and followed, and the available records are reduced and, in ethnographic terms (see Green, Skukauskaite & Baker 2012), turned into data for further analysis.

## Framing the Scenic Work of Uncertainty Reduction

In keeping with a repurposing of ethnomethodology that attends to the *serial* production of local social order, and drawing on the insights available from Chapter 4 in particular, the final step in framing is to attend to the ways in which the past is scenically located in the present. This final step in framing the lived reality highlights the serial nature of local order, and the ways in which individuated actors make the past materially available in the present.

In the first two frames, literate action development was characterized as (1) occurring through the ongoing, joint production of social action and (2) an individuated experience for particular actors under study. At the third step of analysis, then, researchers should have an individuated actor in mind and a particular practice (or practices) to follow through available records-turned-data. Step 3 enables the researcher to see the instances of practice use as deeply scenic by turning to the material work of co-constructing that practice. Through an attention to the material, and a realization of the connections that those materials have to past records of a practice, researchers can identify the new possibilities of objects that are recognized by individuated actors over time.

Researchers can highlight the scenic, material, tactical work of a practice by asking the following questions of the data available from the first two frames:

1. What objects appear to be attended to across particular moments of practice by the individuated actor?
2. How do these objects appear to create new possibilities for action during the highlighted moments of potential dynamic transformation?
3. How might these transformations be materially confirmed in future instances of a practice?

These questions conclude the path to the totality of the literate experience: they, when approached after the conclusion of the first two steps of the process, highlight the transformation of a literate practice from the perspective of the lived reality, and signal to researchers the ways in which the continued transformation of that practice over time might be productively attended to.

These framings are nebulous, but they are purposefully nebulous. At the heart of ethnomethodological study in the tradition of Garfinkel is the rejection of an express methodology. A methodology should be built, in part, on the phenomenon of interest and the site of study for that interest—an intersection, really, of a disciplinary investigation and the site within which that investigation happens. So to prescribe a particular methodology in a form such as grounded theory (Glaser & Strauss, 1967) or ethnography (as framed by Emerson, Fretz & Shaw, 1995) would threaten to occlude an important part of the decision-making process in following the phenomenon of interest across sites, lifeworlds, and the lifespan. Each of the framings articulated here is a productive middle space between site- and participant-responsive methodological choice-making and the larger project of examining literate action development through the lifespan. In Part II, I mobilize this logic-in-use across several sites along the lifespan in order to both test the utility of the totality and begin developing lived reality-grounded concepts from which middle-range theories can later emerge.

# Part II. Tracing Development through the Totality

In Part I, I drew on ethnomethodological research and empirical observation to construct a logic-in-use for studying the lived reality of literate action development. In Part II, I apply this logic-in-use to study the literate action development of six writers at various ages in the lifespan. I conclude Part II by looking across these cases to (1) identify potential concepts that may be worked up into middle-range theories and (2) articulate a vision for seeing the totality as an infrastructure for studying literate action through the lifespan.

In the introduction to this text, I brought up the criteria of *strategic* and *perspicuous* research sites. A research site must be *strategic* in that it shows literate action *in action*, and it must be *perspicuous* by making visible the joint sense-making actions of the literate actors under study. In Part I, the research site selected overlapped in its strategic and perspicuous senses. The literate action studied in Part II, however, is different in a number of ways from the texts in Part I. This is deliberate, in that I want to use the totality at other points in the lifespan to both refine my understanding of it and generate new understandings about literate action development. But these deliberate differences also open up more space between the *strategic* and *perspicuous* research site criteria. Throughout Part II, I make decisions to sacrifice some of one for the other. This introduction to Part II provides a general rationale for my choices, which I will build off of to detail my specific decisions in each chapter.

## A Note on Responsive Abstracting for Part II

In Chapter 1, I drew on the work of Garfinkel (2002) and his use of ticked brackets to articulate the ethnomethodological core of this work: that there is order in the everyday work of social activity, a social order that is always locally produced. Throughout Part I, I followed the ongoing production of social order to identify how individuated development emerged within that order. This work focused largely on ticked brackets, illustrated as ⦃ ⦄. The ticked brackets allowed me to articulate the way in which I saw order as forming scenically, in the moment. In Part II, I continue my search for social order as part of my emergent logic-in-use of the totality.

But the goal of this text is not to uncover social order and its production—instead, I am looking to build and then use a foundational infrastructure for studying literate action development through the lifespan. In Part II, I mobilize the infrastructure of the totality to develop concepts through which middle-range theory can emerge. As we saw in Chapter 1, Garfinkel would characterize this move—from the production of social order to explanatory theory—as this:

$$\leftarrow \rightarrow \rightarrow (\ \ )$$

The arrow in this diagram denotes the methods through which the production of social order is abstracted into formal analytic (FA) conclusions. Garfinkel saw enormous problems with such theorizing, believing that such a move would lose the phenomenon of the production of social order.

Despite Garfinkel's concerns, abstracting from the lived reality is a necessary function of the logic-in-use developed in Part I. Garfinkel's work, focused as it was on groups of people acting together and the practices that emerged from it, had the power of anonymity to support the practices it discovered. The practices for crossing an intersection, for instance, could be confirmed by its anonymous character: everyone acted in such a way to avoid being hit by a car when crossing that intersection. Garfinkel's attention to practices, then, remains focused on the shared aspects of it, and how we can engage in practices to reproduce immortal, everyday society.

Following individuated actors, however, loses some of the explanatory power that the ticked brackets traditionally provide with ethnomethodological work. The individuated take-up of practices in a particular moment is useful for understanding that writer's literate action development, but portable accounts that are useful for teachers and researchers developing lesson plans and research problems cannot easily emerge from such isolated work.

In order to combat this problem, I engage in *responsive* abstracting throughout Part II. Keeping the lived reality at the center of my attention through the totality, I develop concepts that enable one to abstract out of particular situations in ways that are sensitive to the ongoing production of social order from which those concepts emerged. In Chapter 9, I indicate how these concepts can be responsively mobilized into middle-range theories with broader analytical purchase.

## A Note on Methodology for Part II

In Part I, I attended closely to the moment-to-moment literate action of writers. This material attention to literate action allowed me to identify moments of literate action development and build, from those moments, a framework for examining literate action development across wider populations of writers. Though I found this analysis valuable, its success was, in large part, due to the fact that I developed it out of a setting that was both strategic (for my research question) and offered perspicuous detail about the production of social order when the writers I studied were engaged in writing.

The seventh-grade students I studied were at a moment of transition in their lives. Having just moved from a single teacher in sixth grade to multiple teachers in multiple class periods in seventh grade, these students' school-home lives were drastically altered. They now had more bosses and, with them, more homework to attend to. So the writing they often did on their own out of class was pushed aside in order to meet the demands of school. As a result, the writing I saw them perform in the classroom was connected to a broader network of writing activities that dominated, at the time, their writing lives. In contrast, the older writers I study in Part II of this text have complex literate lives that are more difficult to glimpse than that of sixth graders.

The changes in the circumstances of the writers under study necessitate different record collection. Tracing literate action at the moment of its performance ceases to be a useful option, as the cost of following a writer around is too high: such a study would not be able to be continued indefinitely and, if it were, the presence of a camera, or other researcher, or recorder of any kind might (and, in the case of writing in solitude, would) disrupt the everyday production of literate action. As a result, I would destroy the very phenomenon I hoped to study.

In order to keep the phenomenon of interest in my sights, then, I turned to a method of data collection often pushed aside by ethnomethodologists: retrospective interviews. Ethnomethodologists (Garfinkel, 2002) see retrospective interviews as problematic because, in their eyes, the phenomenon of social order is lost in the retelling of it. There are aspects of social order not available to the conscious attention of the actor, and attempts to stimulate recall of those aspects can introduce unavoidable variables: since the interview is itself a production of social order, how can we separate the recall of the production of social order from the production of social order that is the interview?

Despite these problems, however, I suggest that retrospective interviews are rich with possibility for studying the production of social order in literate action. Though certainly rife with potential confounding variables, the payout in terms of records collected on my phenomenon of interest is worth the challenge. By taking up my logic-in-use through records collected via retrospective interviews, I am able to extend and refine my understanding of literate action development from the perspective of the lived reality. Below, I articulate a brief overview of my rationale for moving to retrospective interviews, which I elaborate on further in each chapter as part of my rationale for particular decision-making with particular subjects.

At the heart of my ethnomethodological respecification of the retrospective interview is Schutz's (1945) notion of the *cognitive style*. Schutz, drawing on the work of William James, suggested that "there are several, probably an infinite number of various orders of realities, each with its own special and separate style of existence" (1945, p. 533). Garfinkel's reading of Schutz leads him to conclude that an interview would not grant the researcher access to the cognitive style[5] at work

---

5. Garfinkel's use of the term "cognitive style" in his dissertation and in Seeing Sociologically (2006) is a repurposing of Schutz's phrasing to suggest that one's "cognitive style" emerges with and through interaction. So even in his use of the term, Garfinkel was attempting to work around cognitive explanations of social order and

in the production of a given reality, and that, even if it could, there would be no way to verify that access. The work we do to produce social order, in other words, is not accessible retrospectively. For Garfinkel and the ethnomethodologists who followed him, then, the very act of interviewing *loses* the phenomenon of producing social order.

My recovery of the retrospective interview begins with the assumption that the cognitive style of literate action can, in some circumstances and with the proper (that is, aligned to the phenomenon of interest) interview protocol, reveal the cognitive style of literate action in verifiable ways. My assumption of a cognitive style as accessible via more traditional sociological methods emerges in part from Cicourel's (1964, 2004) reasoning. Cicourel frames what he calls an *ecological validity problem*. This problem is posed as a series of questions:

> To what extent is the content of questions asked commensurate with the socially distributed knowledge possessed by the respondents? Do the questions asked address topics, beliefs, attitudes and opinions the respondents routinely discuss in everyday life during social interaction with others? Further, to what extent can we assume that given the absence of ethnographic information about different communities, we can ignore the extent to which the wording and content of the questions are comprehended similarly by the entire sample? Are the questions, therefore, different from or are they in correspondence or congruent with observing the way respondents express themselves in their daily life encounters with others? (2004)

Cicourel works through this ecological validity problem by avoiding interviews in isolation, and incorporating ethnographic work that helps researchers build ecological validity to the questions posed in interviews (as well as surveys, although that is not part of the data I work with in the coming chapters). As noted above, Cicourel sees the need for interviews to emerge out of the work of everyday life—the questions have to be "congruent" with the ways in which respondents make sense of their daily activity.

Consider, for instance, an interview with a ghost writer, someone writing for other people, such as celebrities who do not have time to pen their own book. A researcher might be interested in how such a writer goes about collecting the material needed for this work, and how evidence is confirmed in the process of producing a text. But drawing on the language of the sentence above would run the risk of skewing the records collected, of leading the interviewee to give infor-

---

focus on interactional work. As he mentions in his article on trust (Garfinkel, 1963), "There is no reason to look under the skull since nothing of interest is to be found there but brains" (p. 6).

mation in the form that is requested by the interviewee, rather than allowing the flow of literate action to shape responses. The interviewer, therefore, would be in a better position to frame interview questions if they began with observing writing in action, the language the writer used when talking with others about their work, and the process through which a text seems to be emerging. This would be a starting point for collecting the language, the activity needed to form questions that will bring forward the lived reality of composing a text.

Ethnographic data of writers writing, as I address above, is problematic with older writers who write through a range of lifeworlds. By substituting several other elements for ethnographic data, however, I suggest that, in the coming chapters, I demonstrate sufficient ecological validity that I am able to glimpse (and confirm) aspects of the lived reality brought to bear on literate action for these participants. For each participant, I make sure to do the following:

1. Conduct multiple interviews over time;
2. Build interviews around objects—texts, computers, readings, etc.; and
3. Triangulate claims among interview segments and objects.

These mechanisms are nothing new to the field of writing research, but their inclusion supports the claims that I make about the lived reality of these participants going forward. In the coming chapters, these mechanisms allow me to develop a uniquely adequate sense of the literate action these writers perform, but relocates the "adequacy" requirement from a broader context such as a classroom to the recurrent iterations of particular practices.

# Chapter 6. Problematizing Transfer and Exploring Agency

The totality of the literate experience offers a productive logic-in-use for thinking through the production of literate action and the way in which development might occur on a moment-to-moment basis within that production. In this chapter, I bring the totality to bear on two new cases of writers, this time two in their early college careers. In doing so, I aim to accomplish the following:

1. Test the totality of the literate experience as a logic-in-use on writers at a different point in the lifespan and with different research methods;
2. Connect the findings in the totality with ongoing discussions in Writing Studies about transfer; and
3. Suggest new insights on transfer that might emerge from my extension of the totality.

I begin this work with a review of existing transfer research and, in particular, the assumptions of transfer researcher that are incommensurate with the framework of the totality—and, by extension, understanding development from the perspective of the lived reality. The central issue of incommensurability that I have identified in my review of transfer research is the assumptions that transfer makes of *What-Comes-Next*. In brief, transfer research has a tendency to make assumptions about *What-Comes-Next* in a variety of ways: in the work of a given course, in the work of subsequent courses, and in the work students do after leaving the university setting. Below, I articulate these assumptions and highlight research that might serve as starting points for building dialogue between my lifespan-oriented research and transfer research.

## What-Comes-Next and Transfer Research

Research on writing development—and, particularly, writing development as participation in social action—offers both roadblocks and possibilities for understanding the ways in which *What-Comes-Next* can be treated as uncertain. Research on the transfer of writing offers further roadblocks and possibilities, albeit ones that are drawn from different traditions and take, as their starting points, different epistemological views. In the next sections, I trace out the ways in which transfer research has assumed a certainty of *What-Comes-Next*. I also identify the ways in which transfer research has begun to pull at the threads of that certainty productively for the lifespan-oriented purposes of my project.

## Transfer Assumptions of What-Comes-Next

Transfer has always been of interest for Writing Studies, but the study of it has taken on new life in recent years. Drawing from a range of theoretical and empirical explorations of transfer research in education, Writing Studies scholars have considered transfer through a variety of frameworks: as a rhetorical act (Nowacek, 2011), as work through threshold concepts (Adler-Kassner, Clarke, Robertson, Taczak & Yancey, 2016; Adler-Kassner, Majewski & Koshnick, 2012), as movement across activity systems (Grijalva, 2016), as consequential transitions (Wardle & Clement, 2016), as remixing and repurposing (Yancey, Robertson & Taczak, 2014), as metacognition (Gorzelsky, Driscoll, Paszek, Jones & Hayes, 2016), as dispositional (Driscoll & Wells, 2012; Reiff & Bawarshi, 2010), as caught up amidst acts of enculturation (Tremain, 2015), and as caught within genre awareness (Clark & Hernandez, 2011; Rounsaville, 2012). These approaches to considering transfer, it should be noted, have all been taken up within the past half-decade or so, during the time leading up to and after the Elon University "Research Seminar on Critical Transitions: Writing and the Question of Transfer," which ran from 2011–2013. Snead (2011) and Donahue (2012) provide interesting and more detailed overviews of the many ways in which transfer has been taken up in the study of writing, and particularly first-year writing. My intent in this section, however, is not to provide a comprehensive overview of writing transfer but to identify the ways in which current trends in transfer study are obscuring the uncertainty of *What-Comes-Next* and, at the same time, single out approaches and studies that may offer useful through lines for shifting attention in transfer toward the uncertainty at the center of the lived reality.

A pursuit of how what-comes-next is stabilized through literature on transfer might be best begun through the Elon Statement on Writing Transfer (2016). As captured in Anson and Moore's *Critical Transitions* (2016), the Elon Statement attempts, among other things, to capture a range of understandings about transfer and situate them in relation to one another (Figure 6.1). This work not only situates multiple approaches to transfer, but also suggests ways in which the uncertainty of *What-Comes-Next* may be obscured.

Figure 6.1 provides a map of how various transfer theories intersect "among knowledge, learners, and contexts" (Anson & Moore, 2016, p. 349). The map attends to the "learner, learner's actions, or learner's processes," the ways in which contexts are described and/or situations are compared, and the ways in which knowledge is constructed and used. Through these three intersecting arenas of transfer theories, the Elon Statement on Writing Transfer suggests relationships among various perspectives on transfer. From the perspective of the lived reality of literate action development (and keeping central to our attention the uncertainty of *What-Comes-Next*), however, nowhere in this model is there an opportunity to bring knowledge, context/situation together through the eyes of the learner. While the Venn diagram structure of the map suggests that CHAT, consequential transitions, communities of practice, threshold concepts, and re-mix might be opportunities to structure these three, these all view the writer from the outside, attending to specific variables, but do not emphasize writers engaging in the production of meaning amid *uncertain* and *emergent* circumstances as I described in Part I.

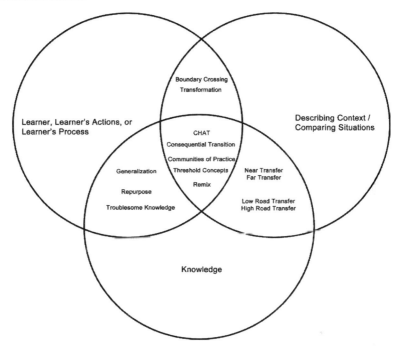

*Figure 6.1. A map of transfer approaches (Anson & Moore, 2016).*

Before exploring in greater detail the problems and possibilities with the ap-proaches to transfer at the center of the map, however, it may be useful to under-stand the eight principles behind understanding (and teaching for) transfer that the Elon Statement proposes. These eight principles offer an overview of the ways in which transfer has been considered in the statement, which can lead to a better understanding of what CHAT, consequential transitions, etc. offer at the center of the map. The eight principles of transfer, according to the Elon Statement, are shown in Table 6.1.

Various components of these principles seem to suggest an awareness of the ongoing uncertainty that writers engaging in transfer are continually walking into. These principles treat prior knowledge as a "complex construct," and suggest that writers must "transform or repurpose that prior knowledge, if only slightly" in their attempt to motivate that knowledge into a rhetorical performance. In these principles, then, there is an attention to the work of individuals taking up prior knowledge in order to make sense of unfolding situations. However, without the totality as a guide, these principles cannot (fully) take on the uncertainty of *What-Comes-Next*. In other words, the rhetorical situation that writers enter into is treated as a given, when in fact it remains to be developed by individuals bringing their prior knowledge to bear on the situation as it is unfolded by those individuals. The very definition of transfer in the first principle—"Writing transfer is the phenomenon in which new and unfamiliar writing tasks are approached through the application, remixing, or integration of previous knowledge, skills, strategies, and dispositions"—takes the task (and the approach to the task) as socially set (rather than constructed, if only in part, by the writer), and the writer is left with nothing to do but bring "previous knowledge, skills, strategies, and dispositions" to bear in different ways.

**Table 6.1. Principles of transfer (Anson & Moore, 2016).**

- Writing transfer is the phenomenon in which new and unfamiliar writing tasks are approached through the application, remixing, or integration of previous knowledge, skills, strategies, and dispositions.

- Any social context provides affordances and constraints that impact use of prior knowledge, skills, strategies, and dispositions, and writing transfer successes and challenges cannot be understood outside of learners' social-cultural spaces.

- Prior knowledge is a complex construct that can benefit or hinder writing transfer. Yet understanding or and exploring that complexity is central to investigating transfer.

- Individual dispositions and individual identity play key roles in transfer.

- Individuals may engage in routinized and transformative (adaptive, integrated, repurposed, expansive) forms of transfer when they draw on or utilize prior knowledge and learning, whether crossing concurrent contexts or sequential contexts.

- Successful writing transfer occurs when a writer can transform rhetorical knowledge and rhetorical awareness into performance. Students facing a new and difficult rhetorical task draw upon previous knowledge and strategies, and when they do it, they must transform or repurpose that prior knowledge, if only slightly.

- Students' meta-awareness often plays a key role in transfer, and reflective writing promotes preparation for transfer and transfer-focused thinking.

- The importance of meta-cognition of available identities, situational awareness, audience awareness, etc., become even more critical in writing transfer between languages because of the need to negotiate language-based differences and to develop awareness about the ways language operates in written communication in each language (Anson & Moore, 2016, pp. 350–351).

Thinking through the lived reality of literate action development, however, suggests that there is a great deal more uncertainty at work in a given writing task than the Elon Statement on Writing Transfer claims. Prior knowledge, tasks, strategies, and dispositions, rather than being constant, can be thought of—through the lens of the lived reality—as regularly being applied anew as a result of the variety of dimensions and environmental variables that each new literate action is constructed from. By treating these elements as stable, the Elon statement obscures the uncertainty of *What-Comes-Next* and, by extension, assumes a non-existent stability regarding the individuated take-up of transfer activity.

This should not be read as a criticism of the Elon statement, but rather an extension that may enable the field of Writing Studies to more deeply consider and work with the concept of transfer. The purpose of the Critical Transitions conference was to establish an understanding of the way(s) in which transfer is, was, and could be taken up, to serve as "an effort to provide a framework for continued inquiry and theory-building" (Anson & Moore, 2016, p. 345) and the Elon statement reflects that purpose. Furthermore, the findings that have emerged from the research that was taken up for the Elon statement—as evidenced by the principles in the statement itself—serve a useful function in expanding our awareness of how we might better conceptualize how students move into and out of postsecondary classes and, in particular, first-year writing courses. However, my pursuit of understanding how writers grow and change over time from a lifespan perspective, centered as it is on the lived reality of literate action development, requires that the uncertainty surrounding each moment of literate action be centrally attended to.

Figure 6.1 seems to indicate that work on CHAT, consequential transitions, threshold concepts, and remix may be ways in which the interrelationships between learner, social context, and knowledge might be most usefully addressed in order to find threads of uncertainty regarding *What-Comes-Next* in transfer literature. However, as I demonstrate below—with studies from Anson and Moore (2016) as examples—CHAT, consequential transitions, and threshold concepts become problematic when considering the uncertainty of *What-Comes-Next*. Each of these is geared too heavily toward socially agreed-upon understandings of literate action, and so fails to offer useful bridges into the lived reality—though, as I show later, the possibilities of "remix" suggest a useful pursuit of threads of uncertainty in the form of genre-based approaches to transfer.

In their chapter, Adler-Kassner, Clark, Robertson, Taczak, and Yancey (2016) focus on threshold concepts, defining them as "portals that learners pass through" and claiming that as learners work their way through those portals, they "change their understandings of something" (p. 18). These changes are "transformative" and "irreversible" (Adler-Kassner et al., 2016, p. 18), serving as critical components of learning to communicate in particular communities of practice. These concepts, Adler-Kassner et al. (2016) argue, are tools through which developing writers can identify the boundaries of the communities of practice that they are caught within, as well as critical components in developing metacognitive awareness about the communities that they are part of.

With this framework in mind, Adler-Kassner et al. (2016) set about identifying five threshold concepts for Writing Studies that are "critical for cultivating students' abilities to assemble and reassemble knowledge-making practices within and across communities of practice" (p. 20):

1.  Writing is an activity and a subject of study;
2.  Writing always occurs in context, and no two contexts are exactly alike;
3.  Reflection is critical for writers' development;
4.  Genre awareness contributes to successful transfer; and
5.  Prior knowledge, experience, attitudes, beliefs set the stage for learning and shape new writing experiences and learning (pp. 20–37)

These threshold concepts, which Adler-Kassner et al. (2016) suggest are methods for helping students think across disciplines, certainly has links to considering the uncertainty of *What-Comes-Next*. However, like the Elon statement, issues like context, genre, and prior knowledge are treated as discrete, concrete entities. Through these concepts, we are not capable (without significant revision) of locating a writer in a moment-to-moment situation in which she is also an actor in shaping past experience and present situation with and through text.

Activity theory has been taken as a way of approaching transfer in a number of studies, even in Anson and Moore's (2016) text. Blythe (2016) unpacks the issue of the "subject" within the activity system, arguing that "future research into transfer and adaptability in writing—studies informed by social theories of activity or genre—must pay more attention to ways that subjects adapt from one situation to another" (p. 51). Here, Blythe is seen treating the situation as apart from the subject working with it, treating the subject as one that needs to adapt, rather than having each adapt to the other.

This tendency by Blythe to see the subject as working with a set situation continues throughout the chapter, although he offers an interesting exploration of the role of subject within the frame of Beaufort's (2007) framework in doing so. Blythe takes greater steps toward expanding the individuated agency of the subject, and his conclusions suggest that the lack of agency of the subject in the construction of social situations may have been the result of his commitment to the terminology of activity theory and cognitive psychology. But this very limitation of Blythe's suggests issues with taking up activity theory as a way of understanding the uncertainty of *What-Comes-Next*.

Wardle and Clement (2016) take up Engestrom's (1987) concept of double binds and Beach's (1999) concept of consequential transitions to make sense of particular moments of "rhetorical challenge" (p. 163). Wardle and Clement (2016) draw from Beach to argue that consequential transitions "weave together changing individuals and social organizations in such a way that the person experiences becoming someone or something new" (Beach, as quoted in Wardle & Clement, 2016, p. 164), and suggesting that these consequential transitions occur when writers are working their way through double binds, or moments of receiving contradictory messages (Engestrom, 1987).

Wardle and Clement's work to unpack the consequential transitions at work in Clement's development as a writer across the bulk of her college education proved useful in understanding the ways in which consequential transitions and double binds serve as shaping agents in Nicole's emerging identity. Even here, however, there is some obscuring of *What-Comes-Next*: it remains difficult to see how the consequential transitions described are crafted by Nicole through her co-construction of the situation. Attending to *What-Comes-Next* more centrally can allow us to see more of the active agency that actors like Nicole have when they work across texts.

The work of Adler-Kassner et al., Blythe, and Wardle and Clement suggest that current attempts to understand transfer through threshold concepts, activity theory, and consequential transitions stabilize *What-Comes-Next*, removing the uncertainty of the unfolding moment by suggesting a stable set of prior knowledge, a stable social situation that research subjects are working with, and a stable sense of identity and self (even if that stability is challenged by the stable social situation that the self walks into). While there may be—particularly in Blythe— some resources that can work to destabilize *What-Comes-Next* through these formats, a more straightforward method to upending *What-Comes-Next* in transfer research is to draw upon research that provides a more dynamic fluidity between prior knowledge and social situation.

## Destabilizing What-Comes-Next in Transfer Research

While the research on transfer, as I indicate through the Elon statement and several chapters of *Critical Transitions* above, stabilizes *What-Comes-Next* in several ways, research on transfer with a base in genre studies has the potential to more squarely attend to *What-Comes-Next*. Genre, rooted as it is in phenomenological sociology (Bazerman, 2013; Miller, 1984), can serve as a tool to orient knowledge, learner, and social context in a way that enables a deeper look into transfer while keeping the uncertainty of *What-Comes-Next* in mind. Genre-based approaches to transfer have located the transfer of *individual* understandings, knowledge, and skills within and across particular social contexts. This approach has been pursued through the take-up of *genre* and *dispositions*, which may serve as useful tools for locating individuated understandings within the movement of understanding from prior knowledge to unfolding situation. I begin with the dynamic models of prior knowledge and dispositions by Yancey, Robertson, and Taczack (2014) and Driscoll and Wells (2012), respectively, to flesh out additional complexities in transfer research that will set the stage for a genre-based elaboration of what transfer is and can do as a concept.

Yancey, Robertson, and Taczak (2014) have explored how individuals take up transfer within different situations across various classes based on prior knowledge. They wonder "how we can help students develop writing knowledge and practices that they can draw upon, use, and repurpose for new writing tasks in new settings" (2014, p. 2), drawing upon thoughts about transfer in recent discussions in Writing Studies, their own experiences with portfolio writing, and recent discussions in higher education about how theory assists with general learning, to explore this issue. Through their study, they develop a model of how students use prior knowledge to apply their understandings to new practices. This model consists of three components. First, students can *remix* their work, meaning that they integrate prior knowledge and new knowledge. Second, students can take on an *assemblage* approach to their work by grafting new knowledge onto previously existing knowledge of composing. Third, students can encounter a *critical incident*, or a problem that "helps [students] retheorize writing in general and their own agency as writers in particular" (Yancey et al., 2014, p. 5). Their approach shows not only the various ways that past knowledge can be brought to bear in a given situation, but how that past knowledge can be transformed. Furthermore, Yancey, et al. have, through their attention to critical incidents, suggested that this past knowledge can be challenged and revised according to the complexities of ongoing social situations. The literate actions we perform, it would seem, are shaped by our knowledge of past knowledge, even as our past knowledge is brought to bear in accordance with the needs of the current situation—something that has a potentially transformative influence on our deployment of that past knowledge in the future.

This work by Yancey, et al. (2014) showcases the role that past experiences play in the transfer of knowledge, and—through the concepts of assemblage, remix, and critical incidents—offers ways to understand how prior knowledge can be transformed by unfolding events, as well as vice versa. Driscoll and Wells (2012) expand the concept of transfer by arguing that "dispositions play an equally essential role" as context and curricula in the development of transfer. They identify five qualities of a disposition. Specifically, dispositions

1. Are a critical part of a larger system that includes the person, the context, the process through which learning happens, and time;
2. Are not intellectual traits but are determinants of how those traits are used;
3. Determine students' sensitivity toward and willingness to engage in transfer;
4. Can positively or negatively impact the learning environment; and
5. Are dynamic and may be context-specific or broadly generalized (Driscoll & Wells, 2012).

They see dispositions such as value, self-efficacy, attribution, and self-regulation as having these five dispositional qualities, and suggest that these dispositions may shape engagement with transfer.

When applied as a lens to previous work on transfer, such as Wardle (2007) and Beaufort (2007), Driscoll and Wells (2012) find "that in many situations where students failed to transfer individual dispositions played a role." Clearly, there are multiple dimensions to transfer beyond prior knowledge—like writing development, there are multiple dimensions of human activity and perhaps environmental variables at work. While dispositions offer more potential insight into thinking about what transfer consists of, it does not, on its own, offer ways to address *What-Comes-Next* in the transfer literature. The dynamic nature of prior knowledge in Yancey et al. (2014) as well as the dynamic nature of dispositions in Driscoll and Wells (2012) shake up the stability of prior knowledge, agency, and social situation that other research has not. In order to incorporate the dynamic nature of dispositions and prior knowledge for the purposes of teasing out threads of *What-Comes-Next*, I turn to recent work with a base in rhetorical genre studies, particularly by Rounsaville (2012) and Nowacek (2011).

Rounsaville (2012), drawing on the work of genre theorists such as Bazerman and Bawarshi, argues that "RGS [rhetorical genre studies] provides a view of genre and genre knowledge that goes beyond conventions such as format, word choice, and various stylistic cues" and, furthermore, that this genre knowledge "compel[s] us to act and write and draw on memory in some ways over others." Rounsaville centers her work in an RGS lineage, drawing on Freadman's theory of genre uptake. The uptake of genres represents the "space of conflicting and discursively informed memory that involves a complex process of selecting and translating prior knowledge" (Rounsaville, 2012) that people work through when engaging in acts of transfer. Much like the dispositions described by Driscoll and Wells (2012) above, genre uptake highlights that there is more to the take-up and transfer of prior knowledge than merely the knowledge itself, that the concept of transfer may be more fragmented than it seems. Genre uptake, however, begins pointing to the outlines of cognitive work that go on while engaging in an act of transfer.

Rounsaville (as well as the people she draws from, such as Reiff, Bawarshi, Freadman, and others) takes her perspective on genre from the work of Bazerman, who—drawing from Schutz (1967)—sees genres as unfinished recipes for action in a given context. That is, in a given setting, a writer perceives and co-constructs a situation that calls forward memory, dispositions, actions, and understandings in patterned ways. Through literate action enabled by these dispositions, actions, and understandings, the writer develops and further perpetuates the situation. In other words, "transfer means more than just the ability to apply one textual convention or strategy to another, less-similar text type" (Rounsaville, 2012). There is a host of understandings of the world that work together in order to engage in the act of transfer, and these understandings are built at least partly on the recipe-like knowledge of genres as well as dispositions. Uptake, for Rounsaville, offers a way to see these aspects working together: "uptake specifies boundary crossing in writing-related transfer of an active, meaning-making site where writers work through and select amongst a range of experiences and knowledges that have been called forth as a result of the unique convergence between prior genre knowledge and local, genred events" (2012). As Driscoll and Wells (2012) demonstrate, this uptake involves more than just knowledge: the space of connection between prior knowledge and local events is infused with dispositional tendencies.

Through the concepts of genre and uptake, then, we can see how prior knowledge is understood, taken up, and used again in a new context through the eyes of the person deploying that knowledge. Furthermore, thanks to the recipe-like work of genres, we can understand, somewhat, how the situation also constructs the way in which past knowledge is deployed (i.e., since genres are recipe-*like*, and therefore not overly deterministic in nature). As we take part in an unfolding situation, we bring the relevant pieces of our past to bear on the current situation. This includes much more than text forms: our understandings of the contexts and social roles, as well as our dispositions toward the genre, roles, and contexts shape our deployment of that prior knowledge.

The work of Yancey, et al, Driscoll and Wells, and Rounsaville have provided interesting threads into upending *What-Comes-Next* in transfer literature. By suggesting that prior knowledge and dispositions are dynamically situated in relation to both one another and the unfolding situation, Yancey et al. (2014) and Driscoll and Wells (2012) have showcased the ways in which the perceived stability of *What-Comes-Next* in transfer literature can be problematic in using it to pursue the lived reality of literate action development. As moments of transfer unfold, those moments transform prior knowledge and dispositions even as those dispositions and that prior knowledge shapes the moment of transfer.

*What-Comes-Next*, as a phenomenon, seems to be a reality balanced on the edge of stability and instability, the known and the unknown. As a situation unfolds, literate actors draw on the prior knowledge embedded in the recipe-like genres in their past experiences to shape the situation and decide what to do next. These genred understandings are shaped by the dispositional tendencies of the literate actor. However, the genred understandings are only recipe-*like*, they are not recipes designed to entirely guide action. The deployment of these understandings by a literate actor is an attempt to construct from the unknown—the continually unfolding moment—a set of understandable circumstances on which to act. As each unfolding moment is rendered understandable (i.e., genred), a new moment arises that requires the further constructive work of the literate actor through genres, dispositions, and prior knowledge.

In this genre-based model of transfer, the writer is always engaged in a process of context construction, with acts that we consider "transfer" consisting merely of more difficult acts of context construction based on the available tools (i.e., past knowledge, dispositions). Nowacek's (2011) work on developing writers as *agents of integration* offers a way of looking at transfer that may provide further insight into this act of context construction. This will help us to more fully translate transfer research into the totality.

Nowacek approaches transfer as an act of recontextualization. This approach works from five principles:

1.  Transfer understood as recontextualization recognizes multiple avenues of connection among contexts, including knowledge, ways of knowing, identities, and goals;

2. Transfer understood as recontextualization recognizes that transfer is not only mere application; it is also an act of construction;

3. Transfer understood as recontextualization recognizes that transfer can be both positive and negative and that there is a powerful affective dimension of transfer;

4. Transfer understood as recontextualization recognizes that written and spoken genres associated with these contexts provides an exigence for transfer; and

5. Transfer understood as recontextualization recognizes that meta-awareness is an important, but not necessary, element of transfer (Nowacek, 2011, pp. 20–30).

Nowacek's approach to the transfer of writing has its roots in the idea of the development of writing. Nowacek sees transfer as a path along a road to integration, something that she supports through the work of Perkins and Salomon (1992), Bakhtin (1986), and Engestrom (1987). Through these authors, Nowacek places transfer at the midpoint between "no transfer" (i.e., inert knowledge, heteroglossia, and double binds) and "integration" (i.e., high road transfer, fully dialogized consciousness, and learning by expanding). Transfer can be considered as the link between these two stages, a developmental moment wherein students learn to approach a certain task in a given setting differently based on reconceptualizations of their past experiences.

Nowacek's approach underscores the complex social aspects of transfer outlined by Driscoll and Wells (2012) and Rounsaville (2012), but calls attention to the myriad levels of conscious attention at work by actors engaged in transfer. By treating students as individual agents of integration working within a complex social world, Nowacek (2011) is able to highlight how "agents' responses"—i.e., their recipe-like genre knowledge "may be cued, but they are not predetermined" (pp. 39–40). That is, each act of transfer is an individuated take-up of potentials for action, not a predetermined performance engaged in by genre-driven dopes: the way in which we make sense of our prior knowledge and take it up in an unfolding situation is shaped but not dictated by either prior knowledge or the unfolding situation. The situation and the prior knowledge inform one another, are cued and enacted through the varying levels of conscious attention paid to the literate act by the literate actor. Recontextualization, it would seem, can happen to both the situation and prior knowledge, and across varying levels of consciousness.

Genre-oriented transfer research highlights several important threads in transfer research that can help us understand how *What-Comes-Next* may be destabilized. The movement of writing from one context to another involves more than just the written text—it involves dispositions, knowledge of social roles, and the varying levels of conscious attention, all of which is caught up in complex dynamic between prior knowledge and the unfolding situation. These findings suggest a constant movement from stable to unstable understandings and social situations, and furthermore that the instability is stabilized through the work of recipe-like prior knowledge and dispositional tendencies as people recontextualize their past and their worlds to engage in literate action.

## One Step More: Removing the Stabilizer in Transfer through the Totality

Nowacek's work—as well as other genre-based research on transfer—offers a productive connecting point to the totality of the literate experience. This transfer research stabilizes *What-Comes-Next* through recipe-like knowledge. This is a cognitive basis of prior knowledge, assuming a stability that the totality does not. In the process of enacting the logic-in-use articulated in Chapter 5, I determined that past practices need to be *scenically* located in the production of social order. So *What-Comes-Next* has to be resolved not by the enactment of a recipe-like knowledge but by possibilities of objects that are mobilized into action. Speaking abstractly, this seems a distinction with a slight difference: the recipe-like knowledge is merely located for the totality in the material realities of a situation, rather than in the mind. In terms of studying literate action development, however, the differences become deeply consequential.

Locating a stability in the knowledge of students can encourage a turn away from the material, moment-to-moment work of constructing social order. By locating transfer in the knowledge that students possess, we turn our research gaze away from the material work of bringing that knowledge to bear in an unfolding situation. So, for instance, a study of how a student in a math class brings a past algorithm to bear on a new problem might focus on what knowledge carried over and, as a consequence, ignore the ways in which that student's fluent work with a familiar notebook and some notes on his cell phone shaped the carry-over of that knowledge.

Nowacek (2011), though attentive to the ways in which transfer is an act of construction, does not provide a mechanism for examining the material work of that act of construction. The recipe-like knowledge that Nowacek turns to instead occludes that work, much like the math student's notebook-and-cell-phone practices, making the scenic production of literate action difficult to see. Without a mechanism for locating how the possibilities of objects are recognized anew in configurations of talk, tools, and texts, writing researchers cannot articulate the connection between individuated literate action development and the collective production of social order.

Furthermore, seeing all acts of transfer as acts of knowing risks a conflation of literate action development with conscious attention—a conflation that, while sometimes fair, does not capture the depth and nuance of some developmental moments. If we take seriously the ethnomethodological work of situational construction as articulated in Part I, then we must seriously consider that certain habits, inclinations, and understandings are not just unmentioned in acts of transfer, but are actually *unmentionable*, particularly at the moment of their enactment: we might be able to do something, but not know how to talk about it (and, indeed, the talking about it would not be able to effectively get at our able-ness in the first place). What I mean here is something more than simply *low road transfer* (Salomon & Perkins, 1988), in which agents automate certain tasks across a range of settings. In the act of socially constructing a situation, there will be indexical references, unspoken assumptions, and the co-operative work of turns at talk (Garfinkel, 1967). These references, assumptions, and turns at talk are far from automated—they are the unacknowledged efforts of actors to work through and participate in social order. Again, our earlier ex-ample of the student in math class engaging with materials around him comes to mind: it is through the coordination of these objects that the past algorithm is rendered present amid his participation in an unfolding situation. To say that this work involves a conscious *knowing how* would be to obscure the complex collaborative work that ethnomethodological efforts identify. The math student is aware in some way of his notebook and cell phone use, but does not recog-nize how the algorithm is caught up in such coordination. The totality allows researchers to consider acts of transfer without the reference frame of *knowing how* needing to be present.

Transfer, then, needs to be examined without the assumptions of know-ing, or the stabilizing influence of recipe-like knowledge. Below, I examine the work that two undergraduate writers do through the logic-in-use of the totality. Through this analysis, I articulate new insights into transfer and how it might be more robustly understood against a background of the ongoing production of social order.

## Literate Action as an Undergraduate: The Cases of May and Lilly

The literate actions of May and Lilly, two undergraduate students at a state uni-versity in the northeastern United States, offer a compelling site for examining the intersections of the lived reality and existing understandings of transfer in fields of Writing Studies, literacy, and education. May and Lilly are both STEM majors participating in a longitudinal study of writing development across the college years. May entered the university as a Marine Biology major and re-mained one until she left the university after her sophomore year. May lived most of her life in New England and all of it prior to college on the east coast of the United States.

Lilly was a Cellular and Molecular Biology major in her freshman year, al-though she shifted her degree focus to veterinary science in her second year. She attended the university with the goal of not only completing her degree but also of participating in a Division I field hockey team. Away from the university, Lilly assists her family as they work on their dairy farm, one of the largest in the northeastern United States. As part of the longitudinal study, I met with May and Lilly each semester, beginning during early Spring semester their freshmen year. These interviews were open-ended, based on a fusion of a literacy history interview (Brandt, 2001), a text-based interview in the sociohistoric tradition (see Roozen & Erickson, 2017), and a study of ESSPs (Prior & Shipka, 2003). In Table 6.2, I list the texts discussed in each interview.

**Table 6.2. Interview texts**

| May's Texts | Lilly's Texts |
| --- | --- |
| **Interview 1** | **Interview 1** |
| High school texts (Google Drive) | Biology 200 Class Notes |
| Biology 100 Notes | Lecture Guides |
| FSN 101 Notes | OneNote pages and tabs |
| SMS 101 Notes | Biology essays |
| English 101 Notes | Introduction to Cellular Biology flashcards |
| Scheduling Notes | Chemistry equations |
| SMS 203 Lab Report | Lab reports |
| SMS 203 Bibliography | Facebook posts |
| SMS 203 Reading Questions | Twitter posts |
| SMS 203 Essays | Instagram posts |
| **Interview 2** | **Interview 2** |
| Maine Policy issues notes | Biology lab reports |
| Ocean temperature and biodiversity notes | Organic chemistry and lab notes |
| Marine Biology essays | Coastal Maine Studies papers |
| Marine Ecology Homework assignments | History of Religion papers |
| Marine Ecology In-class case studies | Microbiology slides |
| Marine Ecology Mid-term | Self-study guides |
| Women, Gender, Sexuality 101 Notes | Lab reports |
| Chemistry notes | Calculus graphs |
| Chemistry worksheets | Letters to grandmother |
| Chemistry lab notes | Writing for the farm |
| Instagram posts | Instagram posts |
| Snapchat posts | Twitter posts |
| Facebook posts | Facebook posts |
| Outing club writing | Email |
| Water polo club writing | Field hockey video notes |

| May's Texts | Lilly's Texts |
| --- | --- |
| Interview 3 | Interview 3 |
| Chemistry quizzes | Organic chemistry lab reports |
| History of Maine Woods essays | Organic history lab notes |
| History of Maine Woods quizzes | Biology lab reports |
| History of Maine Woods final exam | Biology lab notes |
| History of Maine Woods notes | Study guides |
| EES Worksheets | Agenda notes |
| Sudoku puzzles | Women, Gender, Sexuality 101 notes |
| Drawings of writing process and writing activity | Drawings of writing process and writing activity |

May and Lilly offer interesting cases of tracing literate action across a wider swath of the lives of participants than the participants in Emily's classroom did. In my search for research sites that were both *strategic* in relation to my ongoing study of lifespan writing development and offered *perspicuous* settings of the ongoing production of social order, a sequence of retrospective interviews proved effective for getting at both. An initial literacy history interview gave a broader context to ongoing literate action. The texts—and their presence during discussion—served to triangulate claims about literate action, ESSPs, and past narratives of literate performance. The repetitive interviews—regular updates throughout the collegiate career—enabled me to trace the development of literate action over time and, by honing in on particular instances of a practice, unpack the transformation of that practice.

Below, I focus on a particular literate practice and its transformation over time: note-taking activity. For both May and Lilly, I trace their note-taking practice from its initial reference in their first interviews to the work they are doing with it at the conclusion of their sophomore year of college. Both writers signal different kinds of transformations in their literate action: May's engagement with "fidget-writing" becomes a more robust, flexible, and responsive practice as she moves deeper into her undergraduate education, while Lilly's note-taking practices undergo wholesale revision in response to particular circumstances. Both writers, I will show, transform their engagement with the world around them through literate action in various ways, and this variety can provide some new insights into what it means to engage in literate action development.

With the note-taking practice at the center of my attention, I bring to bear the totality of the literate experience in the three framings articulated at the end of Chapter 5. I hope to show how the work of note-taking does not just occur across contexts—it, in part, *creates* those contexts, and its transformation over time signals the work of literate action development. Furthermore, by attending to the lived reality through the totality of the literate experience, we can articulate the lived coherence that lies at the heart of the seemingly inexplicable, enduring changes to practices that writers build their literate action upon throughout their lives.

## Building a Textual Network: May

May grew up around a wide range of writing by all members of her family. She saw her father, a math teacher, do a great deal of inscribing both at home and in the classroom, when she went to school with him. Her mother, who ran part of an apple farm owned by May's grandparents for part of May's youth, was frequently engaged in various kinds of writing that May witnessed. She saw her brother, two years older than her, writing frequently for school. Her grandmother, who babysat her frequently, was often engaged in recipe writing. "I was always really interested in cursive," said May. "So I would just scribble like loop-dee-loops and I thought that was cursive and I'd be like 'OK, mom, what does this say?'"

May also describes herself as a "fidgety person," and used writing to account for her fidgeting on a regular basis. She witnessed her mother—whom she also describes as fidgety—doing similar things while on the phone with people, in particular: "when she's on the phone, she sort of doodles. So whenever she was on the phone I would just see her like do that." May's family has a number of notebooks around the house that people use different pages of for different purposes, and May can identify her mother's doodling on the phone throughout these notebooks.

May's doodling accounts for her fidgeting in a wide variety of social circumstances:

> A lot of times, if I am watching TV, I am a very fidgety person,
> so I always have a notebook and a pen and I'll just write words
> that I hear or if two people are having a conversation I'll just
> write, so I'll just be a jumble of not sentences even, just words.
> That's kind of weird, but I do that, too. So to like have my
> hands be busy, like watching TV or commercials.

This fidget-writing has a number of different "looks" to it, depending on the circumstances. For example, May often ends up writing her name repeatedly as a way to "be doing something with my hands" when she is bored. But perhaps most interesting in terms of her development as a writer is how this fidget-writing became intertwined with the ways in which she organized herself for work during the semester at college. May saw a carry-over from her fidget-writing to planning out her day: "Sometimes, if I had a busy day ahead, I would like write each time and what I'm going to do at that time. So kind of like planning out my day. Just to like organize it, I guess, visually." May's fidget-writing, here, begins to account not just to the demands of the moment (that is, giving idle hands something to do) but to the demands of a complex schedule of tasks for multiple classes.

My study of May's interviews notes this moment as the start of May's transformation of a note-taking practice for the demands of her new life in higher education. May, much like the co-researchers studied by Roozen (2008, 2009a, 2009b, 2010), lives a richly literate life, and is able to draw on a range of practices that work their way through a variety of lifeworlds to accomplish literate action on a regular basis. It seems, as Prior (2018) has argued, that May is *always* transferring her literate practices from one situation to another—she began to take up the fidget-writing she witnessed her mother doing, and turned that toward the work of organizing herself for college work. Below, I bring the totality of the literate experience to bear on this practice of May's, one step at a time, in order to ascertain the ways in which May develops her note-taking practices over a period of two years.

## Framing Ongoing, Joint Action

We can see that May's fidget-writing emerges, for her, from the practices she encounters as a child growing up. The fidget-writing she sees her mother doing on the phone enables her own fidgeting to be pulled into the ongoing production of joint action in conversations, in watching television, in her work for class. Whether it be writing her name, or writing down things that are happening in conversation, on television, or in class, May has used fidget-writing as a way of co-constructing order, of shaping her participation in these situations. We can envision her turns at talk, her participation in the {order} around her, as emerging from an assemblage of actions that involve her doodling.

May's fidget-writing moves with her into the classroom, enabling her to participate in acts of social ordering that come to count as {class} for her, her fellow students, and her teachers. May transforms her fidget-writing from something that simply occupies her hands to something that allows her to move across the various tasks that she needs to accomplish for class: her doodles become class notes, which carry into her independent study, which carry into her assignments as the semester moves along. Figures 6.2, 6.3, 6.4, and 6.5 trace the repurposings of May's doodling to produce order for her not just in a moment but across a range of tasks throughout a period of time.

Figure 6.2, for instance, captures some of the seemingly purposeless "fidget-writing" that May engages in on a regular basis. There appears to be little purpose to the text itself: with the exception of the words "Yellow Stone," in fact, there are no words on the page. But the hearts, the loops, the triangles, the stars are artifacts of a past production of social order in which she could let her "hands be busy" without interfering in the turns at talk and action that constructed the situation. Note the spiral notebook, which was a ubiquitous presence in May's life. May's doodling, here, is not carrying forward in time for her. The production of text kept her hands busy at the moment of writing, and the resulting doodles are not brought to bear in other social situations.

*Figure 6.2. May's doodling, I.*

Figure 6.3, written during the semester, shows May's fidget-writing repurposed in several ways. First, May is not writing in a notebook—this particular schedule is on a Post-It, although May provides several other schedules that are on both loose-leaf paper and pages torn from a notebook. Second, the fidget-writing has now been oriented toward the work of her undergraduate career. This text brings together test dates, assignment deadlines, and study sessions to help May make sense of the coming academic work. The specific, momentary order that this contributed to is lost, but, as May notes in her interviews, such writing serves to "visually" plan her coming work in the nebulousness of her daily academic schedule.

May's fidget-writing can be seen shaping the social order of the classes she takes in Figures 6.4 and 6.5. In Figure 6.4, May's fidget-writing draws her into lifeguard training. Note at the top of the page and along the left-hand margin the squiggles, circles, underscoring, and vertical lines. Here, May's hands are kept busy by the notes of the class, but in the moments where notes are not required, she is able to turn back to her fidget-writing in order to maintain her participation in the ongoing production of local social order.

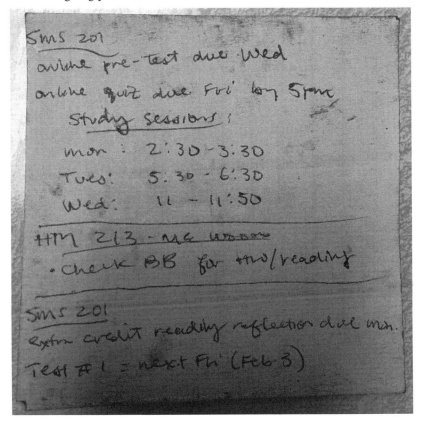

*Figure 6.3. May's doodling, II.*

Figure 6.5, which shows notes from May's biology class, again captures a mixture of note-taking practices and fidget-writing. The doodles in the upper right of the picture show hybrid work of the fidget-writing necessary for May to keep her hands busy and the work of taking notes for class. May orchestrates these two writings together, allowing her to participate in the ongoing, joint action of the class through the work of keeping her hands busy and her notes from the class meeting legible for future study sessions like the ones mapped out in Figure 6.3.

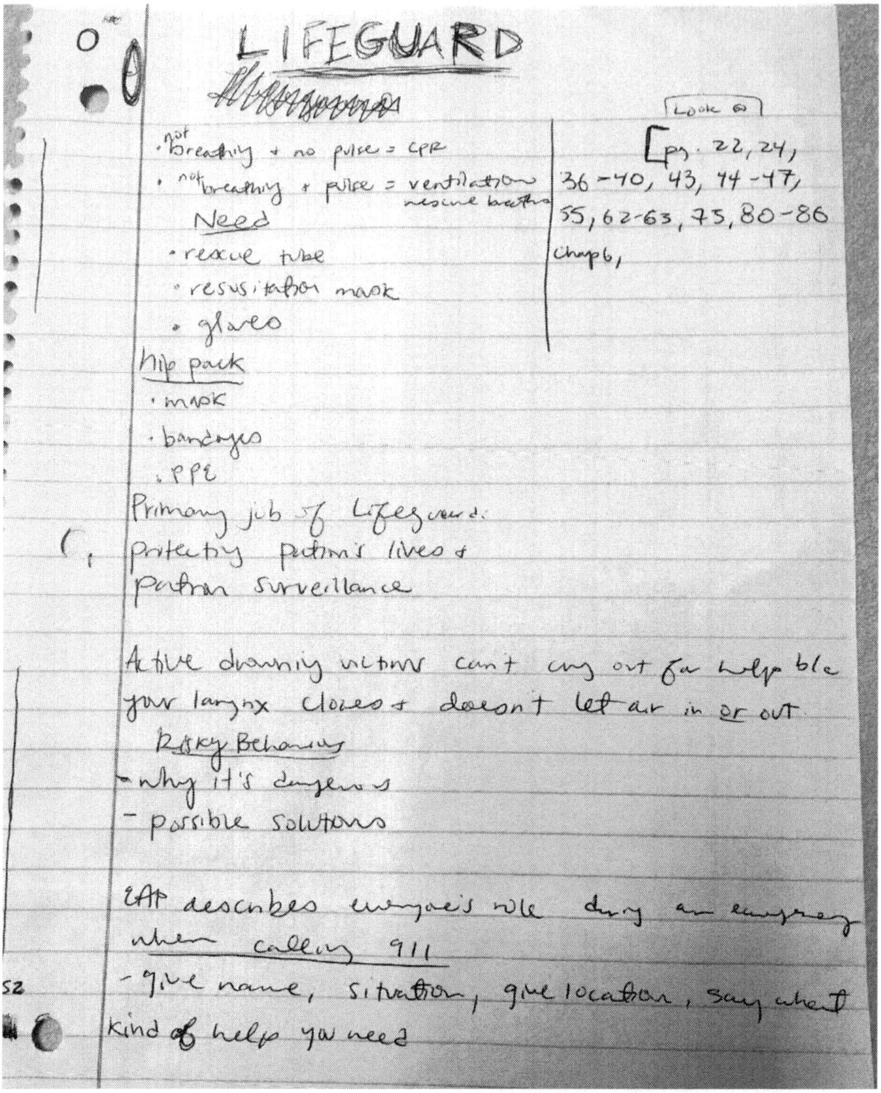

*Figure 6.4. May's doodling, III.*

At this point, May's fidget-writing, even as it transforms into note-taking for classes, can be framed as a turn taken in the ongoing work of joint action. Just as Holly's work of taking out a pen or pencil in Emily's class contributed to the production of social order there, we can envision May's fidget-writing as a mechanism to participate in the ongoing, joint action of the many contexts that it appears to be co-constructing. With this broader work of social action as a starting point, we can begin to frame the individuated actor.

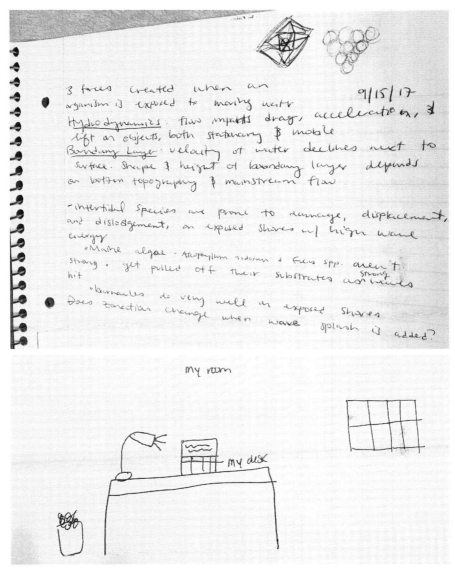

*Figure 6.5. May's doodling, IV.*

## Framing the Individuated Actor

Now that we have a sense of May's fidget-writing and how it is co-constructing the social world around her, we can think about the ways in which those actions contribute to her as an individuated actor in the stretch of circumstances that she employs the practice within. As articulated in Part I, May's engagement with the situation she is participating in is necessarily adumbrated, and the root of that adumbration is the very mechanisms through which she participates in social order. In other words, because she is fidget-writing to co-construct social order, she isn't doing something else. There is an opportunity cost for the fidget-writing-turned-note-taking, as there would be for any other practice. In the second step of tracing the totality, we can see how May's literate action becomes consequential in an individuated way.

A particular focus for tracing out these consequences is through the transformation of her fidget-writing from the "mindless" (in her words) writing during television watching to the planning of her day during the semester. The constant scheduling we see in her writing suggests that May's uncertainty of *What-Comes-Next* is being heightened, the practices she uses to reduce that uncertainty pushed to their limit, and that such practices might have to be repurposed, revised, or in some way changed to address this anomalous amount of uncertainty—what we called "information" in Part I—a heightened level of uncertainty that calls for repurposed practices. We can see the spike in uncertainty in May's consideration of her own patterns of work. Reflecting on the many computer tabs that she has opened in her computer, May notes,

> I'm just sort of scatterbrained. I know I'll have to do all of these
> different things, and I'll work a little bit on something, and
> then a little bit on another thing. I'm always switching back
> and forth, so I'll have everything open.

May's sense of being "scatterbrained" aligns with the work that the scheduling captured in Figure 6.3 seems to be doing for her. The incredible options for action—not just in what she has to do, but what she *can* do—seems to be a challenge for her to work through. The scheduling allows May to reduce her uncertainty in several ways. First, it provides her with tasks to do and an order to do them in, so that she can prioritize the next event in her day. Second, it serves as an organizer of the social order produced *during the act of writing.* In other words, May's co-construction of social order that began with her fidget-writing was also used to reduce the uncertainty of *What-Comes-Next*— that is, to render *information* into a manageable level of uncertainty—both in the co-construction of a moment and, by extension, in the co-construction of future moments.

## Framing the Scenic Work of Uncertainty Reduction

May's fidget-writing-turned-note-writing evidently carries across her life-worlds. She uses it for television, conversation, scheduling, notes in classes, and even some of her extracurricular activity. The third framing for tracing the totality asks how the transformation of a practice by an individuated actor is a scenic accomplishment. How, in other words, were the mechanisms of May's fidget-writing made *materially available* in the ongoing production of social order through these lifeworlds?

The origins of the material availability of such objects can be found in the literate practices of May's household growing up. "At my house," she notes, "we just have a lot of notebooks around the house and everyone just has pages in them from like spans of years ago." The expectation in her house is that opportunities to take notes, to do the kinds of writing that May envisions as a result of her fidgeting, will be available, are lying around, waiting for use when needed by the members of her house.

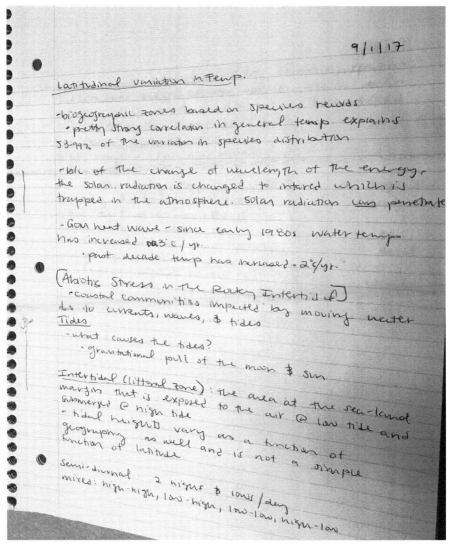

*Figure 6.6. May's note-taking.*

We can see the continuation of this assumption—what we might, drawing on Chapter 5, call envisioning *possibilities of objects*—in the objects that May comes to write her fidget-writing-turned-notes on. Certainly, May engages in writing in notebooks (see Figure 6.6), but she also finds herself scribbling in the margins of pages, on Post-Its, on the materials that she finds at her disposal. May appears to recognize space on various assortments of paper as opportunities for fidget-writing as needed. Rather than carrying a particular notebook or writing implement from one situation into another, May recognizes in the available spaces of various kinds of paper the opportunity to pursue fidget-writing in its multiplicity of appearances. The acts of fidget-writing that May does seems to recognize new associations that such spaces can be connected to—such as note-taking, or schedule-writing—even if the possibilities of the space (that is, to fidget-write) remain consistent.

This recognition of opportunities for fidget-writing serves to help her make sense of her note-taking needs as she moves further into her undergraduate education. May comes to see herself as participating in lecture, in labs, in work at the library, and in the flow of the day during the semester *through* the fidget-writing that she does. This take-up of literate action through fidget-writing on a range of surfaces, for a range of purposes suggests a practice that can proliferate across a range of social action. I refer to this work as *stacking*: May makes available past practices through the recognition of particular possibilities in objects and, by extension, participates in her own literate development and the ongoing production of social order. Experiences using a particular practice (i.e., fidget-writing) are *stacked* on top of one another, adding flexibility and adaptability to such a practice in order to handle future moments of spiked uncertainty. Because of her continued *stacking*, May is able to carry forward her fidget-writing for note-taking, for scheduling, and for a range of other purposes across her early postsecondary experiences. We can compare this flexible act of *stacking* to the bounded practicing of Lilly across the same period of time for a more well-rounded understanding of how practices get instantiated for a next first time.

## Constructing Textual Walls: Lilly

Lilly, like May, came to postsecondary life with a complexly laminated set of lifeworlds that could be oriented to the production of various kinds of texts. Throughout her time in high school, Lilly was an active participant in a range of sports, worked regularly on her family's dairy farm, and was heavily devoted to a challenging course load, particularly as a high school senior. Lilly's writing has always been, in her recounting, deeply shaped by the many lifeworlds that she finds herself balancing. She notes, for instance, that she "used to do writing in my free time like in junior high," but subsequently grew out of it. This "growing out" might be easily attributable to the many demands on Lilly's time: school, sports, work on the family farm, and maintaining a social life.

This complex blend of demands continued upon her transition to college. Lilly, still a member of a sports team—the university's field hockey team—was required to put in a certain number of study hours each week. She also had responsibilities at home that, though not impacting her college life on a daily basis, remained present in her emerging orchestration of her lifeworlds on a moment-to-moment basis. In order to trace Lilly's literate action development through the totality, I turn first to Lilly's note-taking, and then to a particular use of that pattern as recounted to me by Lilly during an interview—Lilly's self-fashioned study guides and flashcards.

## Framing Ongoing, Joint Action

Lilly's individual study habits begin with a participation in ongoing, joint action during her classes. Take, for instance, Lilly's work in her biology class during her freshman year:

> I take notes in class on my computer for bio. And then after class—so this is from the chapter from the book. So I read the chapter we're on and I take notes on here [Microsoft OneNote] because lecture's really vague.

Lilly's practice of self-fashioned study guides and flashcards begins by acting as a member of, in this case, her biology course. Lilly's entry into the classroom, her act of sitting in a seat and making entries into OneNote, co-constructs the work of ⟨class⟩ much in the way that May's fidget-writing did for her.

Lilly's decision to use OneNote is an interesting one, particularly given the range of note-taking applications she has at her disposal and her previous uses of hand-written notes. When I asked her why she chose to use OneNote, she said that "one of the other athletes in class used it," and when she tried it, she found that OneNote offered organizational options suited to the work of the way in which she takes notes. Through configurations of interacting with particular fellow students, then, Lilly was turned toward a particular application that shaped the way in which she comes to act as a member of the classes she is part of. The residue of text left after this participation becomes a tool through which the later work of study-guide building emerges.

Lilly's OneNote entries can be seen as serving two functions. First, they serve as a means of making sense of lectures that she perceives as "vague." Though she finds herself struggling to understand what her instructor is trying to say during the lecture, she is able to triangulate sufficient meaning between the words of the instructor, the words of the PowerPoint slide, and her entries on OneNote. These interacting objects serve to produce, for Lilly, a progression of social order that come to count as ⟨class⟩. This co-construction of ⟨class⟩ is not the same as a co-construction of *meaning* in the notes that she takes: rather, the ways in which Lilly is able to—along with her instructor, the objects in the room, and her fellow students—keep class going is, in part, by keeping her *writing* going in the notes that she produces.

In Lilly's recounting of her note-taking for class, no significant differences emerge between the notes she takes in her college biology class and the classes that come before or with it. Her participation in class is rendered visible by her note-taking activity, and with the exception of beginning to use OneNote, Lilly's pattern of note-taking has not seemed to change. However, if we are to follow the serial production of social order—that is, what Lilly *does* with these notes—out of and then, later, back into the classroom, then a broader pattern of literate action development begins to emerge, particularly around her preparation for tests. Her practices for participating in classroom life, in other words, fail to visibly signal literate action development in the work of class, but lay the groundwork for development to emerge later in her take-up of course materials.

## Framing the Individuated Actor

We can begin to individuate Lilly's note-taking activity as she moves from the classroom to her individual study activities, which take place in a range of places. Figure 6.7 shows Lilly's drawing of the study hall she is required to attend as part of her commitment to her field hockey program on the left, and the desk in her apartment bedroom on the right. In these sites, Lilly brings particular artifacts from the joint production of classroom order into her study and writing sessions.

*Figure 6.7. Lilly's study hall and apartment desk.*

Though Lilly's images are suggestive of these writing and study opportunities as happening in particular places, it is important to realize that they also happen at particular times, and are realized in particular kinds of social order. Lilly arrives at each site with particular tasks to do, and orders the materials about her—the social media on her phone, the distance from other members of the study hall, the availability of light, power outlets, and internet access—to co-construct into being both the site of her academic work and her particular participation in it. Just as in class, Lilly is able to participate in the production of social order, in part, through her notes.

Lilly's notes to enable her to build on the residue of text left from the {class} interactions that she participated in earlier. "I think looking at my notes, looking at what I've starred," says Lilly, "helps me see what we did, how to get that in class." Lilly's return to her notes in a new setting provides her with an opportunity to identify points of confusion, moments when her co-construction of those notes in the re-reading leads to additional information that she has trouble working through. Part of this work involves not only particular spaces (such as the study hall), but the sequencing of tasks over broader periods of time, which allow her to bring in more resources.

A particularly good example of this is the Khan Academy videos that Lilly turns to when needed. As times for major exams draw near, Lilly will "try to go through" her notes to see if she can construct a new understanding of those notes. If not, Lilly can "go and watch Khan Academy videos" to aid the development of new understandings of them. Lilly has a sense that what she is being asked to learn in these classes is not "just knowing how to calculate something" but "knowing the principles of something." Lilly's use of the Khan Academy's videos, then, serve as a response to a new co-construction of her situation for working with her notes: that of building her understanding of the "principles" of the topic she is working with.

In the work of advancing her understanding of the "principles," in addition to the calculations, Lilly will "try to go through" her notes and "build myself a little study guide. I'll try to highlight things I should know, like keywords and stuff." Part of the work of building study guides involves flashcards, something that she begins college using regularly, but it tapers off by the end of her sophomore year:

> I make flashcards. I had to know these enzymes for today so
> I made these flashcards. I would say I haven't used flashcards
> this semester. I don't know why that is. Usually I study with
> flashcards.

At this stage of analysis, what might be considered through other lenses to be good study habits can be seen, through the first two framings, as Lilly participating in the production of social order, and stitching that social order together from one moment to the next. Lilly's notes move from the classroom to study hall and her bedroom desk, and in the co-construction of those spaces

Lilly finds herself in the position of having to make sense of them again. Interestingly, however, it seems that the ongoing production of notes from Lilly's classes lead to some transformation, as Lilly moves away from flashcards later in her work. Lilly seems surprised by it, but later remarks that her new course on Organic Chemistry "is not something you study for with a flashcard." It seems as though Lilly is making the deliberate choice *not* to use flashcards, to enact her practice differently.

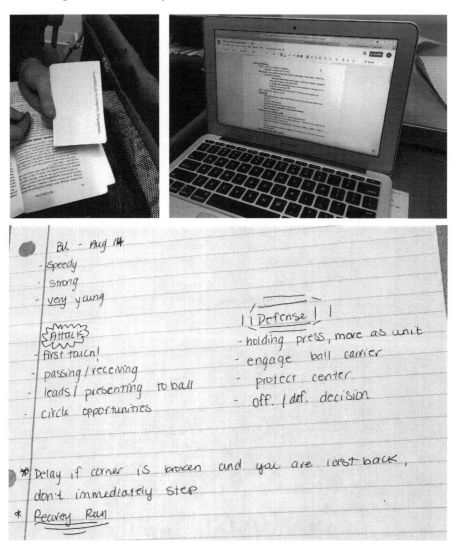

*Figure 6.8. Lilly's note-taking.*

## Framing the Scenic Work of Uncertainty Reduction

In following the note-taking practices of Lilly through her class attendance, her study session attendance, and her work in her apartment, we see that Lilly is constantly doing work to make visible her understandings of various aspects of classroom activity and, doing so, is transforming her note-taking practices. When Lilly arrives at organic chemistry, she struggles to envision the value of her flashcards in her work and responds accordingly, choosing instead to develop her own study guides in the situated moments of literate action that would normally lead to flashcards. In the interactions of her OneNote entries, her notebooks, her lab books, and other resources on her computer, Lilly realizes a new set of possibilities: one in which the work that emerges for her is not a set of flashcards, but rather a more detailed study guide that lets her get at "the function of the enzyme" that she finds herself struggling with so much.

In this realization of new possibilities for action, Lilly is engaged in work that is decidedly different than the *stacking* that we witnessed with May. Instead of building on the work of her flashcards, Lilly repurposes the objects at her disposal for a different kind of work. Seeing the lack of value in flashcards for such a complex topic as she understands it, Lilly *brackets* her flashcard activity. That is, she sets it apart from the current task, identifying the work of building the study guide as antithetical to the work of making flashcards in order to perceive what she sees as a very different kind of problem.

The bracketing work that Lilly does complicates the vision of literate action development that emerged in the first six cases of this study. In those instances of literate action development, particular, enduring changes were made visible, but those changes were additive—an accumulation of transformations in patterns of literate action. Lilly's activity, when framed as *bracketing*, calls attention to the ways in which she deletes particular kinds of literate action and its attendant materials from the scene in order to accomplish her work. Drawing on the language of the totality, I envision Lilly's bracketing decision as the result of a transformed understanding of *What-Comes-Next* in terms of the progression of her preparation for her organic chemistry exam. Aware of the shortcomings of her previous study habit in this particular situation, Lilly strategically reduces the uncertainty of *What-Comes-Next* in order to locate the uncertainty in her understanding of the necessary knowledge for the exam, not the process of working through the content. Such a bracketing action also puts her in the position of being able to carry on with such bracketing in the future, when her teammates see her study guide and ask for some assistance writing their own guides. What Lilly seems to have done here is make a tactical choice for organic chemistry that eventually came to serve as a transformative moment in her note-taking practices.

## Practice Construction: Bracketing and Stacking

May and Lilly's work throughout their two years at the university have engaged in a fair amount of what Roozen (2010) might refer to as repurposing. But a closer analysis through the lens of the totality of the literate experience demonstrates significant, ongoing revisions of these students' understanding of what is asked of them as writers at the university, as well as the resources they perceive themselves as having for going about that work. Notably, these students established patterns of interconnecting writing throughout their lifeworlds in the moments of literate action performance, drawing as necessary across sometimes widely-disparate resources, experiences, and understandings to complete the texts that they need to complete in order to continue the social order of performing as students at a university.

Note that in each of these cases, the work of orchestrating across lifeworlds is scenically available to each actor. When Lilly organizes herself to write in study hall, for instance, the resources she draws across, such as various classes, or the understandings that she developed during discussions in lab, are materially present—they work with other objects to realize arrays of possibility in the unfolding social situation. The realized possibilities also arrive at the study hall via antecedent situations that, when chained together, realize a moving constellation of densely networked talk, tools, and texts that have the moment of the study hall not as an end in mind but a stop along the way to an ever-more-densely constructed network of ever-more-responsive texts.

But these cases do more than outline the logic-in-use developed in Part I: they realize additional complexities that add to our growing understanding of exactly what constitutes the lived reality of literate action development at a stage of life other than early adolescence, and in a setting other than K–12 education. As I suggest in the preface to Part II, the cases in this chapter offer further strategic and perspicuous settings at different stages in the lifespan and in methods of social engagement with and participation in the world. May and Lilly are in different systems of activity and are co-constructing sense of their literate action in new ways. Their adumbrated sense of participation in the ongoing production of social order is causing agency to be shifted to them in ways that the participants traced in Part I did not. May and Lilly are becoming different kinds of participants in different kinds of social settings, for different purposes, and with different co-configurations of talk, tools, and texts at work. This sense of difference from the participants in Part I leads to some interesting questions about the framework of the lived reality, some possible extensions, and some potential limitations.

May and Lilly's work here extended the work of the totality in some interesting ways—their literate action seems to indicate increasingly intricate and, in terms of material, thinly linked sets of situations through which altered recurrence emerges. That is, May and Lilly's increasing agency in daily college life, as compared to the middle school students in the previous study, appear to draw on a wider array of objects across a broader set of circumstances in order to scenically accomplish literate action. Furthermore, the wide-ranging ways in which these scenic accomplishments transform over time suggest that the ebb and flow of literate action development resonate across the lifeworlds that we work through as social actors. This extension usefully troubles the issue of transfer—it suggests that any act of transfer perceived by an institution is part of a broader set of on-going relocalizations of literate action in the life of the actors involved—but it also suggests some questions about how the lived reality operates as a centering influence in the lives of writers. That is, as writers move from one situation to another, dealing with wider or narrower sets of objects and people, how might the lived reality—the means by which *What-Comes-Next* is reduced to perform social action—serve to order, flatten, or otherwise render workable the complex interconnections suggested here? Such questions suggest the need for an explanatory concept. Based on the analysis above, I suggest *circulating agency* as a potential way to render visible to researchers how literate actors come to render *What-Comes-Next* workable.

## Circulating Agency: A Potential Concept

I define *circulating agency* as the work of individuated actors in one moment to create and/or use objects that can be flung into future moments and, through their use, circulate an increased capacity to act back to the individuated actor. This concept is similar in nature to "expansive agency" (Dippre, 2018), but attends more closely to the material work of moving agency without also attempting to capture its results. A straightforward example of such work might be the work I do at the start of a class to write the agenda for the meeting on the board at the front of the room. This act allows me, once class begins, to direct the room from one task to another. My ability to act as a teacher in the classroom has been circulated to the list on the board and, later, back to me. Such a concept can help us think through what we saw May and Lilly doing with their literate action earlier in this chapter.

The language of "circulating agency" resonates with posthuman conceptions of agency. In his review of the term agency in *Keywords in Writing Studies*, Accardi (2015) notes that the commonplace definition of agency "signifies the capacity to act," (p. 1) but goes on to highlight that

> A posthumanist or poststructuralist orientation . . . does not
> locate agency with the subject. According to this lens, agency
> is found circulating in discourse and dispersed into an ever-
> shifting field of power relations (Herndl & Licona, 2007, p.
> 141). In other words, agency cannot be possessed. (p. 2)

Accardi goes on to note that humanist and posthumanist conceptions of agency can be conflated, which, in a sense, is how the concept of circulating agency emerges in my work with May and Lilly's findings. This concept, emergent as it is from the empirical analysis of records-turned-into-data, fits with a situation described by Merton (1968) when articulating the development of middle-range theory through interactions among a discipline and a data set. Beginning with language that is commonly used in the field, I use the intersections of my analysis and particular conceptions of agency to develop a concept that initiates a small difference in understandings of agency circulation from a lifespan perspective, which can "lead to successively more fundamental theoretical differences" over time (Merton, 1968, p. 42). In other words, the bringing together of agency with bracketed and stacked practices creates an opportunity to generate a new conceptualization of agency that is oriented to the demands of studying the lived reality of lifespan literate action development.

We can understand the ways in which May and Lilly bracket and stack their practices by examining the ways in which May and Lilly *circulate agency* to themselves from one situation to the next. This concept draws on a commonplace definition of agency—the capacity to act—as understood through a posthuman lens: nonhuman objects *also* have the capacity to act on a situation. But this definition departs from typical posthuman representations of agency in that the agency circulates *back to* particular individuated actors as they work to co-construct social order. We can think of May's fidget-writing in class, then, not as a way of passing time but as a way of participating in the production of social order that both counts as classroom activity and is integrated with the serial production of local, social order that she is co-constituting throughout her lifespan.

Consider the broader context of the work that May is co-constructing when she engages in such fidget-writing in class. In preparation for class, May packs a bag with the material she will need: computer, notebook, pens, etc. The notebook and pen, having bearing on the situation (Latour, 2005) of their own, move into the space of the classroom with May: they arrive in a bag, are set up at a space in a lecture hall, and become available to May as she participates in the ongoing production of social order. They are *scenically available* objects through which particular possibilities can be recognized, and May can recognize the possibility of fidget-writing with them. In the packing of her bag for attending class, May has circulated the possibility of acting through fidget-writing into her notebooks and pens, which in their movement from her dorm to the lecture hall become available again to her for use.

The circulation of agency, then, refers to the ways in which objects are imparted with particular possibilities of use by individuated actors and then rendered scenically available in future situations of co-configured talk, tools, and texts. In other words, we circulate capacities to act in particular ways back to ourselves with particular objects that we make available for use from one situation to the next. This concept offers interesting questions for studying lifespan literate action development. For instance, how might the mechanisms of circulation change over time? In what ways might May and Lilly, in their development through adulthood, come to re-orchestrate the talk, tools, and texts around them so that different materials—or new possibilities in similar materials—give them the capacity to act in future moments of literate action? Future studies can dimensionalize further the concept of circulating agency, and by extension allow it to develop as the core of a middle-range theory of lifespan literate action development.

## Implications for Transfer Research

Tracing the complex, material work of the situated transformations of talk, tools, and texts that endure across situations suggest productive complexities for understanding research on writing transfer. As indicated above, the agency of writers as they move from one situation to another can usefully complicate the ways in which we consider transfer. How might the circulation of agency in classroom discussion, for instance, enable the transfer of literate practices and knowledge for some, but not others? How might it help writing instructors think about the degree to which students are working to enact their own understandings, shape the course through their own visions of how it should unfold? If, as Prior (1998, 2010, 2017), Roozen (2010), Roozen and Erickson (2017), and others suggest, we look to the multidimensional literate lives of students, how might we more carefully account for that work in our emerging studies of writing transfer?

Writing researchers have conclusively demonstrated that transfer is, if nothing else, an extremely complex phenomenon. The work of May and Lilly does little to simplify this complexity, but it does suggest that looking to the social ordering that occurs in any given moment of transfer are worth attending to in order to understand the ways in which acts that we, as teachers and researchers, consider transfer happen. Making future sites of transfer study more attentive to the members' methods for constructing social situations, as well as how those methods resonate with seemingly unrelated lifeworlds of literate action, would bring valuable insights to our emerging understandings of transfer.

An important aspect of the chapter that stands out for thinking about transfer is the role that agency plays for the students who are co-constructing social order not only in their classrooms but in the chains of social action that lead into and away from those classrooms—into the study habits they engage in, the interactional orders they take up as they talk about the concepts, formula, tools, etc., presented in a given class, and the practices they bring to bear on making sense of that material. The ways in which students transfer knowledge, activities, skills, etc., into and out of particular classes is shaped by the ways in which they work out their sense of *What-Comes-Next* both in the moment of the class and in their engagement with the material of that class during out-of-class assignments. Attending to the ways in which agency is circulated to, through, and back to students from one moment to the next throughout the semester—and the materials through which that agency is circulated—will be important to understanding, in a more fine-grained manner, the ways in which certain practices are bracketed or stacked from one course to the next.

The essential contribution, perhaps, of this chapter to ongoing research on transfer is the vision of the ongoing *work* of the social world within which any given classroom is caught up. If we cease to see a future class as a standalone entity and instead as something that must be co-constructed with the particular students we are interested in studying, then the complex work that goes into the concepts, practices, etc., that educators hope to bring from one moment to the next may be more fully recognized and worked with in future studies of transfer. Envisioning the production of a class meeting as interactive social work—and work that is deeply interconnected with the many other lifeworlds that participants engage in—is the first step in a more robust, interactionally-aware understanding of transfer that is both attentive to social complexity and productive for educators to think through in terms of curricular design.

## Expanding a Vision of Lifespan Literate Action Development

The three steps of uncovering the totality of the literate experience as articulated in Chapter 5 served as a sufficient starting point for studying the literate action development of Lilly and May. As the study of their literate action expanded across lifeworlds and over greater spans of time, it became clear that we needed a concept to account for out how the materials that were available for the take-up of a particular practice were made scenically available to them from one moment to the next and, furthermore, the role they had in making such material available. Tracing the material presence of this agency across events and over a two-year period has provided this study with the first of several tools in studying literate action development through the logic-in-use of the totality.

But the necessity of the concept of agency and its circulation suggests that perhaps attention is needed for yet another. The study of Lilly and May, though beneficial in stretching the totality as a logic-in-use into a different age span and set of social conditions, is hardly the end of the road: Lilly and May, as well as the methods of record collection used with them, may highlight more expansive literate action across a wider range of lifeworlds, but their literate lives have every chance of growing more complex over time. The agency that is circulated back to them can transform in myriad ways over time, as they become caught up within many other literate practices throughout the complexity of their lives.

In order to continue to test the potentiality of the logic-in-use that is the totality, I turn, in the next chapter, to a set of writers, Tom and John, in their thirties and forties. I have selected these writers not merely because of their age but because of the complexity of the practices with which they are engaged, and the histories behind those practices that have shaped their use over time.[6] The length

---

6. Though the complexity and history of the practice is, itself, connected to their age: it is difficult to develop literate practices as complex as John and Tom do without a sustained series of literate practice production from which to build them.

of time that these writers have engaged with their practices offers another opportunity: one of developing a sense of how identity is constructed through the circulation of agency. May and Lilly, though effective participants for tracing agency, were not strategic sites for following the production of identity as I will come to define it in the next chapter. Tom and John, in addition to adding complexity our current understanding of the totality, can serve as a strategic site for tracing the work of identity with and as part of literate action over time.

# Chapter 7. Circulating Agency and Emergent Identities

In Chapter 6, I outlined some issues with transfer, as well as some roots in transfer research that may be productively explored through the totality. Further research into the cases of May and Lilly uncovered a concept that emerged through the examination of a wider span of time and lifeworlds—the circulation of agency—that was revealed in the tracing of the bracketing and stacking of individuated uses of practice for a next first time. In this chapter, I study the cases of two writers further along in their careers (and their lifespans) than May and Lilly. John and Tom are writers in their 30s and 40s, respectively, who were, at the time of my work with them, pursuing graduate degrees in creative writing at a university in the northeastern United States. My work with them through the totality of the literate experience confirmed the utility of looking toward agency and its circulation to understand the lived reality of literate action development, but also suggested an additional concept: identity. Below, I articulate an ethnomethodological position on identity, which I then orient toward the issue of literate action development. I then draw on that refined position to make sense of identity in my studies with Tom and John.

## Finding Agents for our Agency: Ethnomethodological Perspectives on Identity

Understanding the ongoing recirculation of agency through the studies of May and Lilly in Chapter 6 is related to an under-examined aspect of the emerging understanding of the lived reality in this text: identity. A significant amount of attention has been focused on how people use practices to make sense to themselves and others about what they are doing, but the ways in which this work is transformed into who they are becoming—that is, how identities form and reform as a result of that work—has remained unaddressed. While this aspect of literate action development has remained occluded in the cases so far, part of the reason for this occlusion may be the roots of this text in ethnomethodological study, which traditionally eschews issues of identity and selfhood.

Identity is caught up within the notion of *whole persons*, a concept that is pushed aside in ethnomethodological studies because of EM's focus on remaining a rigorously empirical enterprise. Whole persons cannot be seen acting in a given social situation: they are, for ethnomethodologists, as fictitious as whole corporations. One is unable, in a given moment, to see either operating. When we see an individuated actor doing work in a social situation, we are seeing one aspect, one facet, of a complex social being—one, in fact, that is never finalizable, never able to be rendered "whole" in a way that would not leave out some unfinished aspect of the person-in-process.

Just like whole persons, identity is not finished, not finalizable, and difficult to discern in the ongoing production of social order as an ethnomethodological respecification in the traditional sense. That is, *perspicuous settings* may be found in which people discuss their identities, talk it into being, but tracing identity across settings becomes more challenging in less perspicuous circumstances. As the study of Tom and John shows in this chapter, however, identity is a powerful shaper of literate action. What is needed, then, is a conceptualization of identity that is situated within the ongoing production of social order, even if not as perspicuously available as a traditionally-respecified EM understanding would suggest.

Such a conceptualization of identity would have to be *practiced* into being, just as any other aspect of producing social order. An identity must be practiced into the ongoing production of social order if we are to have an understanding of identity at all. Through the study of Tom and John, below, I attend to the tactical work of identity construction and build, from that tactical action, an understanding of the role that identity comes to play in lifespan literate action development.

Tom and John, in their 40s and 30s respectively, are creative writers in an MA program in northern New England at the time of the study. Both of these writers have been involved in a range of writing situations, from stand-up comedy in Las Vegas (John) to submarine maintenance in the U.S. Navy (Tom). Both of these writers also engaged in extensive notebook writing practices across the bulk of these writing experiences. The transformations of these notebook writing practices over time reveal not only the complex lifeworlds that Tom and John are part of but the ways in which their identities as writers have transformed in their interactions with and through that complexity.

The focus of the interviews—with the exception of John's first interview—were focused on these writers' notebook writing practices. John's interviews were caught up within a separate study of his development as a teaching assistant (Dippre, 2016). My first interview with John, a literacy history interview based on Brandt's (2001) methodology, was part of that initial study. Interviews 2 and 3 emerged from John's growing interest in talking about his writing process. Below, I identify the traces of identity work that emerged from my study of their literate action.

## Submarines and Short Stories: Tom's Notebook Writing

Tom's notebook writing has a history that stretches back to his youth in northern New England. Tom always envisioned himself as someone who would become a writer, but struggled to take on that label for himself:

> My father's a minister. And for some reason, whether it was the
> type of school I grew up in, or that my father was constantly
> writing, I always assumed I would be a writer of some sort.

> When I was younger, I had this idea that I needed to get older
> before anyone would take me seriously as a writer. So I did
> attempt occasionally to keep journals. I was really bad at it. It's
> humorous to look back on.

Tom's initial sense of identity might be as a *potential future writer* in his younger years: he sees himself, looking back on his life, as having prepared for the work of being a writer in halting, uncertain ways. This halting development as a writer was caught up in conflicting circumstances that led him away from college and into the U.S. Navy after his freshman year.

> I went to school for theology and English initially, switched it
> to English once I got there. I lasted one year in college the first
> time, when I was eighteen. So I joined the navy. I dropped out
> of college because my parents didn't have that much money.
> And they were taking out loans, and I was taking out loans,
> and I didn't see that college was doing anything for me that
> was worth the cost of that much debt. So I joined the navy as
> a sort of job training. I was assuming that I'd get some sort of,
> that whatever I did in the navy would be the equivalent of a
> college degree, which it did turn out to be for life.

Tom's movement from college to the U.S. Navy seemed, on the surface, to impact his work as a writer. But as our interviews unfolded, we discovered that Tom actually wrote regularly during his time in the service, and the notebook writing that he did, though adapted to life aboard a submarine, continued a complex set of practices that would eventually carry him into an MA program with a focus in creative writing. Tom notes of his time in the Navy that

> It turns out that I still wrote, looking back on it I still wrote all
> the time. I just didn't ever think of it, I never thought of myself
> as a writer until much later. I'm still hazy about the term. It's a
> term that has some baggage for me. I'm not sure why.

Despite Tom's struggles to identify himself as a writer, he found himself regularly engaged in writing in various kinds of notebooks for various purposes. These writing experiences spanned both space and purpose: Tom wrote in submarines, in the business world, and in school; for his own entertainment, to track budgets in his family, and for to keep track of ideas. Below, I focus in particular on the ways in which Tom goes about using lists over time in order to understand how his literate action develops.

## Framing Ongoing, Joint Action

The earliest records of Tom's list-keeping in the Navy—he had a notebook that he kept before entering boot camp that he would later return to, but personal items were not allowed during basic training—can be found in his notebooks for his advanced coursework, what he referred to as "A School" (Figure 7.1). Here, Tom's lists are shaped by the curriculum of the coursework that he is involved in. Tom notes that this tightly focused writing—both the lists in Figure 7.1 and the subsequent writing for the rest of his volume—are not typical of the work that he will later do. He notes that this is "the most professional thing I've ever done," as he sees his later notes as deeply laminated[7] with other aspects of his life that these notes don't take up.

Tom's initial work in A School is seen by him, in retrospect, as professional in a way that his later writing fails to take up. Applying the *ongoing, joint action* framing to Tom's work suggests that this difference is not the result of past discipline or a future laziness, but a production of social order through which past practices were not rendered scenically available in the then-existing configurations of talk, tools, and texts. 'A School,' a specialist training school that follows on the heels of basic training, continued the work of separating Tom from previous practice use. The combination of past notebook writing practices being scenically unavailable and the present work of A School as tightly restricted according to the demands of the Navy.

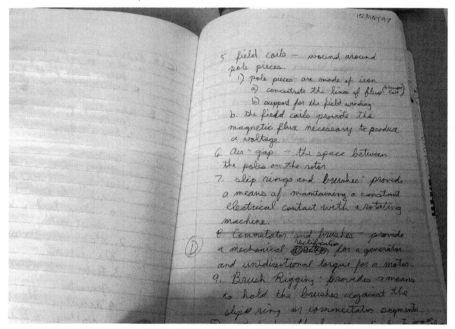

Figure 7.1. Tom's A School notes.

---

7. Tom actually used the word "laminated" several times in our discussion, a reference to Prior and Shipka's (2003) work, which Tom read as part of a methods course in his MA program.

In other words, like the note-writing of Lilly and May, Tom's notebook writing here is caught up within the ongoing production of order in a class, albeit a different kind of class. Tom's A School notebooks are almost strictly shaped by the demands of A School—his participation in ongoing, joint order brackets his past practices. But in the work that follows those classes—his work on submarines, for instance, and his eventual move to the private workforce and then, eventually, graduate work—we can see him begin to integrate his professional writing with practices of participating in the ongoing, joint order of other lifeworlds.

## Framing the Individuated Actor

The initial notes of Tom from his early work in the Navy gives way, in his later notebooks, to a range of other lists. His notebooks—even those that he carries with him in his tours on submarines—carry within their pages lists of movies, of activities, of budget items, and—of course—of various tasks for work. Figure 7.2 is a particularly clear example of the ways in which Tom's lists come to be laminated with a variety of purposes within the space of the same page. As of the writing included in Figure 7.2, Tom has come to see the list as an important practice, a mechanism of ongoing uncertainty reduction. Tom uses lists to keep track of movies and jokes he wants to remember when he is ashore, and to keep track of his tasks when he is on a shift.

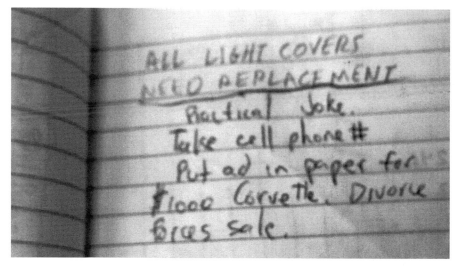

*Figure 7.2. The co-presence of Tom's lists.*

In his later work, however, Tom sees cause to repurpose the act of lists in his movement to the computer. The writing in Figure 7.3 occurs after Tom has completed his work in the Navy and has moved on to graduate school. Tom describes the lists that he developed in his older notebook writing as having migrated from the space of a handwritten notebook to the Notes feature that Macbooks offer. This shift emerges out of the demands of his new circumstances: the lists that Tom composes are not merely for his own entertainment, but for the work of developing stories that will later come to compose his MA thesis. In one of his interviews, Tom registers surprise that he was continuing to use such a durable practice: ". . . that's actually the same exact thing I used to do, but I'm just doing it online now, I just never connected the two."

*Figure 7.3. Tom's Macbook notes.*

Much like Lilly in Chapter 6, Tom sees an increased uncertainty when bringing existing practices to bear on a particular problem. By bringing his practice of listing items to his electronic notes, Tom now has easy access to his ideas for writing, and can more effectively draw on those when in the space of composing stories for his MA thesis. The sometimes-nebulous nature of writing a master's thesis has now been rendered at least partly familiar, transformed from information into another instance of *What-Comes-Next.*

## Framing the Scenic Work of Uncertainty Reduction

Tom's work to transform his practice of listing into this MA thesis can be materially traced across several mechanisms, each of which made the task of writing his thesis somewhat less cumbersome. Though Tom's transformation of his practice began with the realization of possibilities in a notebook and ended with the realization of possibilities in a Notes function of a Macbook, Tom's recognition of new possibilities in the object of the laptop involved at least one intermediary: the iPod.

While in graduate school, Tom bought an iPod for himself, one that had a WiFi connection and a Notes feature on it as well. It was here that Tom recognized new possibilities for action in the iPod. The iPod, much like the notes that Tom had and very *unlike* the laptop he would later turn to, could be carried in his pocket: it was an unobtrusive addition to his life that he could turn to with similar ease to his notebook. In other words, the addition of the iPod provided Tom with essentially the same arrays of possibilities for writing lists as his notebook did.

The realization of the "sync" function on his iPod, however, kickstarted a more dramatic set of transformations in the array of possibilities that Tom recognized in the objects through which lists were developed. The ability that Tom had to make the notes on his iPod available on his Macbook eased the work of moving from lists of notes into the short stories that would constitute his MA thesis. This greater ease was somewhat hampered later by a failure of the syncing app that Apple offers, but by then Tom had begun to enter his notes directly onto his laptop. By rearranging the materials through which Tom made his lists, he was able to more fluidly move from his lists to his story writing, and thus render the uncertainty of his production of thesis writing more manageable.

## Concept in Use: The Circulation of Agency

The work of Tom to move from his notebook lists to his laptop lists signaled a transformation of his literate action and, it seems, an enduring one—or at least one that endured across the entirety of the thesis. In the previous chapter, however, we saw that the reduction of uncertainty is not the final step in understanding the totality. As writers move from one moment to the next, from one situation to the next, researchers need to understand *how* that which is scenically available in a moment comes to be there. How, in other words, are literate actors able to circulate agency back to themselves from one moment to the next? Tom has certainly stacked his literate practices in productive ways, moving with effectiveness from the production of social order through notebook writing to the production of social order through note-writing on his laptop. But how was Tom able to make this transition possible? How does Tom possess the agency to make this move, the ability to bring a particular concatenation of talk, tools, and texts to bear in the production of his short stories?

Locating Tom's agency best starts, as we saw in Chapter 6, not in a particular object or moment but in an ongoing circulation of objects from one moment to the next. If we think back to the initial lists in Tom's notebook during A School, we see Tom initially following the work of his classes. But as time goes on, the work that he has to do—for his advanced training, for his work on submarines, for his undergraduate work—become saturated with other aspects of different lifeworlds: movies he wants to see, quotes he wants to remember, plans for the future, traces of the past. Tom's work to splice together the notebook practice of writing lists enables him to envision his work of listing in his notebook as flexible, as multiply effective. When the time comes to write a thesis, then, he turns to the practice that he sees as beneficial to this thinking, as an ongoing accompaniment to his consistent production of social order over a twenty-year span: list writing.

As Tom moves from one instance to the next, as he finds himself no longer writing lists for himself but working through the challenges of composing an MA thesis, he envisions the chapters of his thesis not as components of a larger whole but as a list: a table of contents that needs to be articulated. The list, which is a natural space for the lamination of multiple lifeworlds, provides Tom with the flexibility to identify creative ideas that will lead to interesting short stories and, by extension, thesis chapters. Tom brings the idea of the list forward as he is working through the challenge of turning the nebulousness of the thesis into something that he values, something that he can have authorship over. By bringing the list to bear, by reducing the uncertainty of the thesis, Tom gains agency over the authorship of the thesis, is able to develop a sense of what it looks like, and the work that needs to get done in order to make that vision real.

It should be noted that not all attempts to circulate agency back toward himself were successful. For instance, when Tom returned to his Navy notebooks after leaving the service, he ran across parts of jokes that, at the time, he had hoped to remember. Present-day Tom, however, was unable to recall the whole joke for most of them, and had to turn to his fellow veterans on Facebook to see if some of the gaps could be filled in (not all were). This degradation of a move to circulate agency back to oneself through literate action poses an interesting complication in how agency is and can be effectively circulated over time, particularly long stretches of time.

Overall, however, from one moment to the next, Tom draws on the list in order to keep writing—and, by extension, social order—going. When he reaches the work of his MA thesis, Tom once again draws on the list, this time to both reduce the uncertainty of writing a thesis and have an agentive stake in the construction of that document. This circulation of agency toward a particular product can be productively complicated with the work of John, below, as he draws on his notes to circulate agency back toward himself across a range of lifeworld interactions.

## Manual Labor and Creative Writing: John's Notebook

John, like Tom, was a graduate student in a creative writing MA program in northern New England when I met him. John was a middle child in a household that had two parents with advanced degrees, as well as other relatives who were writing regularly for work in PR firms and publishing houses. John is very aware of the idiosyncratic path toward the identity of a writer that he has crafted throughout his life. His early life was split between an interest in athletics and an interest in academics. He grew up in what he describes as "affluent suburbs. Not outrageously so, but I was fortunate." Remarking that, when you are young, "it's important who you can bike to," John noted that all of his friends growing up were extremely interested in athletics. While John was also interested in athletics, he describes himself as "definitely the kid who brought a book to the sleepover, and got ripped on." Even with such an early interest in reading, and the literate acts he was frequently exposed to, John does not mark the start of his life as a writer until age nineteen, when he "got up one night and started writing a book." Describing it as a "crime novel" that was "a mash of what I'd been reading for fun mixed in with some of the more bizarre things I'd been learning for school," John seems to sense a change in his literate life from that moment on: "ever since then, I worked on writing."

John finished his BA in philosophy with a history minor at a university in New England, and immediately turned to what he terms manual labor—painting houses, working for moving companies, etc.—for his primary income while working on writing in his spare time. Both his writing and his manual labor have their origins in his college life, with John painting houses in the summer while taking a creative writing class in his sophomore year.

Manual labor is an important part of John's life. He spent six years working full time because "that was dignified in a way that I couldn't give up." He saw it as something that he "wanted to be able to do" and that he would be "really in trouble if I didn't understand this world" of social action that was very different from what he would encounter in the white-collar world. John's work to make manual labor and writing integral parts of his life come together in his notebook writing practices, as well as the various transformations that his literate action around and through those practices go through. In particular, I identify the genesis of his practice of writing down definitions of words in a notebook and trace it through a range of iterations over time.

## Framing Ongoing, Joint Action

When John was in college and majoring in philosophy, he found himself discussing the *Nicomachean Ethics* in a class about Aristotle. His professor used a word—"stochastic"—that he had not heard before. Even though he had never come across it before, John was struck by the fact that it seemed to be something he *should* know, and so he wrote it down with the intention of looking it up later.

In this moment, John was participating in the social construction of order in the classroom. Though no record of it exists, the position of his body in space, the movements of his hand over the page, and—perhaps most of all—the way in which he let pass the mention of a word that he did not know enabled the class to continue to understand both what was going on (class) and what to do next (continue the discussion of *Nicomachean Ethics*). Much like May's fidget-writing, or Lilly's note-taking, John's scrawling of a word that he wanted to look up later did two things: it perpetuated ongoing, joint action in the moment and created an object that could be incorporated in to the later production of social action.

## Framing the Individuated Actor

The word "stochastic" followed John out of the classroom quite literally, on the slip of paper that he wrote it on. This word was quickly followed by others, which he dutifully wrote down when he stumbled across and would later define in a handwritten record of words that he kept in a binder (Figure 7.4). The work of the class becomes individuated in the future production of social order by John when he chases down the words that he wishes to learn more about.

We can locate John, as an individuated actor, in his development of this particular practice of literate action. John's adumbrated participation in a particular class meeting or the reading of a particular text leads to the presence of information in the normal flow of *What-Comes-Next* through a word that John cannot make sense of. Drawing on his practice of defining words that he doesn't understand through the integrated work of note-card writing and binder use, John is able to reduce information into a manageable instance of *What-Comes-Next* and, by extension, keep writing going.

*Figure 7.4. John's binder of definitions.*

John's process developed over time, from just generating individual definitions to a system that allowed John to write down interesting words on notecards, then later define them more fully in his notebook. When John enrolls in graduate school, his professional life begins to change. The manual labor recedes into the background, and the bulk of the working day is taken up by writing and writing-related tasks. This transforms the social action that John's definition work co-constructs, and John finds himself doing some of that work on a computer. However, since John "almost always keep[s] a paper journal," the notecard-to-handwritten-definition process remains largely intact. Instead of bringing his binder with him wherever he goes to do work, John keeps the binder at his office desk, where definitions of new words can be managed.

## Framing the Scenic Work of Uncertainty Reduction

John's system of definitions serves, for him, as a way of offloading some of the challenges of reading academic work. "It's become familiar to me," says John. "It allows me to keep reading if I don't know a word, because I know I will." John's acts to *keep reading going* through words he has not encountered before are made scenically visible by the presence of the binder of words he has. Because of this binder, "rare is the word that will stop me in the middle of a short story."

John's binder—and the notecards in it—co-construct a space for deep engagement with texts in his office. While leaving the binder in his office does not prevent John from reading and writing in other places, the presence of John's binder creates opportunities for engaging with text that he cannot find elsewhere. In other words, the texts that John reads are recognized as having new possibilities in them because of the situated work of a net of objects at John's desk—including John himself. John's past practice of writing definitions is made materially present by the definitions already in the binder, and the blank notecards and pages make materially available the investigation of new words in John's continued work of reading.

## Concept In Use: The Circulation of Agency

John's work to define new words over time has transformed into an object that pulls him into positions of agency in future acts of reading. John can keep reading after jotting down a note on a notecard to define a word later or, if he needs to, he can stop what he is doing and begin writing up a definition. "If there's a word I know I want to get," he says, "I'll find it quickly." Any given re-use of the system is responsive to the demands of the reading. Referring to his readings for a Writing Studies graduate course, John notes that "I would look up words as I went. It would prevent me from getting through if I didn't know *heteroglossia*, for instance." John's definition-writing activity did not just allow him to reduce uncertainty in a given moment of keeping writing going: it gave him a flexible practice that could be pulled—via the notebook that he kept his definitions in—into a range of reading situations that would give him agency over how he took up developing an understanding of new words.

John's practice of defining new words over time also shows us the possibility that attempts to circulate agency back to oneself can fail. Though John conscientiously attends to his definitions, he occasionally forgets the definitions of words, or remains unsure how to pronounce them. Sometimes, John will write down the definition of a word only to realize that he has already included it in his binder. Such moments of disruption in the work of this practice offers John opportunities to revise that practice, but so far John has seen his work of defining words as effective enough to continue doing.

## Dimensionalizing Agency Circulation: Extensions and Complications

The broader spans of time that Tom and John's literate practices offer show a few extensions and complications of how agency might be circulated. In Chapter 6, I defined "circulating agency" as the ways in which objects are imparted with particular possibilities of use by individuated actors and then rendered scenically available in future situations of co-configured talk, tools, and texts. For May and Lilly, this meant the ways in which note-taking practices were rendered available—or deliberately rendered unavailable—in the work of co-constructing the social order of the classroom, the dorm conversation, or the field hockey film session. Tom and John's enactment of notebook practices across a wider span of years—over twenty for Tom, and over ten for John—unveils more of the challenges of circulating agency back to oneself in the serial production of local social order. When Tom is making lists on a submarine, for instance, the lists allow him to, eventually, have the capacity to act toward finding movies he is interested in watching when on shore leave. But across longer stretches of time, his notebook practice degrades in its effectiveness—consider, for instance, his inability to remember the partial jokes he has listed.

John similarly signals some degradation in his notebook practice when he finds himself unable to remember words he defined, or writing them down more than once. In these instances, the uncertainty of *What-Comes-Next*, though reduced in the moment of the initial use of the notebook practice, is elevated in an unexpected manner in a later instance. Such instances trigger further work of uncertainty reduction. For John, this means returning to his definitions. For Tom, this means reaching out to fellow veterans to find more information on the jokes. In each of these instances, the failure of a practice to make scenically available particular possibilities in an array of objects triggers new literate action, new opportunities to circulate agency to oneself in a future moment of literate action.

The complications of John and Tom's literate practices over a longer period of time suggest that bracketing and stacking—that is, the work of circulating agency to oneself through the use of practices—is not entirely within the control of the individuated actors under study. There are opportunities for complication that can disrupt a given instantiation of a practice and, in doing so, perhaps provide an opportunity for further literate action development by transforming such a practice. The details of the potential barriers to agency circulation are a worthwhile problem for further research to examine. What is it that interferes problematically with taking up objects that are circulated back to oneself for action? How might researchers best characterize the break in that circulation so that the hiccups, detours, and challenges to literate action development might be further understood? In the next chapter, I draw on case studies of two older writers to enrich our understanding of these boundaries.

## Bracketing and Stacking Toward Identity (Re)Construction

Tracing the agentive work of Tom and John, and their various stacking and bracketing of practices as they transformed their notebook writing over time, suggests that the logic-in-use of the totality may be ready to uncover another productive concept. As both Tom and John developed their literate action through notebook writing, their agency circulated back to them again and again through the objects that they co-constructed and came to, eventually, recognize new possibilities in. The work of agency circulation, however, brought with it some language suggesting that both actors were doing more than simply circulating agency back to themselves. In the process, they seemed to be working out, in some broad sense, who they were—that is, in the moment of literate action they are recounting— and its relationship to who they were during the course of the interview.

Tom provides particularly clear insights into this kind of serial work of identity construction—or, more accurately, (re)construction. He notes his lifelong movement toward an identity as a writer, even if he is uncomfortable, as of our interviews, with calling himself that. Tom's surprise with seeing the continued return of particular practices across a range of media suggest a transformed understanding of on several occasions a sense of embarrassment when looking back on some of his older writing, noting that "I'm not the same person" as he was when particular moments of writing happened. This suggests a shift in how Tom identifies himself over time, and suggests further that within the circulation of agency, a kind of identity work is going on that is also caught up in the ongoing work of producing social order.

John's work on developing a sense of identity throughout his writing experiences are more subtle, but nonetheless present. Note the ways in which John feels called toward the work of what he terms "manual labor," and the ways in which he gravitates in his writing toward an audience of readers who might be caught up within that audience. Tom's growing sense of identity shaped not only his sense of a future audience, but also the ways in which he goes about stacking and bracketing his practices. While an MA student, John takes on summer work painting houses while also wrapping up his graduate study, bringing in his past practice of working in the day and returning to his writing afterward (to quote John: "If you paint [houses] all day, you're ready for some Deleuze"). The way that his writing and his own split between academia and manual labor intertwine suggest an interesting role of identity construction in the ongoing circulation of agency.

Tom and John's work, then, seem to expand the consequentiality of the practice bracketing and stacking that May and Lilly were engaged in. It would seem that such work does more than circulate agency: it also provides a mechanism for identity construction—or, in the sense of everything happening for "another first time," perhaps (re)construction is a better way to make sense of that identity work. Just as agency and its circulation proved a valuable concept for making sense of the ways in which May and Lilly stacked and bracketed their practices, identity (re)construction offers a productive concept for seeing how individuated actors come to construct presentations of themselves in patterned ways over time, and how those patterns change.

Examining identity (re)construction means attending to the ways in which actors situate themselves in relation to both texts and the production of texts. For Tom and John, this means locating their sense of selves in relation to the notebook writing they decide to share. Of course, because of the nature of the interviews and their structure, what we see of identity (re)construction is always partial—that is, we only have at our disposal the writing that the actors chose to bring with them, as John and Tom did. But even in such necessarily partial records, acts of identity (re)construction can be identified, traced, and situated in relation to one another. In the next chapter, I draw on a study of writers in their 60s and 80s to increase the robustness of this concept, as well as agency, for understanding literate action development through the lifespan.

# Chapter 8. Complicating Agency and Identity in a Moment

The previous two chapters worked out concepts from the application of a portable logic-in-use—the totality of the literate experience—that allows for the study of the lived reality of literate action development with a broad range of records and across a widely ranging amount of time. The totality, as it stands at the end of Chapter 7, has studied transformations that resonated in varying ranges, from across a unit of blog writing to across multiple decades of using a particular practice, with two productive concepts—agency and identity—emerging from it. In this chapter, I create a stress test for these concepts by studying the literate action of two writers in their 60s (Michelle) and 80s (James) through the totality. These case studies are effective sites (that is, strategic) for complicating these concepts, and for several reasons:

1. Both write frequently, and write in a range of modes for a range of audiences;
2. Both have long histories of writing; and
3. Both are at an age that is largely understudied in writing research (see Bowen, 2018).

Because both Michelle and James are highly active writers, their complex literate lives will provide a host of material for the three framings to make sense of. Their long histories of writing will cause the two concepts—agency and identity—to stretch beyond the histories examined in Chapters Six and Seven. And their age—as well as the understudied nature of that age in Writing Studies—provides a useful opportunity to test the benefit of the totality beyond increasing the field's knowledge of lifespan literate action development. The insights that emerge from this chapter may impact positively future writing interventions for older writers.

## Age Studies and Literate Action Development

Age studies is a subject of growing importance, particularly in the United States. By 2030, over 20% of the U.S. population will be over age 65 (Bowen, 2018)—a milestone in the demographic history of the country. But older writers have been a heretofore understudied population in Writing Studies. Writing researchers have often remain focused on school-aged writers, with some investigation into workplace writing (i.e., Spinuzzi, 2008). Bowen (2018) likens the situation of studying older writers as being both present in our research and absent from "overt analysis" (p. vii). In earlier work (Dippre, 2018), I signaled the importance of understanding agency in the lives of older writers, suggesting that it was a "central concern of age studies" (p. 77) and that contemporary understandings of the agency of writers is caught up within cultural discourses—what Bowen (2011) has called a *curriculum of aging*.

Investigating the literate action development of older writers with the logic-in-use of the totality offers an interesting opportunity to study older writers with tools that enable us to sidestep the *curriculum of aging* that shapes so much contemporary thought about older writers. The totality has the potential to shed light on the complex ways in which older writers go about achieving agency through the performance of literate action. But, furthermore, the totality has the potential to show how that agency is connected to the other aspects of social order that older writers participate in. More importantly, perhaps, is the potential contribution to age studies that can be gained from looking not just for literate action in older writers, but the ways in which that literate action *develops* over time. Attending to literate action development in older writers, just as we might for college writers, upends the narrative of decline that so often comes with old age, and recasts the work of that segment of the lifespan as a potential site of transformation.

## Cast Bullet Shooting, Identity, and Time: James' Newsletter

James is a retired engineer in his 80s. James' career was a widely varied one, involving military service, the interstate highway system, and academia. James' switch to academia occurred after finishing a Ph.D. at MIT and being hired by a local university. While at the university, James moved through a host of academic and administrative positions. Finding a need to express himself in retirement—in particular, by telling stories that would help his grandchildren "find out what kind of characters we were," John enrolled in a writing course then offered by the local "senior college"—a statewide program dedicated to enriching the lives of older members of the population. James would end up self-publishing two books as a result of the writing he began in that course.

In addition to his biographical writing, James was an active member of a cast bullet shooting organization. James had been involved in the sport of cast bullet shooting for years, and in that time had developed what he referred to as a "contrarian" stance on a number of topics. When it comes to cast bullet shooting, according to James, "there's tons of old stories about what you need to do and what you don't need to do. About half of them are not true." As a member of the cast bullet organization and a frequent author in their newsletter, James was provided with opportunities to build on his "contrarian" nature by acting as a "devil's advocate" against commonly-held-but-flawed beliefs about cast bullet shooting. James believes in evidence-based work, that he needs to "[build] up a case, an argument about why we shouldn't bother to do some of those things" when challenging commonly-held beliefs:

> Take . . . cast bullets. One of the things that looks logical, is that
> you get a bunch of bullets that are not all identical, they're pret-

ty identical, and one of the logical things is to weigh them and make sure the ones you shoot in matches weigh just the exactly the same. And I too used to do that . . . I'm a Depression baby, and I'm tight, and I cast a bunch of bullets, and the ones that were light or heavy . . . I start shooting them as well, in competition with the others. I found out they shot just as well . . . over the years I tested that again and again. So that's something that's absolute, ironclad rule is to always weigh your bullets to the nearest one tenth of a grain. And I don't weigh my bullets at all, and I sometimes beat all these guys that are weighing their bullets. So I'm kind of obnoxious about writing it down (laughs).

In this interview segment, we see James positioning himself as a contrarian within the world of cast bullet shooting, and doing so through the empirical testing of a potential hypothesis. Such work by James is nothing new—in past roles as a college professor, an administrator, and a member of his disciplinary organization, James has taken contrarian positions to generally accepted understandings to great effect.

## Framing Ongoing, Joint Action

James' recounting of his cast-bullet writing can be seen as participating in several instances of ongoing, joint action. Part of this joint action begins with his writing in his office at home. Here, James participates in the ongoing work of the cast bullet association that he is involved in. As an active member of this organization, James is responsible for participating in the organization of competitions, as well as communication via a regular newsletter. The work of writing up the newsletter—up to and including his "contrarian" columns—involves a coordination of multiple people sending in new items, advertising for material and competitions, and preparing for publication. The production of the newsletter, in other words, is a recurrent phenomenon in the lives of those participating in it, including James.

The production of those columns, then, is synchronized in time, space, and focus with the broader work of the cast bullet newsletter. James, in other words, is not *only* taking a contrarian position on a topic: he is doing so amidst the production of a newsletter with particular demands of time, space, and the needs of the organization. James' work to take a contrarian stance needs to be understood as emerging from and integrating with this relationship.

## Framing the Individuated Actor

James' participation in that ongoing work as a "contrarian" emerges from several sources. At the core of this particular contrarian point of view is James' sense of himself as a "Depression baby," and his subsequent disinclination to throw away what he sees as perfectly good bullets because he is "tight." Finances are deeply intertwined with James' perception of his role as the leader of the cast bullet association. He envisions the association as needing to bring in new, young members—members who may not be able to afford to spend money making bullets that they then throw out.

This intertwining of what he perceives as the finances of potential new recruits to cast bullet shooting and his own experiences of "sometimes beat[ing] all these guys that are weighing their bullets" shapes James' individuated participation in the social action that generates the newsletter. Because James has come to see the problems with throwing away "perfectly good bullets," and because he connects those problems to recruitment barriers in the cast bullet association, James comes to see the space of his column as an opportunity to dissuade readers from these notions.

If we examine this work by James through the concepts of the totality, we can see James taking an adumbrated stance on the economy of throwing away what he sees as perfectly good cast bullets. This adumbrated perspective leaves James faced with information about *What-Comes-Next* not only in his column writing, but in this work of cast bullet shooting. In bringing his past practice of testing a hypothesis, the added information of throwing away bullets is reduced into a manageable *What-Comes-Next*, from which James can develop his column. The transformation in individuated action that becomes visible here, in other words, is the pivoting of James' work outside of his cast bullet shooting hobby to inside of it, so that such practice can now be used to make sense of the demands of his cast bullet shooting life.

## Framing the Scenic Work of Uncertainty Reduction

James' work to both envision these problems and see his column as a way of getting at those problems in the ongoing production of the newsletter can be traced to the scenically available material that is at his disposal when writing. While James is at his office, he has at his disposal the data he has collected in order to investigate the claims that he has come to see as, over time, not holding up. If we examine Figure 8.1, we can see James' pattern of activity that bring him to the site of writing up his column.

In the first step, James is testing out his concern with weighing bullets, and writing down the results of his work. In the second step, James works up an analysis of his data, and in the third step, James communicates that via the newsletter. The record of James' shooting experiments is transformed into data for his analysis over time, and across several stages, so that he can eventually be at his desk and, with the results of his work at hand, produce a newsletter that allows him to proffer his "contrarian" point of view on weighing cast bullets.

Figure 8.1. James' collection of records.

## Concept in Use: The Circulation of Agency

The scenic availability of James' results when he is writing up his newsletter is the result of an ongoing circulation of agency through objects and back to him. We can think of this circulation of agency as working across a range of lifeworlds into the moment of textual production, but for the purposes of this analysis, we can trace the circulation starting with the weighing of the bullets. James begins his work with the decision *not* to throw away bullets because of weight differences. When he envisions a lack of discernable differences between his own results and the results of those that weigh their bullets, he begins to build a set of records about his results with unweighed bullets. These records become scenically available from one step to the next, moving with James as he develops further his contrarian stance.

The "contrarian stance" and the unweighed bullets seem to be, here, an intersection across multiple lifeworlds. James' history as a Depression baby and his history as being willing to buck several trends in his professional life converge on his decision not only to use unweighed bullets but to conduct research confirming his own assumptions that such a choice is practical and feasible *and* to publish that work to his association, and this convergence moves from one scene to the next with the interrelated inscriptions of records, analysis, and writing. James stacks his practices deliberately, over time, in order to shape the development of his regular column.

## Concept in Use: Identity (Re)Construction

This circulation of agency, as we saw in Chapter 7, brings with it an opportunity to (re)construct—for another first time—an identity (or identities, as the case may be). In this instance, James re-constructs himself as a "contrarian" in his stance on cast bullet shooting—and, importantly, a contrarian that has supporting data. Just as he was able to muster support for his contrarian arguments as a professor and a university administrator, James was also able to show data of his shooting experiences that support his contrarian claims against weighing bullets. James is not being a contrarian for the sake of being one, but rather is pointing out an overlooked set of data that other, like-minded individuals participating in the lifeworld of cast bullet shooting are not attending to. In developing this contrarian perspective, the literate action of James' profession and the needs of his personal hobby intersect, leading him to produce new texts for new audiences that repurpose and reconstruct an identity ("contrarian") in response to novel circumstances.

Just as the writing identities of Tom and John, James' identity as a contrarian is situated: it is re-constructed in a moment as part of the ongoing work of producing social order. But in tracing James' identity throughout the review of his work with cast bullet shooting, I noticed a different trend than I did when interviewing Tom or John. Tom and John project a fragmented sense of identity construction, and give the impression of varying degrees of identity transformations over time. James, on the other hand, sees stability in his identity as a contrarian. Perhaps his stacked practices—which are not broken by boot camp, for instance—allow him to develop a more continuous sense of development over time than either Tom or John. Or perhaps James' age—that is, the distance between the interview and his past identities-in-action—obscures the ongoing transformations of identity over time. My next case, Michelle, may provide additional insight into this.

## Poetry and Bird Sanctuaries: Michelle's Newsletters

Michelle, an active member of a number of organizations throughout the state, has led a varied and interesting life. Michelle earned her Ph.D. at Harvard University, and spent ten years on the faculty of a local school of education. She left this position in the mid–2000s, although much of the active life she had around that position continued after she left.

Writing was perhaps more necessary for Michelle than it was for some of the other participants because of the activities of which she was part. The organizations that Michelle gave her time to were, largely, far-flung. For instance, Michelle spent considerable time supporting a bird sanctuary, which rescued birds around the state through a winding network of sites and volunteers. This involved a great deal of driving, and a great deal of communicating with people at long distances.

In order to foster a sense of community, Michelle organized a weekly newsletter for the group, one that included everything from poetry to breaking news.

This provided members of the sanctuary with ways to communicate with one another, to feel as if they were part of a community even if it was a community highly separated by the surprisingly large state of Maine. The composing practices that Michelle engages in are reflective of both the need to reach such a widely-dispersed constituency and the limit demands of her writing time. Because Michelle is on the road so often, the writing that she does is often composed in her head. This mental composing later ends up in handwritten notebooks of poetry. Michelle often writes about birds, and occasionally this poetry ends up in one of her newsletters. However, much of her poetry is not directed at a particular audience. She does the writing primarily for herself, a way to capture an image, or an idea, but purely for her own benefit.

Michelle's newsletters serve as an interesting blend of what might be termed her "personal" writing (the poetry that she does for herself) and more public writing, since the newsletters can serve as a place for her to make her personal writing public. This curious blend reaches back into her early writing experiences. Michelle grew up as part of a family that had a rich history of literate activity. Michelle's parents regularly read stories and poetry to their children at night, encouraging them to memorize poems along the way. Michelle's family was also engaged with local literate culture, as Michelle's parents and siblings on several occasions wrote to the local newspaper. This kind of movement—from writing for the family to writing for the public—is similar to the movement that Michelle's poetry occasionally makes.

## Framing Ongoing, Joint Action

Much like James, Michelle is involved in regular newsletter activity, although her newsletters are multiple and are published significantly more regularly—on a weekly basis, for her bird sanctuary newsletter. This work of producing a weekly newsletter is at the intersection of a far-flung network of ongoing, joint social action. Michelle's organizations are strung throughout a large, rural state: Maine has roughly the square mileage of Indiana, with about 20% of the population. The newsletters that Michelle puts together, then, are ways of stitching together the actions of people from a range of areas in the state for particular purposes: bird rescue and needlework.

The bird sanctuary in particular is dependent on the newsletter in order to keep members of the organization informed of the goings-on of the rest of the network that they may not be aware of. Since the work of the organization involves a great deal of driving, and one-on-one handoffs of rescued birds, the entire organization—or even large segments of it—are never in the same place at the same time. The newsletter, then, helps social actors locate their individual acts within a larger framework of organizational action. Their participation in the newsletter, such as sending in news items, or pictures, or poems, co-constructs this widespread communication.

## Framing the Individuated Actor

At the center of this work is Michelle, who collects all of the news items that come in as a response to her call for news items. Michelle, as seen in Figure 8.2, is in her office, engaged in the work of making the newsletter real. But her work to make the newsletter real is shot through with her own materially-present histories of engagement, the ways in which she arrives at the process of writing this newsletter. Michelle articulates her individuated work of the newsletter as follows:

> So basically begins with the panic attack. Shit, it's Monday, I forgot! (Laughs) No, I didn't forget, but I had been traveling and I realized oh my gosh and I'd been doing a bird run every day since we got back from our trip and sort of being there was not part of it, kind of much more in the foreground than the writing. So I talked to _____, oh what's new, what have I missed . . . you know so I'd have a little bit of news to put in the newsletter. Then I sit down and I'm checking the emails that I've gotten from people about their bird stories and whatever from the last challenge. And then I'm thinking okay now what else are they going to want to know about in this newsletter or what do I need to tell them. So then I'm very intensely writing and that's where the cats are bothering me (laughs) . . . and then once it's typed up I read it over, often I read it aloud, I don't know I just have that oral delivery that you know it has to sound right, not just look right on the page. And then I push the send button.

Michelle's organization of herself and the material around her for the action of writing the newsletter reduces the uncertainty in the *What-Comes-Next* of producing text. By locating herself within a particular time frame ("Shit, it's Monday"), and in certain co-configurations of actors to make determinations about the general content of the newsletter, Michelle creates and then takes up particular possibilities of action.

Michelle arrives at her desk to do this writing on the heels of already participating in the co-construction of the bird sanctuary in a variety of ways. One of the ways in which she participates is by bringing rescued birds from one site to another, often through long drives through rural Maine. During this process, Michelle passes the time by mentally drafting poems—often about birds, and often related to the particular bird being rescued at the time. This poetry composing and memorizing relates to her family's tradition of memorizing poems in her youth. Once out of the car, Michelle often writes these poems down for later use.

Both the poetry and the drive shape the ways in which Michelle comes to act in individuated ways during the co-construction of the newsletter. Michelle comes to see the newsletter not just as a site for reporting news on the organization, but for celebrating the work of bird rescue and, by extension, birds themselves. Michelle creates space in the newsletter to share the poetry that she develops about birds—not just hers, but that of others who might be interested in submitting their work. Michelle's individuated history, her patterns of interaction with language and her ways of making sense of the long rides involved with bird rescue, bring her into the work of newsletter writing with a particular, individuated approach to the uncertainty of the blank page that is the newsletter when she begins writing it.

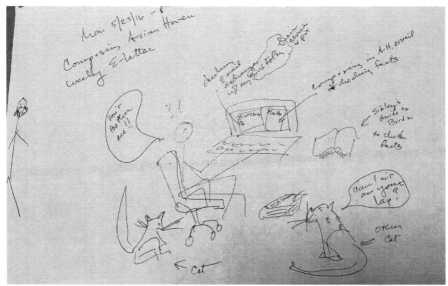

*Figure 8.2. Michelle writing a newsletter.*

## Framing the Scenic Work of Uncertainty Reduction

Michelle's scenic work of writing the newsletter—the pattern of activity through which the newsletter is made real—begins with her "Oh, shit!" moment, when she realizes it is Monday and that the newsletter has to go out. Figure 8.3 depicts Michelle's 12-step process of getting to "send." In this work, Michelle makes scenically available the news about the organization via her email, the poems available for publishing via her book of poetry writing, and the notes that she has collected throughout the week from her interactions with others. The notes, poems, and emails coalesce into a scenically available set of data that she can use to populate the space of the newsletter, allowing her to "fill in" the "Shit, it's Monday" moment, turn by turn, until the letter is ready to be sent out.

The scenic availability of such a range of materials suggests a long-term sedimentation of literate action, beginning with the literate histories of Michelle's family as a child, running through her professional life as a scholar and a teacher, and situated, now, in the work of managing a complex network of bird sanctuaries through a regular newsletter. Michelle's weekly newsletter, in other words, emerges through scenically available materials that arrive at Michelle's office courtesy of long, complex, and intertwined patterns of use and engagement. This scenic complexity offers useful complications for understanding agency and its circulation throughout the course of the lifespan.

*Figure 8.3. Michelle's process of writing the newsletter.*

## Concept in Use: The Circulation of Agency

Michelle, much like James, is able to circulate agency to her in the production of the newsletter through the chains of interactions that led her to her office and the act of writing. By coming to see the space in the car ride as an opportunity to construct poetry, Michelle has, in her office, as scenically available, material for making the newsletter. Furthermore, the availability of that poetry leads her to see part of the space of the newsletter as a space for poetry—something taken up not only by her, but by others in the organization as well. The chain of activity from mental composing in a car, to writing down the poems in a journal, to drawing on that journal as part of the scenically available tools at her disposal allow for her to have tools at her disposal for shaping the newsletter.

The work that Michelle does to keep the newsletter running suggests that the circulation of agency might be better understood if it were to take into account the ways in which agency could accumulate to particular individuals across instances of agency's circulation. Dippre (2018) explored this accumulation of agency, referring to it as *expansive agency*, but Michelle's work with the newsletter does not suggest expansiveness. Rather, it suggests a deepening of agentive prowess that is brought to bear in particular moments of textual construction. Future research into the circulation of agency from a lifespan literate action development perspective can render more robust our language for understanding how agency grows, changes, and transforms.

## Concept in Use: Identity (Re)Construction

The circulation of agency also brings with it opportunities for identity (re)construction. As Michelle composes her newsletter for a next first time, she does so in a way that takes up her existing sense of identity as a language user: one attending carefully to language, committed to "playing with words" in a variety of ways. The play with language is not limited strictly to the poetry section of the newsletter, but rather carries across the range of decisions that brings the newsletter into being: spacing, organization, and even the reporting of news items offer Michelle a chance to build on her sense of playing with words in ways that further (re)construct her identity.

Like James, Michelle's sense of identity appears far more durable than the identity (re)construction witnessed in Tom and John's cases. Michelle's participation in complex social organizations through writing—and her leadership of it, when necessary—are enacted in ways that perpetuate a sense of willingness to toy with language that stretch back to her earliest childhood memories. Michelle, however, offers some further insights on the potential causes behind this smoothing out of identity transformations. In her far-flung work with the bird sanctuary, Michelle has had a great deal of agency circulated to her: the work of the newsletter shapes not just her own understandings of the organization, but the understandings (and subsequent actions) of others participating in this organization. Perhaps this expanded ability to circulate agency to oneself provides opportunities, over time, for the more conflicted aspects of identity (re)construction to be chipped away, leading to the development of relatively smooth, or linear understandings of self.

# Revised Understandings of Agency and Identity

Throughout Part II, the concepts of circulating agency and identity (re)construction have been rendered more robust—that is, they have begun to do more work in providing explanations of how literate action develops through the lifespan. Michelle and James provide some further extensions and complications of both of these concepts. Below, I summarize the new insights that Michelle and James provide, and I articulate a revised understanding of these concepts that future research can take up and further develop.

In Chapter 7, the concept of circulating agency was complicated by degradations in the take-up of objects with the re-use of a particular practice: when Tom could not remember the full jokes, for instance, or when John forgot definitions (or that he wrote down the definition of a word earlier). These degradations brought up the question of what barriers arise to the circulation of agency? How does agency, when circulated through objects in one instance back to oneself in a future instance, become problematic?

The cases of Michelle and James demonstrate that the issue is not one of time—that is, the distance in time between the initial circulation and take-up of an object for agentive action does not necessarily, and by itself, have a bearing on how the possibilities of that object are recognized. James, for instance, circulates agency to himself through a long history of engagement with cast bullet shooting and participation in a cast bullet shooting organization. James is able to avoid the degradation of agency circulation through more and more deeply interconnected objects: that is, the work he does to circulate agency to himself in one moment stretches out through time and space not with one object but with a constellation of them, so that his return to writing in a future moment has multiple avenues for agentive uptake. Michelle performs similar work with her own constellation of objects for writing her weekly newsletter. The uncertainty of *What-Comes-Next* is reduced not by a particular object but by the mutually-definitional work of her cats, her computer, her dictionary, her notebook, and other objects in her office.

Amid this circulation of agency, the individuated actors studied in Part II demonstrate multiple moments of identity (re)construction. But the identity work of Michelle and James are notably different from that of Tom and John. Tom and John locate themselves within competing lifeworlds, both co-present and situated along complex pasts. Michelle and James, on the other hand, articulate their positions within a broader, more consistent trajectory of selfhood. James sees himself as a contrarian in his cast bullet writing, but sees that as yet another instantiation of locating himself as a contrarian in yet another social situation. Michelle's poetry writing—the process of memorizing, writing down, and publishing in a newsletter her poems about particular birds—is a continuation of her sense of herself as one who plays with words. This smoothing out of identity (re)construction in relation to past moments of literate action suggests a complexity to recognizing one's identity within a range of histories of lifeworld engagement that would shape the lived reality of a given moment of literate action and, subsequently, the rambling path of development that can follow from that moment. These increasingly sensitive understandings of agency circulation and identity (re)construction offer productive ways of building accounts of literate action development throughout the lifespan. Agency circulation and identity (re)construction, as concepts, have become more robust as they were studied across spans of five or six decades, and can be complicated further with future studies of writers at other ages and in different social, economic, and literate circumstances.

## Evaluating the Totality of the Literate Experience

The concept of the totality of the literate experience has helped us trace the literate action of Michelle and James across a wide swath of lifeworlds and through a long history. It did so while also interpreting heretofore unexplained phenomena in the lives of older writers. Finally, in the course of its use, the totality uncovered additional characteristics of the concepts of identity and agency that will benefit future lifespan-oriented research into these concepts. It would seem, then, that the totality of the literate experience is a flexible framework, adaptable to the study of literate action at a variety of scales, from the moment-to-moment to the year-to-year. It provides useful insight into both specific segments of the lifespan and large swaths of years. In the next chapter, I expand more fully on the consequences of treating the totality as a logic-in-use, as an infrastructure upon which a complex, yet coherent theory of literate action development through the lifespan can eventually emerge.

# Conclusion. Renovating Our Worlds

In this chapter, I bring together the various insights into literate action development through the lifespan that the eleven cases earlier in this book highlighted. First, I bring together the several threads that have developed about the lived reality of literate action development. From there, I expand my orienting of literate action theory toward development. I close the chapter by articulating the next steps in treating the work of this text as a *foundational infrastructure* for studying lifespan literate action development.

## The Totality of the Literate Experience: A Summary

As I mention in the introduction, tracing writing development through the lifespan is challenging for two reasons: (1) the complex sets of affairs that individuals write through as they live their lives; and (2) "writing" proves, upon detailed inspection, to be too "contextually thin" of a unit of analysis for careful study (Prior, 1998, p. xi). In order to provide a consistent lens through which I could view literate action at all stages of the lifespan, I turned to the *lived reality* of development—the ongoing, moment-to-moment, lived work of engaging in activity with developmental consequences. In order to shore up the limitations of writing as a unit of analysis, I turn to *literate action* to describe the focus of my analysis. My pursuit of the *lived reality of literate action development*, then, attempts to build both a robust unit of analysis and a lens that will hold constant through the entirety of the lifespan. *Development*, in the sense of this project, refers to sustained transformations of patterns of literate action amid situations recognized by the actor as *recurrent*.

A logic-in-use for making sense of and analyzing literate action development from the perspective of the lived reality involves five interlocking concepts: practices, *What-Comes-Next*, information, object possibilities, and adumbration. This framework is put into action at the level of the local production of social order. That is, in each passing moment, co-configurations of people, talk, tools, and texts are mobilized to create social situations from and through which actors can make sense of both what they are doing in a moment and what they need to do next. In order to do this, members of a situation produce *practices*—socially recognizable actions that inform themselves and others what it is that they are doing. These practices are sometimes part of projects—that is, goal-oriented work—but practices are also ends in and of themselves: they are the tactical work we do to keep social action (in this case, literate action) going.

Practices are also a way of reducing uncertainty. In any given moment of our lives, we are largely uncertain of what the next moment will bring. But the work of practices reduces that uncertainty: the simplest things such as acts of handing

(Scollon, 2001) or a greeting can allow members of a situation to make assumptions about the next moment, what I refer to in Chapter 2 as *What-Comes-Next*. Part of the work of practices is to manage the uncertainty of *What-Comes-Next*. So long as practices continue to maintain a reduced uncertainty of the next moment, social action—and, by extension, literate action—can be (re)produced unproblematically.

But sometimes the *What-Comes-Next* brings forward an anomaly, something that existing practices cannot resolve, cannot work into the ongoing production of social order. Drawing on the language of Garfinkel (2008), I refer to this as *information*. Information, as I am using it, is the anomalous aspects of *What-Comes-Next* that practices must be altered to make sensible, usable for individuated actors. Resolving information requires the adaptation of practices for a next-first-time, and this adaptation, as seen particularly clearly in Chapter 7, can be a productive trigger for literate action development.

Members of situations work through the anomalies that information provides through recognizing new arrays of possibilities in objects. In daily interaction, this work of recognizing an object's possibilities are overlooked. A book I am discussing in class is now a container of words requiring interpretation; now that I am back in my office it becomes a paperweight for student papers; now that I am leaving for home it becomes an irritant that makes it difficult for me to snap my briefcase closed. All objects have multiple social possibilities, and these possibilities are realized through the concerted co-configurations of objects in social situations. That is, a book in a classroom is treated as a container of words requiring interpretation not only because of my understanding of the book but because of the way in which the bodies in the classroom, the desks in the room, the language of the syllabus, and the schedule of the academic year conspired to make the class a site where the book could be treated as a book. When members of a situation have to deal with information, they recognize new arrays of possibilities in objects in order to transform that information through newly reconfigured practices.

All of the descriptions above work to bring us to an understanding of members' methods as they make sense of a given social situation. But these concepts, on their own, only attend to the work of members in a general sense—we do not have the language needed to see, in an individuated manner, the ways in which specific actors in a given social interaction take up practices, work through the anxiety of *What-Comes-Next*, and reduce information via the recognition of new possibilities in objects. Each individuated actor in a group, however, has an *adumbrated* perspective on the work of the group. Individuated understandings that emerge from perspectival co-configurations of actors, talk, tools, and texts in any given moment can lead to significantly different rambling paths of development even in the writing lives of actors who have, in Schutz's (1967) words, *grown older together* in a sustained chain of situations.

These five concepts, working together, can reveal the complex, individuated, moment-to-moment work of participation in social order through literate action. As individuated actors with adumbrated perspectives in a given social situation enact practices to reduce the uncertainty of *What-Comes-Next*, they recognize new arrays of possibilities of objects in order to transform the anomaly of information and, by extension, transform their practices as well. Should these transformed practices be sustained through situations which these actors define as recurrent—that is, as happening to them for a next-first-time—then development can be said to have happened.

At the end of Chapter 5, I mobilized these concepts into a portable logic-in-use that I refer to as the *totality of the literate experience*, which has three framings: (1) ongoing joint action; (2) individuated actors; and (3) the scenic reduction of uncertainty. In Part II, I brought this logic-in-use to bear on the study of six writers at different points in the lifespan. These analyses revealed two concepts for understanding and articulating literate action development through the lifespan: agency and identity.

## The Totality as Foundational Infrastructure

At the start of this text, I argued for the need for a foundational infrastructure of literate action development through the lifespan. The totality of the literate experience, as a logic-in-use to get at the lived reality of literate action development, is meant to serve as that infrastructure. From this starting point, it becomes possible to develop new understandings of literate action, new explanations of data that serve as *middle range theories* of lifespan literate action development.

The term "theory of the middle range" was used by Robert Merton in his review and critique of the state of sociological study. Merton was concerned that sociology—a discipline that, at the time of Merton's career, was still in its infancy compared to the hard sciences—was rushing too hard to catch up with other fields. He critiqued "grand theories" as being applicable both everywhere and nowhere because of the lack of specifics and gaps in their explanatory power. Likewise, he critiqued theories of the narrow range for their lack of applicability outside of the specific circumstances of their study. Merton was looking for theories of the middle range, or theories that provide specific information for wider circumstances than the area of study but avoid becoming so generalized as to lack utility in any given specific application of that theory.

This "middle range" concept has been explored in the field of writing studies by Bazerman (2008). In his reflection on historical studies of writing, Bazerman (2008) argues that "middle range theory seems appropriate to pursue in writing studies, given the complexity of writing—linguistically, psychologically, technologically, socially, historically, and even economically and anthropologically" (p. 4). A theory of the middle range—or an approach to studying writing that is tightly anchored to the available data and yet still connected to many more sites of writing than are shown in this text—is a useful and practical tool for both understanding and studying literate action development. I envision middle-range theory as a necessary tool for building, over time, a theory of lifespan writing development that is both complex enough to account for the complexity of writing and coherent enough to be mobilized into teaching, research, and further theorizing. This can be best exemplified by working with the concepts that emerged from the work of Part II—agency and identity. To be sure, these concepts are not yet middle-range theories. Rather, each is "*merely* an image for thinking about a component" of literate action development through the lifespan (Merton, 1968, p. 42, emphasis in original). Such concepts have the potential to develop into full-fledged middle-range theories because of both their origins and the analytical purchase that they represent.

One of the primary criteria for candidacy as a middle-range theory is the way in which a concept emerges. First, these concepts "have not been logically *derived* from a single all-embracing theory" (Merton, 1968, p. 41). The totality of the literate experience, as a logic-in-use, is not a theory. Rather, it is a set of framings for examining a phenomenon of interest (literate action development through the lifespan) from a particular perspective (the lived reality of the individuated actor doing the developing). The totality does not predict or explain: it only serves as a focusing agent that keeps the lived reality at the center of analysis. The concepts that emerged in Part II are the result of applying this logic-in-use to data. For these concepts, "the proof is in the using" (Merton, 1968, p. 41). When we use these concepts to make an empirical study literate action development, we can see things that we might not otherwise see.

Though the words attached to these concepts are commonplace in writing research, the ways in which they are used in this text—that is, through the totality—are different. "The difference," Merton (1968) argues, "is initially a small one—some might say so small as to be insignificant—but the shift in the angle of vision leads to successively more fundamental theoretical differences" (p. 41). Agency and identity, as concepts, are understood through the totality of the literate experience. Therefore, they are oriented to literate action as it emerges from the ongoing work of social order, and the broader patterns that emerge from it. As these concepts emerged from an analysis of the lived reality of the participants of Part II, they brought with them specific, if small, changes. The circulation of agency, while linked to a posthuman tradition, calls attention to the ways in which *human* agents circulate agency *back to themselves* in their selection of practices for the co-construction of a given context for action. The (re)construction of identity, while resonating with the production of a situated self, is slightly tweaked to attend to the ways in which that (re)construction is scenically pulled together. These changes are, indeed, slight, but they suggest—as indicated in Chapter 8—the start of what will become deeply transformed understandings of both concepts.

Agency and identity, then, are useful concepts for developing middle-range theories of lifespan literate action development. But, again, they are images, not robust theories, at the moment. As Merton (1968) suggests, this image "is a beginning, not an end, for it leads directly to certain analytical problems" (p. 42). The concepts should suggest problems, and potentially hypotheses, through which future writing researchers may develop more robust realizations of these concepts and, with it, middle-range theory. Though still images rather than theories, these concepts, in the work they did throughout Part II, have begun to suggest interesting problems and potential hypotheses that may be followed to make them more robust theories for use.

The work of agency through three different segments of the lifespan offered a handful of interesting problems. For instance, in the cases of Lilly and May, there is no clear explanation of their selection of practices in a given moment: the decisions for bracketing and stacking remain largely opaque, excepting perhaps those obvious reasons. But these reasons are retrospective. There is no evidence of the production of order in the classroom, in the field hockey film room, that suggests what pulled Lilly toward note-taking in one instance and away in the other. How does Lilly's realization get realized in the moment? *Does* it get realized in the moment, or are there aspects of the production of social order that do such work only to be later effaced as a straightforward rationale?

This issue suggests a problem (the mechanisms through which things are bracketed and stacked are unclear), some specifics for what might make for a strategic research site (a place that provides evidence of the moment-to-moment work of practices in use, as well as access to the histories behind and around them), and a level of perspicuity needed for the production of social order (turns at talk may need to be directly visible). It is not the only such interesting problem that is offered by the concept of agency, which suggests that agency may be at the basis of a rich middle-range theory. I continue to refer to agency as a concept, however, because not enough of these interesting problems have been answered to allow the concept to predict or explain with sufficient power the work of literate action development.

Identity, like agency, offers interesting problems for take-up by those interested in literate action development through the lifespan. In the process of balancing a working life of manual labor and a personal life that involves writing in a range of ways— short stories, stand-up comedy, screenplays, and reflective writing—John used a range of notebooks to coordinate his action, stacking and bracketing practices where necessary to (re)produce an identity that allowed him to, in various moments and activities, manage groups of workers, compose screenplays, develop "bits" for his stand-up comedy acts, and encounter difficult readings in graduate courses. Through recurring iterations of such work, John worked out a complex, ever-revised sense of himself as a worker, a student, a writer, etc.

Various aspects of John's life lead these identities to overlap, integrate, and intertwine as he (re)produces his identity scenically over time, but little is known about what brings about these particular moments. How might we locate particular characteristics of points of development not just for John, but for writers like John, who are consistently investigating, tying and retying their connections across a range of lifeworlds? Like Lilly, John's case offers a problem (how might points of significant identity (re)construction be located throughout the lifespan?), indications of what research sites may have strategic value (sites of literate action that lie at the intersection of multiple identity (re)constructions), and perspicuity needs (perhaps a significant moment bookended by recent retrospective interviews). These next steps might be followed by future research to work identity up into a middle-range theory from a lifespan perspective.

Agency and identity, as shown above, offer useful central concepts for eventual middle-range theories that emerge from a study of lifespan literate action development through the logic-in-use of the totality. I mention above that I envision the totality acting as a foundational infrastructure, and these concepts show the potential of this infrastructure in action. Below, I elaborate on the totality as an infrastructure by connecting it to existing issues in the emerging work of lifespan writing research.

## Using the Infrastructure: Furthering the Missions of Lifespan Writing Research

Although much has been done recently to understand and frame lifespan writing research, there is much work that remains. First, the incredible complexity of writing through the lifespan, as a research object, must be brought to heel. This will require studies that follow participants throughout the entirety of the lifespan, which in itself will necessitate coordination of researchers as they study writing across multiple nations, ethnic backgrounds, socioeconomic circumstances, etc. It is this work that the *Writing through the Lifespan Collaboration* has set itself toward (see Dippre & Phillips, in press).

Second, lifespan writing research must engage with the here-and-now demands of the field, of the careers of emerging researchers (as emerging researchers will be in high demand in order to trace such a long-range research trajectory), the pressing questions of writing in a changing world, and the immediate problems of multi-disciplinary, multi-institutional, and multi-site collaboration. In short, lifespan writing researchers must address the immediate needs of the field and the problems of writing while *simultaneously* engaging in a long-term pursuit of studying writing through the lifespan. I have aimed, throughout this text, to develop a foundation that would allow lifespan writing researchers to aim toward both of these goals.

The totality of the literate experience, as a portable logic-in-use, is a way to re-envision literate action development, to locate evidence of it through a variety of records and trace instances of it across wide swaths of time while keeping a steady frame of the lived reality of that development. Such a logic-in-use can keep up with the challenges of studying writing in a range of different times and places: it is flexible enough to be adaptable to limits and possibilities offered by various research sites, and it is durable enough to allow findings to maintain coherence across such local adaptations. This combination of flexibility and durability provides a productive starting point for a life-long and life-wide tracing of literate action development.

But the totality can also act as a foundational infrastructure for more pressing, immediate needs. Early-career researchers interested in understanding lifespan literate action development can use such a foundation to launch shorter-term, more focused studies of particular populations and set their results in conversation with other researchers interested in other segments of the lifespan who also have lifespan orientations. This would solve two problems at once: early-career researchers can address the demands for publication that they are under, and problems, questions, and concerns about writing for specific populations or segments of populations can be targeted and addressed with a lifespan orientation in mind.

One particular need that is both long-term and short-term is uncovering useful approaches for interdisciplinary work. A forthcoming volume (Dippre & Phillips, in press) provides some groundwork for interdisciplinary approaches, but the totality also provides a potential way forward. The totality can serve as a broader structure, a point at which various disciplines can pull their insights together. Having a connecting point for emergent concepts and middle-range theories also means having a way of identifying what is not yet known, and what *needs* to be known. The totality, in other words, can serve as a spark for discussing and agreeing upon shared priorities for future research. Importantly—at least in my vision of research—the totality does not dictate future research, leaving open possibilities for serendipitous findings, research sites, and breakthroughs. Rather, the totality, in its role as an orienting mechanism both creates the groundwork for a shared vision of research priorities and leaves open the possibility of startling and evocative new insights. Below, I suggest some next steps that might be best taken advantage of for building interdisciplinary efforts in lifespan writing research.

## Steps toward Interdisciplinary Work

In this section, I attend to the interdisciplinary possibilities that emerge from the totality and its treatment as an infrastructure for studying lifespan literate action development. Below, I attend to three areas of research that have as yet been minimally attended to in this text: interiority, functional systems of activity, and cohorts of writers across wide swaths of time. These starting points may usefully connect to ongoing work in recent issues of *Writing and Pedagogy*, *Literacy in Composition Studies*, and an edited collection of lifespan writing research (Dippre & Phillips, in press).

## Attending to Interiority

Throughout this text, I have remained focused on the scenic production of social order and, through it, insights into development. I have deliberately sidestepped cognitive explanations of social action that was not scenic—that is, cognition that was not evident as being distributed through particular arrays of objects. The ties across materials in the production of literate action were demonstrably empirical, in following with ethnomethodology's radically empirical tradition. However, this should not be read as a complete rejection of cognitive activity. On the contrary, I envision cognitive and neurological studies of literate action to be important as twenty-first century writing research unfolds, and have merely positioned this project as providing a framework from which future cognitive research can move forward in ways that continue to attend to the contexts in which cognition occurs.

Future research on writing development from cognitive, psychological, or neurological perspectives can benefit from beginning with the lived reality in mind and, by extension, the situated work of cognition, interiority, and synaptic firings. If we are to think about writers as developing via a participation in the ongoing production of local social order, how does that transform the ways in which we make sense of the ways in which cognition activates? Coulter (1991), writing about cognition from an ethnomethodological perspective, argues for a *praxiological* approach to cognition, one in which memories are not *"themselves neurally-encoded phenomena"* but rather "neural structures, states or events as enabling, facilitating the *situated production of memory-claims* (to oneself or others) in all their variety" (p. 188, emphasis in original). How might longitudinal studies of cognition in writing be productively attended to using the lived reality as a starting point? What might emerge from an understanding of cognition that began as distributed and worked inward, into the mind, rather than outward from the firing of neurons, the activations of concepts, or the steps of cognitive acts?

## Attending to Functional Systems of Activity

Throughout this text, I have attended as tightly as possible to the lived reality of literate action development. This focus occluded the wider literate activities that this lived reality was caught up within so that a portable frame of analysis could be devised that would carry through the lifespan and across lifeworlds. The broader, mutually constitutive systems of literate activity would have lost the phenomenon of the lived reality. However, now that the lived reality has been productively established as a logic-in-use, researchers can begin building out from the lived reality to wider functional systems of activity.

In my use of the term "functional systems of activity," I am drawing primarily on the language of Prior (1998) and have at heart the systems of activity that he describes in his text. However, this term could also be taken more generally to mean any analysis of activity and genre systems, such as those proposed by Russell (1997), Engestrom (1987), and others. These analyses have been typically located within particular sites, such as higher education or health care centers, but, with the lived reality as a starting point, the tracing of multiple, interacting systems of genre and activity through the lifespan of individuated actors can become possible. The key problem of studying functional systems of activity throughout the lifespan is the massive amount of data that emerges from it: individuals move through countless systems of activity throughout their lives, and tracing those systems and their interaction makes data collection challenging and data reduction incredibly problematic. With the totality, however, researchers may be able to more easily engage in productive data reduction that attends to the lived reality without losing the phenomenon of development as haecceitically situated.

## Attending to Cohorts and Timespans

In the process of developing a framework for attending to literate action development from the perspective of the lived reality, I have not had the opportunity to look to wider collections of writers across broader swaths of history. Future research might benefit from taking a "life course" approach to studying literate action development across wider segments of time. "Life course" studies, which has its home in sociology, attends to sociological patterns of development within broader patterns of historical change. Elder (2008), for instance, attends carefully to the impact of the Great Depression and World War II on the life course trajectories of men and women of various generations. Beginning with the totality of the literate experience, future researchers may productively locate the lived reality of literate action development within emerging historical threads and the ongoing production of sociological change.

The life course studies expansion of this foundational infrastructure is most directly at odds with the ethnomethodological base of this work. It is interesting to note that in neither recent publications on life course research and methods (Elder & Giele, 2009) nor in wider surveys of the field of sociology (Bryant & Peck, 2007) did ethnomethodology or any of the branches of sociology near it come into contact with life course studies. The "micro" level attention, as some sociologists (see Coser, 1975) erroneously call it, does not seem to fit into the wider, "macro" level attention of life course studies. Despite this disconnect, however, the accomplishments, concepts, and theories of life course research may still prove to be useful in elaborating upon the totality.

## A Lifespan Perspective as a Starting Point

At one of the first virtual meetings of the *Writing through the Lifespan Collaboration*, Diana Arya remarked in passing that understanding how writing develops through the lifespan was "where we should have started" in building curricular frameworks for writing all along. At the end of this text, I cannot help but think of a lifespan perspective as exactly that: a starting point, a new beginning from which our many understandings of writing, writing development, and writing activity come to be understood anew. The field's metrics for tracking development, talking about development, and understanding development have been and continue to be temporally bound by the limitations of our most expansive longitudinal studies. But examining literate action development through the logic-in-use of the totality may offer a productive way out of these bounds, of seeing the connections between moments of literate action and broader patterns of transformation, of renovated worlds of literate action. By seeing moments and patterns interacting and unfolding on a sea of ongoing, joint action, writing researchers may develop a flexible, responsive understanding of what it means to engage in literate action development not in a particular setting, or in a particular kind of genre, but as an integral part of what it means to be human in contemporary society.

# References

Adler-Kassner, L., Clark, I., Robertson, L., Taczak, K. & Yancey, K. B. (2016). Assembling knowledge: The role of threshold concepts in facilitating transfer. In C. Anson & J. Moore (Eds.), *Critical transitions: Writing and the question of transfer* (pp. 17–48). The WAC Clearinghouse; University Press of Colorado. https://wac.colostate.edu/books/perspectives/ansonmoore/.

Adler-Kasser, L., Majewski, J. & Koshnick, D. (2012). The value of troublesome knowledge: Transfer and threshold concepts in writing and history. *Composition Forum, 26*(Fall). https://compositionforum.com/issue/26/troublesome-knowledge-threshold.php.

Al-Saji, A. (2004). The memory of another past: Bergson, Deleuze and a new theory of time. *Continental Philosophy Review, 37*, 203–239. https://doi.org/10.1007/s11007-005-5560-5.

Alwin, D. F. (2012). Integrating varieties of life course concepts. *The Journals of Gerontology, Series B: Psychological Sciences and Social Sciences, 67*(2), 206–220. https://doi.org/10.1093/geronb/gbr146.

Andrews, R. & Smith, A. (2011). *Developing writers: Teaching and learning in the digital age.* McGraw-Hill.

Applebee, A. A. (2000). Alternative models of writing development. In R. Indrisano & J. R. Squire (Eds.), *Perspectives on writing: Research, theory, and practice* (pp. 90–110). International Reading Association. https://doi.org/10.1598/0872072681.4.

Applebee, A. N. & Langer, J. A. (2013). *Writing instruction that works: Proven methods for middle and high school classrooms.* Teachers College Press.

Arminen, I. (2008). Scientific and "radical" ethnomethodology: From incompatible paradigms to ethnomethodological sociology. *Philosophy of the Social Sciences, 38*(2), 167–191. https://doi.org/10.1177/0048393108315300.

Artemeva, N. (2009). Stories of becoming: A study of novice engineers learning genres of their profession. In C. Bazerman, A. Bonini & D. Figueirido (Eds.), *Genre in a changing world* (pp. 158–178). The WAC Clearinghouse; Parlor Press. https://wac.colostate.edu/books/perspectives/genre/.

Atkinson, P. (1988). Ethnomethodology: A critical review. *Annual Review of Sociology, 14*(1), 441–465. https://doi.org/10.1146/annurev.soc.14.1.441.

Attewell, P. (1974). Ethnomethodology since Garfinkel. *Theory and Society, 1*(2), 179–210. https://doi.org/10.1007/bf00160158.

Bakhtin, M. M. (1986). *Speech genres and other late essays.* University of Texas Press.

Barton, D. & Hamilton, M. (2012). *Local literacies: Reading and writing in one community.* Routledge. https://doi.org/10.4324/9780203125106.

Bawarshi, A. & Reiff, M. (2010). *Genre: An introduction to history, theory, research, and pedagogy.* Parlor Press; The WAC Clearinghouse. https://wac.colostate.edu/books/referenceguides/bawarshi-reiff/.

Bazerman, C. (1988). *Shaping written knowledge.* University of Wisconsin Press. https://wac.colostate.edu/books/landmarks/bazerman-shaping/.

Bazerman, C. (1999). *The languages of Edison's light*. MIT Press. https://doi.org/10
.7551/mitpress/4130.001.0001.

Bazerman, C. (2001). Writing as a development in interpersonal relations. *Journal for the Psychoanalysis of Culture & Society 6*(2), 298–302.

Bazerman, C. (2004). Speech acts, genres, and activity systems: How texts organize activity and people. In C. Bazerman & P. Prior (Eds.), *What writing does and how it does it* (pp. 315–346). Routledge. https://doi.org/10.4324/9781410609526.

Bazerman, C. (2008). Theories of the middle range in historical studies of writing practice. *Written Communication 25*(3), 298–318. https://doi.org/10.1177/07410
88308318025.

Bazerman, C. (2013a). *Literate action: A theory of literate action* (Vol. 2). The WAC Clearinghouse; Parlor Press. https://wac.colostate.edu/books/perspectives/liter
ateaction-v2/.

Bazerman, C. (2013b). Understanding the lifelong journey of writing development. *Infancia y Aprendizaje, 36*(4), 421–441. https://doi.org/10.1174/021037013808200320.

Bazerman, C. (2015). A genre-based theory of literate action. In N. Artemeva & A. Freedman (Eds.), *Genre studies around the globe: Beyond the three traditions* (pp. 80–94). Trafford Publishing.

Bazerman, C. (2016a, August). *The puzzle of conducting research on lifespan development of writing abilities*. Working paper presentation at the Dartmouth Research Institute. Hanover, New Hampshire.

Bazerman, C. (2016b, August). The puzzle of conducting research on lifespan development of writing abilities. Plenary talk at the 50th Anniversary Dartmouth Conference. Hanover, NH.

Bazerman, C. (2018). Lifespan longitudinal studies of writing development: Heuristic for an impossible dream. In *The Lifespan development of writing* (pp. 326–365). National Council of Teachers of English.

Bazerman, C., Applebee, A., Berninger, V. W., Brandt, D., Graham, S., Matsuda, P. K., Murphy, S., Jeffrey, J. V., Rowe, D. W. & Schleppegrell, M. (2017). Taking the long view on writing development. *Research in the Teaching of English, 51*, 351–360.

Bazerman, C., Applebee, A., Berninger, V. W., Brandt, D., Graham, S., Jeffrey, J. V., Matsuda, P. K., Murphy, S., Rowe, D. W., Schleppegrell, M. & Wilcox, K. C. (Eds.) (2018). *The lifespan development of writing*. National Council of Teachers of English.

Bazerman, C., Applebee, A., Berninger, V. W., Brandt, D., Graham, S., Jeffrey, J. V., Matsuda, P. K., Murphy, S., Rowe, D. W., Schleppegrell, M. & Wilcox, K. C. (2018). The challenges of understanding developmental trajectories and designing developmentally appropriate policy, curricula, instruction, and assessments. In *The lifespan development of writing* (pp. 369–382). National Council of Teachers of English.

Bazerman, C., Applebee, A., Berninger, V. W., Brandt, D., Graham, S., Jeffrey, J. V., Matsuda, P. K., Murphy, S., Rowe, D. W., Schleppegrell, M. & Wilcox, K. C. (2018). Toward an understanding of writing development across the lifespan. In *The lifespan development of writing* (pp. 20–54). National Council of Teachers of English.

Bazerman, C. & Prior, P. (2005). Participating in emergent socio-literate worlds: Genre, disciplinarity, and interdisciplinarity. In R. Beach (Ed.), *Multidisciplinary perspectives on literacy research* (pp. 133–178). Hampton Press.

Beaufort, A. (2000). Learning the trade: A social apprenticeship model for gaining writing expertise. *Written Communication, 17*(2), 185–223. https://doi.org/10.1177 /074108830001702002 .

Beaufort, A. (2004). Developmental gains of a history major: A case for building a theory of disciplinary writing expertise. *Research in the Teaching of English, 39*(2), 136–185.

Beaufort, A. (2007). *College writing and beyond: A new framework for university writing.* Utah State University Press. https://doi.org/10.2307/j.ctt4cgnko.

Benson, D. & Hughes, J. (1991). Method: Evidence and inference—evidence and inference for ethnomethodology. In G. Button (Ed.), *Ethnomethodology and the Human Sciences* (pp. 109–136). Cambridge University Press. https://doi.org /10.1017/cbo9780511611827.007.

Berninger, V., Vaughan, K., Abbott, R. D., Begay, K., Coleman, K. B., Curtin, G., . . . Graham, S. (2002). Teaching spelling and composition alone and together: Implications for the simple view of writing. *Journal of Educational Psychology, 94*(2), 291–304. https://doi.org/10.1037/0022-0663.94.2.291.

Bloome, D., Power Carter, S., Morton Christian, B., Otto, S. & Shuart-Faris, N. (2005). *Discourse analysis and the study of classroom language and literacy events.* Lawrence Erlbaum. https://doi.org/10.4324/9781410611215.

Blythe, S. (2016). Attending to the subject in writing transfer and adaptation. In C. Anson & J. Moore (Eds.), *Critical transitions: Writing and the question of transfer* (pp. 49–68). The WAC Clearinghouse; University Press of Colorado. https:// wac.colostate.edu/books/perspectives/ansonmoore/.

Bologh, R. W. (1992). The promise and failure of ethnomethodology from a feminist perspective. *Gender and Society, 6*(2), 199–206. https://doi.org/10.1177/08912439 2006002004.

Bolter, J. & Grusin, R. (1999). *Remediation: Understanding new media.* MIT Press.

Boscolo, P. (2014). Two metaphors for writing research and their implications for writing instruction. In B. Arfe, J. Dockrell & V. Berninger (Eds.), *Writing development in children with hearing loss, dyslexia, or oral language problems: Implications for assessment and instruction* (pp. 33–45). Oxford University Press. https:// doi.org/10.1093/acprof:oso/9780199827282.003.0003.

Bourdieu, P. (1977). *Outline of a theory of practice.* Cambridge University Press. https://doi.org/10.1017/cbo9780511812507.

Bowen, L. M. (2011). Resisting age bias in digital literacy research. *College Composition and Communication, 62*(4), 586–607.

Bowen, L. M. (2018). Composing a further life: Introduction to the special issue [Special Issue, Composing a Further life]. *Literacy in Composition Studies, 6*(2), vi–xxvi. https://doi.org/10.21623/1.6.2.1.

Boyle, C. (2015). An attempt at a practitioner's manifesto. In P. Lynch & N. Rivers (Eds.), *Thinking with Bruno Latour in rhetoric and composition* (pp. 202–218). Southern Illinois University Press. https://doi.org/10.1080/07350198.2016.1107933.

Brandt, D. (1990). *Literacy as involvement: The acts of writers, readers, and texts.* Southern Illinois University Press.

Brandt, D. (1992). The cognitive as the social an ethnomethodological approach to writing process research. *Written Communication, 9*(3), 315–355. https://doi.org/1 0.1177/0741088392009003001.

Brandt, D. (2001). *Literacy in American lives.* Cambridge University Press. https:// doi.org/10.1017/cbo9780511810237.

Brandt, D. (2015). *The rise of writing: Redefining mass literacy.* Cambridge University Press. https://doi.org/10.1017/cbo9781316106372.

Brandt, D. & Clinton, K. (2002). Limits of the local: Expanding perspectives on literacy as a social practice. *Journal of Literacy Research, 34*(3), 337–356. https://doi.org /10.1207/s15548430jlr3403_4.

Brodkey, L. (1987). Modernism and scene(s) of writing. *College English, 49*(4), 396–418. https://doi.org/10.2307/377850.

Brooke, R. (1987). Underlife and writing instruction. *College Composition and Communication, 38*(2), 141–153. https://doi.org/10.2307/357715.

Bryant, C. D. & Peck, D. L. (Eds.). (2007). *21st century sociology: A reference handbook.* Sage.

Butler, C. W., Gardner, R. & Fitzgerald, R. (2009). Branching out: Ethnomethodological approaches to communication. *Australian Journal of Communication, 36*(3), 1–15.

Cairns, D. (2013). *The philosophy of Edmund Husserl.* Springer. https://doi.org/10 .1007/978-94-007-5043-2.

Callon, M. (1986). Some elements of a sociology of translation: Domestication of the scallops and the fishermen of St. Brieuc Bay. In J. Law (Ed.), *Power, action, and belief: A new sociology of knowledge?* (pp. 196–233). Routledge.

Camp, H. (2012). The psychology of writing development—and its implications for assessment. *Assessing Writing, 17*, 92–105. https://doi.org/10.1016/j.asw.2012 .01.002 .

Carlin, A. P. (2015). Re-Assembling a corpus: Garfinkel's ethnomethodology and intellectual history. *Symbolic Interaction, 38*(1), 156–160. https://doi.org/10.1002/symb .144.

Caron, C. O. (2013). *Reflexivity at work: Making sense of Mannheim's, Garfinkel's, Gouldner's, and Bourdieu's sociology* (Publication No. NR94525). [Doctoral dissertation, Carleton University]. ProQuest Dissertations and Theses Professional.

Chung, C. & Pennebaker, J. (2007). The social functions of function words. In K. Fiedler (Ed.), *Social communication* (pp. 344–359). Psychology Press.

Cicourel, A. V. (1964). *Method and measurement in sociology.* The Free Press.

Cicourel, A. V. (1973). *Cognitive sociology: Language and meaning in social interaction.* The Free Press.

Cicourel, A. V. (2004). "I am NOT opposed to quantification or formalization or modeling, but do not want to pursue quantitative methods that are not commensurate with the research phenomena addressed": Aaron Cicourel in conversation with Andreas Witzel and Günter Mey. *Forum: Qualitative Social Research, 5*(3). http://www.qualitative-research.net/index.php/fqs/article/view/549/118.6.

Cicourel, A. V. (2016). Response to Smith and Atkinson. *International Journal of Social Research Methodology, 19*(1), 111–120. https://doi.org/10.1080/13645579.2015.1068008.

Clarke, A. E. (2003). Situational analyses: Grounded theory mapping after the post-modern turn. *Symbolic Interaction, 26*(4), 553–576. https://doi.org/10.1525/si.2003.26.4.553.

Clark, I. (2016). Genre, identity, and the brain: New insights from neuropsychology. *The Journal of General Education: A Curricular Commons of the Humanities and Sciences, 65*(1), 1–19. https://doi.org/10.5325/jgeneeduc.65.1.0001.

Clark, I. L. & Hernandez, A. (2011). Genre awareness, academic argument, and transferability. *The WAC Journal, 22*, 65–78. https://wac.colostate.edu/docs/journal/vol22/clark.pdf .

Cole, M. (2005). Cross-cultural and historical perspectives on the developmental consequences of education. *Human Development, 48*, 195–216. https://doi.org/10.1159/000086855.

Corbin, J. & Strauss, A. (2008). *The basics of qualitative research* (3rd ed.). Sage. https://doi.org/10.4135/9781452230153.

Coser, L. A. (1975). Presidential Address: Two methods in search of a substance. *American Sociological Review, 40*(6), 691–700. https://doi.org/10.2307/2094174.

Coulter, J. (1983). Contingent and a priori structures in sequential analysis. *Human Studies, 6*(4), 361–376. https://doi.org/10.1007/bf02127769.

Coulter, J. (1991). Cognition: Cognition in an ethnomethodological mode. In G. Button (Ed.), *Ethnomethodology and the human sciences* (pp. 176–195). Cambridge University Press. https://doi.org/10.1017/cbo9780511611827.009.

Czyzewski, M. (1994). Reflexivity of actors versus reflexivity of accounts. *Theory, Culture & Society, 11*, 161–168. https://doi.org/10.1177/026327694011004006.

Davidson, C. (2012). Ethnomethodology and literacy research: A methodological "road less travelled." *English Teaching, 11*(1), 26.

De Certeau, M. (1984). *The practice of everyday life.* University of California Press.

Denzin, N. K. (1991). Back to Harold and Agnes. *Sociological Theory, 9*(2), 280–285. https://doi.org/10.2307/202091.

DiCicco, B. & Gibson, D. R. (2010). More than a game: Sociological theory from the theories of games. *Sociological Theory, 28*(3), 247–271. https://doi.org/10.1111/j.1467-9558.2010.01377.x.

Dippre, R. (2016, July). Trajectories of GTA development: How teaching assistants take up and think through a "writing about writing" approach to English 101. Presentation at the Council of Writing Program Administrators Annual Conference. Raleigh, North Carolina.

Dippre, R. (2018). Faith, squirrels, and artwork: The expansive agency of textual coordination in the literate action of older writers. *Literacy in Composition Studies 6*(2), 76–93. https://doi.org/10.21623/1.6.2.6.

Dippre, R. & Phillips, T. (Eds.). (In press). *Approaches to lifespan writing research: Steps toward an actionable coherence.* Utah State University Press.

Dobrin, S. (2007). The occupation of composition. In C. Keller & C. Weisser (Eds.), *The locations of composition* (pp. 15–36). SUNY Press.

Donahue, C. (2012). Transfer, portability, generalization: (How) does composition expertise "carry?" In K. Ritter & P. Matsuda (Eds.), *Exploring composition studies: Sites, issues, and perspectives*. Utah State University Press. https://doi.org/10.2307 /j.ctt4cgjsj.12.

Dowling, M. (2007). From Husserl to van Manen: A review of different phenomenological approaches. *International Journal of Nursing Studies, 44*, 131–142. https:// doi.org/10.1016/j.ijnurstu.2005.11.026.

Driscoll, D. L. & Wells, J. H. M. (2012). Beyond knowledge and skills: Writing transfer and the role of student dispositions in and beyond the writing classroom. *Composition Forum, 26*(Fall). https://compositionforum.com/issue/26/beyond -knowledge-skills.php.

Duncan, D.J. *River teeth: Stories and writings*. The Dial Press.

Duranti, A. (2010). Husserl, intersubjectivity, and anthropology. *Anthropological Theory, 10*(1–2), 16–35. https://doi.org/10.1177/1463499610370517.

Durkheim, E. (1895). *The rules of sociological method*. The Free Press.

Dyson, A. H. (1983). The role of oral language in early writing processes. *Research in the Teaching of English, 17*(1), 1–30.

Dyson, A. H. (2008). Staying in the (curricular) lines: Practice constraints and possibilities in childhood writing. *Written Communication, 25*(1), 119–159. https://doi .org/10.1177/0741088307309552.

Dyson, A. H. (2013). *ReWRITING the basics: Literacy learning in children's cultures*. Teachers College Press.

Eberle, T. S. (2012). Phenomenological life-world analysis and ethnomethodology's program. *Human Studies, 35*, 279–304. https://doi.org/10.1007/s10746-012-9219-z.

Elder, Jr., G. (1998). The life course as developmental theory. *Child Development, 69*(1), 1–12. https://doi.org/10.2307/1132065

Elder, Jr., G. & Giele, J. Z. (2009). Life course studies: An evolving field. In G. Elder, Jr. & J. Z. Giele (Eds.), *The craft of life course research* (pp. 1–24). Guilford Press.

Emerson, R. M., Fretz, R. I. & Shaw, L. L. (1995). *Writing ethnographic fieldnotes*. Chicago: University of Chicago Press. https://doi.org/10.7208/chicago/97802262 06851.001.0001.

Emirbayer, M. & Maynard, D. W. (2011). Pragmatism and ethnomethodology. *Qualitative Sociology, 34*, 221–261. https://doi.org/10.1007/s11133-010-9183-8.

Engestrom, Y. (1987). *Learning by expanding*. Cambridge University Press. https:// doi.org/10.1017/cbo9781139814744.

Erickson, F. (1982). Taught cognitive learning in its immediate environment: A neglected topic in the anthropology of education. *Anthropology and Education Quarterly, 13*(2), 149–180. https://doi.org/10.1525/aeq.1982.13.2.05x1831k.

Erickson, F. (2004). *Talk and social theory*. Polity Press.

Evans, K. (2003). Accounting for conflicting mental models of communication in student-teacher interaction: An activity theory analysis. In C. Bazerman & D. Russell (Eds.) *Writing selves/writing societies* (pp. 393–497). The WAC Clearinghouse; Mind, Culture, and Activity. https://wac.colostate.edu/books/perspectives /selves-societies/.

Faigley, L. (1992). *Fragments of rationality: Postmodernity and the subject of composition*. University of Pittsburgh Press. https://doi.org/10.2307/j.ctt7zwbhf.

Fallace, T. (2015). The savage origins of child-centered pedagogy, 1871–1913. *American Educational Research Journal, 52*(1), 73–103. https://doi.org/10.3102/0002 831214561629.

Fele, G. (2012). Harold Garfinkel, 29 October 1917–21 April 2011. *Human Studies, 35*(2), 153–155. https://doi.org/10.1007/s10746-012-9221-5.

Fenstermacher, S. (2016). The turn from "what" to "how": Garfinkel's reach beyond description. *Symbolic Interaction, 39*(2), 295–305. https://doi.org/10.1002/symb .222.

Freedman, A. & Smart, G. (1997). Navigating the current of economic policy: Written genres and a distribution of cognitive work at a financial institution. *Mind, Culture, and Activity, 4*(4), 238–255. https://doi.org/10.1207/s15327884m ca0404_3.

Frei, R. (2011). Identity, narrative, and lived experience after postmodernity: Between multiplicity and continuity. *Journal of Phenomenological Psychology, 42*, 46–60. https://doi.org/10.1163/156916211X567488.

Frie, R. & Coburn, W. J. (Eds). (2011). *Persons in Context: The Challenge of Individuality in Theory and Practice*. Routledge. https://doi.org/10.4324/9780203869321.

Gallant, M. J. & Kleinman, S. (1983). Symbolic interactionism vs. ethnomethodology. *Symbolic Interaction, 6*(1), 1–18. https://doi.org/10.1525/si.1983.6.1.1.

Garfinkel, H. (1963). A conception of, and experiments with, "trust" as a condition of stable concerted actions. In O.J. Harvey (Ed.) *Motivation and Social Interaction* (pp. 187–238). Ronald Press.

Garfinkel, H. (1964). Studies of the routine grounds of everyday activities. *Social Problems 11*(3), 225–250. https://doi.org/10.1525/sp.1964.11.3.03a00020.

Garfinkel, H. (1967). *Studies in ethnomethodology*. Prentice Hall.

Garfinkel, H. (1991). Respecification: Evidence for locally produced, naturally accountable phenomena of order, logic, reason, meaning, method, etc. in and as of the essential haecceity of immortal ordinary society (I)—An announcement of studies. In G. Button (Ed.), *Ethnomethodology and the Human Sciences* (pp. 10–19). Cambridge University Press. https://doi.org/10.1017/cbo9780511611827.003.

Garfinkel, H. (2002). *Ethnomethodology's program: Working out Durkheim's aphorism*. Rowman & Littlefield.

Garfinkel, H. (2006). *Seeing Sociologically: The Routine Grounds of Social Action*. Paradigm. https://doi.org/10.4324/9781315632186.

Garfinkel, H. (2007). Lebenswelt Origins of the Sciences: Working out Durkheim's Aphorism: Book Two: Workplace and documentary diversity of ethnomethodological studies of work and sciences by ethnomethodology's authors: What did we do? What did We learn? *Human Studies 30*(1), 9–56. https://doi.org/10.1007 /s10746-007-9046-9.

Garfinkel, H. (2008). *Toward a Sociological Theory of Information*. Paradigm. https:// doi.org/10.4324/9781315631516.

Garfinkel, H. & Sacks, H. (1986). On formal structures of practical actions. In H. Garfinkel (Ed.), *Ethnomethodological Studies of Work* (pp. 160–193). Routledge.

Gee, J. P. & Green, J. L. (1998). Discourse analysis, learning, and social practice: A methodological study. *Review of Research in Education 23*: 119–169. https://doi.org/10.2307/1167289.

Gibson, J. (1986). *The ecological approach to visual perception*. Taylor & Francis. https://doi.org/10.4324/9781315740218.

Giddens, A. (1984). *The constitution of society*. University of California Press.

Gilleard, C. & Higgs, P. (2016). Connecting life span development with the sociology of the life course: A new direction. *Sociology, 50*(2), 301–315. https://doi.org/10.1177/0038038515577906.

Ginev, D. (2013). Ethnomethodological and hermeneutic-phenomenological perspectives on scientific practices. *Human Studies, 36*, 277–305. https://doi.org/10.1007/s10746-013-9264-2.

Ginev, D. (2014). Radical reflexivity and hermeneutic pre-normativity. *Philosophy and Social Criticism, 40*(7), 683–703. https://doi.org/10.1177/0191453714536432.

Glaser, B. & Strauss, A. (1967). *The discovery of grounded theory: Strategies of qualitative research*. Transaction. https://doi.org/10.4324/9780203793206.

Gleeson, D. & Erben, M. (1976). Meaning in context: Notes towards a critique of ethnomethodology. *The British Journal of Sociology, 27*(4), 474–483. https://doi.org/10.2307/590186.

Godbee, B. (2012). Toward explaining the transformative power of talk about, around, and for writing. *Research in the Teaching of English, 47*(2), 171–197.

Goffman, E. (1963). *Behavior in public places*. The Free Press.

Goffman, E. (1983). The interaction order. *American Sociological Review, 48*(1), 1–17. https://doi.org/10.2307/2095141.

Goodnow, J., Miller, P. & Kessel, F. (Eds.). (1995). *Cultural practices as contexts for development* (New Directions for Child Development, No. 67). Jossey-Bass. https://doi.org/10.1002/cd.23219956703.

Gorzelsky, G., Driscoll, D. L., Paszek, J., Jones, E. & Hayes, C. (2016). Cultivating constructive metacognition: A new taxonomy for writing studies. In C. Anson & J. Moore (Eds.), *Critical transitions: Writing and the question of transfer* (pp. 215–246). The WAC Clearinghouse; University Press of Colorado. https://wac.colostate.edu/books/perspectives/ansonmoore/.

Graham, S. (1999). The role of text production skills in writing development: A special issue—I. *Learning Disability Quarterly, 22*, 75–77. https://doi.org/10.2307/1511267.

Graham, S. (2018). A writer(s)-within-community model of writing. In *The Lifespan Development of Writing* (pp. 272–325). National Council of Teachers of English.

Green, B. (2008). The social beyond words: The case of Harold Garfinkel. *New Literary History, 39*(4), 957–969. https://doi.org/10.1353/nlh.0.0060.

Green, J. & Bloome, D. (2004). Ethnography and ethnographers in and of education: A situated perspective. In J. Flood, S. B. Heath & D. Lapp (Eds.), *Handbook of research on teaching literacy through the communicative and visual arts* (pp. 181–202). Macmillan. https://doi.org/10.4324/9781410611161.

Green, J., Skukauskaite, A. & Baker, D. (2012). Ethnography as epistemology. In J. Arthur, M. Waring, R. Coe & L. V. Hedges (Eds.), *Research methods and methodologies in education* (pp. 309–321). Sage.

Grijalva, R. A. (2016). Minding the gap: Writing-related learning in/across/within multiple activity systems. In C. Anson & J. Moore (Eds.), *Critical transitions: Writing and the question of transfer* (pp. 139–160). The WAC Clearinghouse; University Press of Colorado. https://wac.colostate.edu/books/perspectives/ansonmoore/.

Hak, T. (1995). Ethnomethodology and the institutional context. *Human Studies, 18*(2), 109–137. https://doi.org/10.1007/bf01323206.

Hammersley, M. (1989). The problem of the concept: Herbert Blumer on the relationship between concepts and data. *Journal of Contemporary Ethnography, 18*(2), 133–159. https://doi.org/10.1177/089124189018002002.

Hammersley, M. (2018). *The radicalism of ethnomethodology: An assessment of sources and principles.* Manchester University Press. https://doi.org/10.7228/manchester/9781526124623.001.0001 .

Haswell, R. (1991). *Gaining ground in college writing: Tales of development and interpretation.* Southern Methodist University Press.

Hayes, H., Ferris, D. R. & Whitaus, C. (2016). Dynamic transfer in first-year writing and "writing in the disciplines" settings. In C. Anson & J. Moore (Eds.), *Critical transitions: Writing and the question of transfer* (pp. 181–213). The WAC Clearinghouse; University Press of Colorado. https://wac.colostate.edu/books/perspectives/ansonmoore/.

Heap, J. L. (1984). Ethnomethodology and education: Possibilities. *The Journal of Educational Thought, 18*(3), 168–171.

Hilbert, R. A. (1990). Ethnomethodology and the micro-macro order. *American Sociological Review, 55*(6), 794–808. https://doi.org/10.2307/2095746.

Hilbert, R. A. (1995). Garfinkel's recovery of themes in classical sociology. *Human Studies, 18*(2), 157–175. https://doi.org/10.1007/bf01323208.

Hillocks, G. (2002). *The testing trap: How state writing assessments control learning.* Teachers College Press.

Ho, W. C. (2008). The transcendence and non-discursivity of the lifeworld. *Human Studies, 31,* 323–342. https://doi.org/10.1007/s10746-008-9098-5.

Honeyford, M. A. & Boyd, K. (2015). Learning through play. *Journal of Adolescent & Adult Literacy, 59*(1), 63–73. https://doi.org/10.1002/jaal.428.

Husserl, E. (1960). *Cartesian meditations: An introduction to phenomenology* (D. Cairns, Trans.). Martinus Nijhoff.

Husserl, E. & Lauer, Q. (1956). Philosophy as strict science. *CrossCurrents, 6*(4), 325–344.

Hutchins, E. (1995). *Cognition in the wild.* MIT Press.

Ivanic, R. (1998). *Writing and identity: The discoursal construction of identity in academic writing.* John Benjamins. https://doi.org/10.1075/swll.5.

James, W. (1890). *Principles of psychology.* Henry Holt. https://doi.org/10.5962/bhl.title.47583

Johnson, R. (1997). Audience involved: Toward a participatory model of writing. *Computers and Composition, 14,* 361–376. https://doi.org/10.1016/s8755-4615(97)90006-2.

Johnson, T. R. (2011). How student writers develop: Rhetoric, psychoanalysis, ethics, erotics. *Journal of Advanced Composition, 31*(3/4), 533–577.

Jones, R. L. & Corsby, C. (2015). A case for coach Garfinkel: Decision making and what we already know. *Quest, 67*(4), 439–449. https://doi.org/10.1080/00336297.2015.1082919.

Kaplan, A. (1964). *The conduct of inquiry: Methodology for behavioural science.* Routledge. https://doi.org/10.4324/9781315131467.

Kellogg, R. T. (2008). Training writing skills: A cognitive developmental perspective. *Journal of Writing Research, 1*(1), 1–26. https://doi.org/10.17239/jowr-2008.01.01.1.

Kerschbaum, S. (2014). *Toward a new rhetoric of difference.* National Council of Teachers of English.

Kessen, W. (1986). *The rise and fall of development.* Clark University Press.

Killgallon, D. & Killgallon, J. (2000). *Sentence composing for elementary school: A worktext to build better sentences.* Heinemann.

Korbut, A. (2014). The idea of constitutive order in ethnomethodology. *European Journal of Social Theory, 17*(4), 479–496. https://doi.org/10.1177/1368431013516057.

Koschmann, T. (2012). Early glimmers of the now familiar ethnomethodological themes in Garfinkel's *The perception of the other. Human Studies, 35*(4), 479–504. https://doi.org/10.1007/s10746-012-9243-z.

Kunitz, S. & Markee, N. (2017). Understanding the fuzzy borders of context in conversation analysis and ethnography. In S. Wortham, D. Kim & S. May (Eds.), *Discourse and Education* (pp. 1–13). Springer International. https://doi.org/10.1007/978-3-319-02243-7_8.

Latour, B. (1991). *We have never been modern.* Harvard University Press.

Latour, B. (2005). *Reassembling the social.* Oxford University Press.

Lave, J. & Wenger, E. (1991). *Situated learning: Legitimate peripheral participation.* Cambridge University Press.

Lee, A. (2004). Thinking about social theory and philosophy for information systems. *Social Theory and Philosophy for Information Systems, 1*, 1–26.

Lemke, J. L. (2000). Across the scales of time: Artifacts, activities, and meanings in ecosocial systems. *Mind, Culture, and Activity, 7*(4), 273–290. https://doi.org/10.1207/s15327884mca0704_03.

Lester, M. & Hadden, S. C. (1980). Ethnomethodology and grounded theory methodology: An integration of perspective and method. *Journal of Contemporary Ethnography, 9*(1), 3–33. https://doi.org/10.1177/089124168000900101.

Liberman, K. (2007). *Husserl's criticism of reason: With ethnomethodological specifications.* Lexington Books.

Liberman, K. (2013). *More studies in ethnomethodology.* SUNY Press.

Livingston, E. (1987). *Making sense of ethnomethodology.* Taylor & Francis.

Livingston, E. (2003). Reading ethnomethodology's program. *Research on Language and Social Interaction, 36*(4), 481–486. https://doi.org/10.1207/s15327973rlsi3604_7.

Lotman, Y. (1990). *Universe of the mind: A semiotic theory of culture.* Indiana University Press.

Lynch, M. (1993). *Scientific practice and ordinary action.* Cambridge University Press. https://doi.org/10.1017/cbo9780511625473.

Lynch, M. (1999). Silence in context: Ethnomethodology and social theory. *Human Studies, 22,* 211–233. https://doi.org/10.1023/a:1005440501638.

Lynch, M. (2000). Against reflexivity as an academic virtue and source of privileged knowledge. *Theory, Culture, and Society, 17*(3), 26–54. https://doi.org/10.1177/02632760022051202.

Lynch, M. (2001). Ethnomethodology and the logic of practice. In T. R. Schatzki, K. Knorr Cetina & E. von Savigny (Eds.), *The Practice turn in contemporary theory* (pp. 131–148). Routledge.

Lynch, M. (2006). Cognitive activities without cognition? Ethnomethodological investigations of selected "cognitive" topics. *Discourse Studies, 8*(1), 95–104. https://doi.org/10.1177/1461445606059559.

Lynch, M. (2011). Harold Garfinkel (29 October 2017–21 April 2011), A remembrance and reminder. *Social Studies of Science, 41*(6), 927–942. https://doi.org/10.1177/0306312711423434.

Lynch, M. (2012a). Garfinkel stories. *Human Studies, 35,* 163–168. https://doi.org/10.1007/s10746-012-9222-4

Lynch, M. (2012b). Revisiting the cultural dope. *Human Studies, 35*(2), 223–233. https://doi.org/10.1007/s10746-012-9227-z

Lynch, M. (2015). Garfinkel's legacy: Bastards all the way down. *Contemporary Sociology, 44*(5), 604–614. https://doi.org/10.1177/0094306115599356a.

Lynch, M. (2016, June). *Radical ethnomethodology.* Position paper for meeting at Manchester Metropolitan University. Manchester, UK.

Lynch, M. (2017, July). Garfinkel, Sacks, and formal structures: Collaborative origins, divergences, and the vexed unity of ethnomethodology and conversation analysis. Keynote address at the International Institute for Ethnomethodology and Conversation Analysis. Otterbein College, Westerville OH.

MacKenzie, S.V. & Harris, W.J. (2008). National board-certified teachers: Can they make a difference in Maine schools? *Maine Policy Review, 17*(1), 94–106.

Mangrum, F. G. & Mangrum, C. (1995). An ethnomethodological study of concerted and biographical work performed by elderly persons during game playing. *Educational Gerontology: An International Quarterly, 21*(3), 231–246. https://doi.org/10.1080/0360127950210304.

McCarthy, L. P. (1987). A stranger in strange lands: A college student writing across the curriculum. *Research in the Teaching of English, 21*(3), 233–265.

McCutchen, D., Teske, P. & Bankston, C. (2008). Writing and cognition: Implications of a cognitive architecture for learning to write and writing to learn. In C. Bazerman (Ed.), *Handbook of Research on Writing* (pp. 447–465). Lawrence Erlbaum.

Medway, P. (1996). Virtual and material buildings. *Written Communication 13*(4), 473–514. https://doi.org/10.1177/0741088396013004002.

Mehan, H., Wood, H. (1975). *The reality of ethnomethodology.* John Wiley & Sons.

Merton, R. (1968). *Social theory and social structure.* The Free Press.

Merton, R. (1987). Three fragments from a sociologist's notebooks: Establishing the phenomenon, specified ignorance, and strategic research materials. *Annual Review of Sociology, 13,* 1–28. https://doi.org/10.1146/annurev.so.13.080187.000245.

Micciche, L. (2014). Writing material. *College English, 76*(6), 488–505.

Miller, C. (1984). Genre as social action. *Quarterly Journal of Speech, 70,* 151–167. https://doi.org/10.1080/00335638409383686.

Miller, C. (1994a). Genre as social action. In P. Medway & A. Freedman (Eds.), *Genre and the new rhetoric* (pp. 23–42). Taylor & Francis. https://doi.org/10.4324/9780203393277.

Miller, C. (1994b). Rhetorical community: The cultural basis of genre. In P. Medway & A. Freedman (Eds.), *Genre and the new rhetoric* (pp. 67–78). Taylor & Francis. https://doi.org/10.4324/9780203393277.

Mitchell, C. J. (1984). Typicality and the case study. In Ellen, P. F. (Ed.), *Ethnographic research: A guide to general conduct* (pp. 238–241). Academic Press.

Moore, J. & Anson, C. (2016). Introduction. In C. Anson & J. Moore (Eds.), *Critical transitions: Writing and the question of transfer* (pp. 3–16). The WAC Clearinghouse; University Press of Colorado. https://wac.colostate.edu/books/perspectives/ansonmoore/.

Mullins, N. C. (1973). The development of specialties in social science: The case of ethnomethodology. *Science Studies, 3*(3), 245–273. https://doi.org/10.1177/030631277300300302.

Nowacek, R. (2011). *Agents of integration: Understanding transfer as a rhetorical act.* National Council of Teachers of English.

Ogien, A. (2013). Garfinkel reading mead. What should sociology do with social naturalism? *Österreichische Zeitschrift Für Soziologie, 38*(1), 97–113. https://doi.org/10.1007/s11614-013-0099-x.

Ogien, A. (2016). Durkheim as a sociologist of knowledge: Rudiments of a reflexive theory of the concept. *Journal of Classical Sociology, 16*(1), 7–20. https://doi.org/10.1177/1468795X13497139.

Olson, C. J. (2012). Practicing histories. *Advances in the History of Rhetoric, 15,* 1–8. https://doi.org/10.1080/15362426.2012.657041.

Otto, K. (2016). Dual Enculturation: A Comparison of Five L2 Students Writing for One General Education Course (Publication No. 10159756) [Doctoral Dissertation, University of California, Santa Barbara]. ProQuest Dissertations and Theses Global.

Pearlman, J. (2018). *Football for a buck: The crazy rise and crazier demise of the USFL.* Houghton Mifflin.

Pennycook, A. (2010). *Literacy as a local practice.* Routledge.

Perri, T. (2014). Bergson's philosophy of memory. *Philosophy Compass, 9,* 837–847. https://doi.org/10.1111/phc3.12179.

Pigg, S. L. (2014a). Emplacing mobile composing habits: A study of academic writing in networked social spaces. *College Composition and Communication, 66*(2), 250–275.

Pigg, S. L. (2014b). Coordinating constant invention: Social media's role in distributed work. *Technical Communication Quarterly, 23*(2), 69–87. https://doi.org/10.1080/10572252.2013.796545.

Pigg, S. L. (2015). Distracted by digital literacy: Unruly bodies and the schooling of literacy. In L. Lewis (Ed.), *Strategic discourse: The politics of (new) literacy crises.* Computers & Composition Digital Press. https://ccdigitalpress.org/strategic.

Pollner, M. (1991). Left of ethnomethodology: The rise and decline of radical reflexivity. *American Sociological Review, 56*(3), 370–380. https://doi.org/10.2307/2096110.

Pollner, M. (2012a). The end(s) of ethnomethodology. *American Sociologist, 43*(1), 7–20. https://doi.org/10.1007/s12108-011-9144-z.

Pollner, M. (2012b). Reflections on Garfinkel and ethnomethodology's program. *American Sociologist, 43*(1), 36–54. https://doi.org/10.1007/s12108-011-9146-x.

Prior, P. (1998). *Writing/disciplinarity.* Lawrence Erlbaum. https://doi.org/10.4324/9780203810651.

Prior, P. (2008, February). *Flat CHAT? Reassembling literate activity.* Presentation at Writing Research Across Borders. Santa Barbara, California.

Prior, P. (2014a). Combining phenomenological and sociohistoric frameworks for studying literate practices: Some implications of Deborah Brandt's methodological trajectory. In J. Duffy, J. N. Chrisoph, E. Goldblatt, N. Graff, R. Nowacek & B. Trabold (Eds.), *Literacy, economy, and power: Writing and research after literacy in American lives* (pp. 166–182). Southern Illinois University Press.

Prior, P. (2014b). Semiotics. In C. Leung & B. Street (Eds.), *The Routledge companion to English studies* (pp. 160–173). Routledge. https://doi.org/10.4324/9781315852515.ch11.

Prior, P. (2015, March). *Becoming a biologist: Tracing trajectories of writing and disciplinarity across the lifespan.* Paper presentation at the Annual Convention of the Conference on College Composition and Communication. Tampa, Florida.

Prior, P. (2016, August). *The units-of-analysis problem for writing research: Tracing laminated trajectories of becoming a biologist.* Presentation at the 50th Anniversary Dartmouth Conference. Hanover, New Hampshire.

Prior, P. (2017, March). *Girl talk, slider bars, and self-medicating monkeys: Taking up ethnomethodology in research on academic writing.* Presentation at the Conference on College Composition and Communication. Portland, Oregon.

Prior, P. (2018). How do moments add up to lives: Trajectories of semiotic becoming vs. tales of learning in four modes. In R. Wysocki & M. P. Sheridan (Eds.), *Making future matters.* Computers & Composition Digital Press. http://ccdigitalpress.org/makingfuturematters.

Prior, P. & Hengst, J. (Eds.). (2010). *Exploring semiotic remediation as discourse practice.* Palgrave Macmillan. https://doi.org/10.1057/9780230250628.

Prior, P. & Shipka, J. (2003). Chronotopic lamination. In C. Bazerman & D. Russell (Eds.) *Writing selves/writing societies.* Fort Collins, CO: The WAC Clearinghouse and Mind, Culture, and Activity. https://wac.colostate.edu/books/perspectives/selves-societies/.

Psathas, G. (1995). *Conversation analysis: The study of talk-in-interaction.* Sage.

Qualley, D. (2016). Building a conceptual topography of the transfer terrain. In C. Anson & J. Moore (Eds.), *Critical transitions: Writing and the question of transfer* (pp. 69–106). The WAC Clearinghouse; University Press of Colorado. https://wac.colostate.edu/books/perspectives/ansonmoore/.

Quere, L. (2012). Is there any good reason to say goodbye to "ethnomethodology"? *Human Studies, 35*(2), 305–325. https://doi.org/10.1007/s10746-012-9234-0.

Rawls, A. W. (1985). Reply to Gallant and Kleinman on symbolic interaction vs. ethnomethodology. *Symbolic Interaction, 8*(1), 121–140. https://doi.org/10.1525/si.1985.8.1.121.

Rawls, A. W. (2005). Garfinkel's conception of time. *Time & Society, 14*(2–3), 163–190. https://doi.org/10.1177/0961463X05055132.

Rawls, A. W. (2008). Harold Garfinkel, ethnomethodology, and workplace studies. *Organizational Studies, 29*(5), 701–732. https://doi.org/10.1177/0170840608088768.

Rawls, A. W. (2009). An essay on two conceptions of social order: Constitutive orders of action, objects and identities vs aggregated orders of individual action. *Journal of Classical Sociology, 9*(4), 500–520. https://doi.org/10.1177/1468795X09344376.

Rawls, A. W. (2011a). Garfinkel, ethnomethodology, and the defining questions of pragmatism. *Qualitative Sociology, 34*, 277–282. https://doi.org/10.1007/s11133-010-9185-6.

Rawls, A. W. (2011b). Wittgenstein, Durkheim, Garfinkel, and Winch: Constitutive orders of sensemaking. *Journal for the Theory of Social Behaviour, 41*(4), 396–418. https://doi.org/10.1111/j.1468-5914.2011.00471.x.

Rawls, A. W. (2013). The early years, 1939–1953: Garfinkel at North Carolina, Harvard, and Princeton. *Journal of Classical Sociology, 13*(2), 303–312. https://doi.org/10.1177/1468795X13477292.

Rawls, A. W. & Mann, D. (2010). The thing is . . . what is our "what"?": An ethnographic study of a design team's discussion of "object" clarity as a problem in designing an information system to facilitate system interoperability (MITRE Technical Report 10–2594). The MITRE Corporation. Retrieved from: https://www.mitre.org/sites/default/files/pdf/10_2594.pdf.

Rawls, A. W. & Mann, D. (2015). Getting information systems to interact: The social fact character of "object" clarity as a factor in designing information systems. *The Information Society, 31*(2), 175–192. https://doi.org/10.1080/01972243.2015.998106.

Register, M. E. & Herman, J. (2006). A middle range theory for generative quality of life for the elderly. *Advances in Nursing Science, 29*(4), 340–350. https://doi.org/10.1097/00012272-200610000-00007.

Reiff, M. & Bawarshi, A. (2011). Tracing discursive resources: How students use prior genre knowledge to negotiate new writing contexts in first-year composition. *Written Communication, 28*(3), 312–337. https://doi.org/10.1177/0741088311410183.

Rifenberg, J.M. (2016). The performance of literate practices: Rhetoric, writing, and stand-up comedy. *Journal of the Assembly for Expanded Perspectives on Language, 22*, 78–91.

Robertson, L., Taczak, K. & Yancey, K. B. (2012). Notes toward a theory of prior knowledge and its role in college composers' transfer of knowledge and practice. *Composition Forum, 26*(Fall). https://compositionforum.com/issue/26/prior-knowledge-transfer.php.

Rogers, M. F. (1983). *Sociology, ethnomethodology and experience.* Cambridge University Press.

Rogoff, B., Baker-Sennett, J., Lacasa, P. & Goldsmith, D. (1995). Development through participation in sociocultural activity. In P. J. Miller, F. Kessel & J. J.